THE
CRUELLEST CUT

THE CRUELLEST CUT

IRISH WOMEN WHO KILL

ANTHONY GALVIN

Gill & Macmillan

Published by Gill & Macmillan Ltd
Hume Avenue, Park West, Dublin 12, Ireland
with associated companies throughout the world
www.gillmacmillan.ie

© Anthony Galvin, 2009
ISBN 978 07171 4675 8

Type design: Make Communication
Typesetting and Print Origination: Carrigboy Typesetting Services
Printed and bound in the UK by JF Print Ltd

This book is typeset in Linotype Minion and Neue Helvetica.

The paper used in this book comes from the wood pulp of
managed forests. For every tree felled, at least one tree is
planted, thereby renewing natural resources.

A CIP catalogue record for this book is available from the British
Library.

5 4 3 2 1

CONTENTS

INTRODUCTION

In 1990, when I was still a junior reporter on the *Limerick Leader*, one of our photographers returned from a grisly assignment. He had been out to Southill, one of the rougher estates in a rough city, to take a photograph of a grieving young widow. Her husband had been blasted to death in a shotgun attack the previous day, and she was appealing for any information about his attacker.

It was a routine appeal: we see them all the time in the papers after families have been robbed of their loved ones. But something wasn't right.

'I think she had something to do with it,' the photographer told a disbelieving newsroom. We laughed at him.

'That's why you take the pictures, and we write the stories,' someone joked. We all knew that women didn't kill people—that was men's work.

But a few days later Majella Boland, aged twenty-three, was charged with conspiracy to commit murder. She had paid a local thug, Declan Malone, the princely sum of £200 to blow away her husband. Women do kill, and can be surprisingly vicious about it.

Women kill for the same reasons men kill. They kill out of greed, for revenge, to protect themselves or their loved ones. They kill to get themselves out of embarrassing situations, or to keep their dirty secrets hidden. Some even kill for fun.

But they also kill for their own individual reasons: they kill because they see it as the only way out of an abusive relationship; they kill their children in a fit of despair; they kill if the world has dumped on them for years, and they have had a history of abuse, and they have finally taken too much—they have reached snapping point.

Just because women kill less often than men doesn't mean that they can't be every bit as vicious when they get the urge. They can make the men look like choirboys.

Jack the Ripper was not the first serial killer: that dubious honour goes to a woman. Hungarian Countess Elizabeth Báthory (1560–1614) was a sadist who took great pleasure in torturing and abusing her servants. During one vicious attack on a girl she was sprayed with blood and became convinced that it had improved her complexion! This was the only catalyst she needed, and over the next number of years she tortured and killed an unknown number of young women. Because of her isolation and her social position she was protected, but eventually the tales became too lurid, and the Hungarian court was forced to move against her.

When the authorities stormed her castle the sights they saw matched the most gruesome stories about her. Bones littered the basement: one woman was found dead, and another dying; several women were in chains, evidently being fattened up for the slaughter.

Báthory was tried and convicted of eighty murders, but the true number is believed to have been somewhere between three hundred and six hundred. King Matthias pushed for the death penalty, but Countess Elizabeth had powerful relations, and was instead placed under house arrest for the rest of her life. She was bricked up in a suite of rooms, with only a small slit left open through which she could receive food. After four solitary years she gave up the ghost and joined her victims.

No Irish woman killer matches the ferocity of Europe's first lady of death, but there are several remarkable tales in the annals of Irish murder. Some Irish women have killed more than once, including a teenage girl in the midlands who drowned two toddlers in her care over the course of a summer. She killed for the most trivial of reasons; her mistress had taken an outfit from her, because she was too fond of the boys. Her story is told in this book.

Everyone else in this book (with the exception of Mary Keegan, who killed twice, and Margaret McCole, who couldn't quite finish off her victim) killed just once, but I believe their stories are interesting. Violence in women is a subject that has been ignored for too long. We love reading about crime, but it is 'glamorous' crime that attracts us—gangland hits, armed robberies, random serial killers. Most women kill in a domestic setting, which is why we tend to forget just how vicious women can be. And there are fewer women in jail than men.

When choosing cases for this book I had a number of criteria in mind—but I cheerfully broke my own rules when I felt a case merited it. My first rule was that the killers had to be violent. You will find no poisoners here, no women who hired men to do their dirty work—every killer between these covers got her hands dirty. One or two had help, but they all played a major hands-on role in the killings of which they were convicted. That is why Majella Boland is not here. Even had Sharon Collins succeeded in killing her partner, PJ Howard, with the hitman she recruited over the internet, she would not have made it into this book either.

My second rule—and this was very arbitrary—was that I confined my research to the Republic. Several juicy murderesses in Northern Ireland could have claimed inclusion, but you have to draw the line somewhere or the book would have become an unwieldy monster.

My third rule was that the cases had to be fairly recent. I am with Henry Ford, the American industrialist and car manufacturer, who said: 'We want to live in the present and the only history that is worth a tinker's dam is the history we made today.'

For me history begins with the moon landing, because it is the first major event I remember. But I kept everything in these pages a lot more current than that. All the cases are from the nineties and the noughties; some come from last year. But of course, there are exceptions. Mary Cole killed in the 1920s, but she was only fourteen at the time, and she killed twice in as many months: that qualifies her for inclusion. I also included another case from the 1920s, but only because it had interesting parallels with the most notorious murder (male or female) of recent years.

The Scissors Sisters, Charlotte and Linda Mulhall, shocked us all when they chopped up their mother's lover, dismembering him and removing his head, which was never found. But they weren't the first to do that: two sisters and a brother killed their older brother because he was a domineering bully, and they wanted the farm. That was back in the twenties, in Clonakilty, County Cork. They were even more careless about the disposal of the body than the Mulhall sisters. The Mulhalls threw Farah Noor's body parts into the Royal Canal, where they remained in clear view of the city. If they hadn't taken the precaution of hiding his head they might have been caught even more quickly than they were. The O'Learys were even more careless. They chopped up their brother and left the bits scattered around the farm in the hope that local dogs would do the rest. The dogs didn't oblige, and the O'Learys were convicted of murder. Their story is here, alongside the Mulhalls'.

The psychology of killers is an intriguing subject. Why do some people snap while others in similar circumstances just take a Valium or go for a long walk to calm down? Forensic psychiatrist Dr Brian McCaffrey, who has testified in several high-profile cases down the years, was gracious enough to share his insights on some of the cases in this book.

I divided the women who killed their children into three categories: the sad; the mad; and the bad.

The sad are the depressives, those who kill their children (and often themselves) in moments of deep despair. They think it is the right thing, that dying is preferable to the pain of going on. Mary Keegan, who killed her two children in Dublin in 2006, was depressed at the time. Sometimes depression can come on suddenly, but often it can be there in the background, undiagnosed and untreated for years; yet with treatment it is a relatively simple problem to fix. Depression often first sets in after a birth—the baby blues—and post-natal depression can blight the rest of a woman's life if left to fester.

'Post-natal depression is very serious, both from a suicide point of view and from a danger of killing children. The sad thing is that it can be very treatable,' says Dr McCaffrey.

Sometimes depression lasts a lifetime, and runs from generation to generation. Dr Lynn Gibbs, who spent decades battling mental illness, saw her mother commit suicide; then she saw her daughter develop symptoms of anorexia. It was too much for her to bear, and she drowned her sixteen-year-old daughter.

The second category of child killers is the mad. Some people suffer an episode of insanity and kill their child because the voices inside their heads are telling them to, in a psychotic episode that might be caused by schizophrenia or by drugs. Schizophrenic killers are far less likely than depressive killers to take their own life. Jacqueline Costello, who killed her eight-year-old son Robert in Mullinavat, County Kilkenny, is typical of this type of killer. Mary Prendergast, who killed her grown-up daughter because the Virgin Mary spoke to her through a dripping toilet, is a little more unusual, but definitely falls into the 'mad' category.

The bad are the worst of all. These people have no excuses: they are not depressed; they do not suffer from a mental illness; they are just appalling human beings. The woman at the centre of the Roscommon incest case is a recent example, but the bad have always been with us. In this book we look at two women whose appalling treatment of their children led, either directly or indirectly, to death.

Some cases are included because the human story behind them is fascinating. This is a significant factor, because not all murders are interesting. As a young reporter, the first murder I covered was that of a middle-aged man in Moyross, Limerick. It was a domestic matter, a murder over a woman, and the murderer had taken the train from Dublin to kill his victim. The case was cleared up in days, and there was nothing of note to remember. If one witness had not changed his mind about a quote he had given me, and then struck me over the head with an umbrella, I probably wouldn't remember the case at all.

But the case of Tracey Butler, killed by her close friend Deborah Hannon, and Hannon's accomplice Suzanne Reddan, was completely different. I have forgotten none of it. The story had all the ingredients of a best-seller—a love triangle, a double murder, and a blonde teenage killer. At the time I thought the story deserved a book. Now it is included in one.

The case of Kelly Noble is another fascinating one, which confirms the words of American writer Frank Herbert: 'There is no escape—we pay for the violence of our ancestors.' This tragic teenager saw her mother jailed for killing her abusive father. A few short years later she joined her mother in prison, after killing a young mother in Laytown, County Meath. Read the story and decide for yourself whether Kelly Noble was a bad person, or simply in the wrong place at the wrong time; and whether her upbringing had left her with any resources other than violence to cope with the situation she found herself in.

Una Black killed her neighbour over a dog he was minding for her. A young girl, only fifteen, used a shotgun on her best friend's husband because of what he was doing to his wife. Kathleen Bell stabbed her partner to death because he chose to taunt her about a particularly brutal episode in her past. She was pushed beyond her limits.

There can be a fine line between murder and a couple of bruises. Under the right circumstances a small knock can kill someone; but occasionally a beating with a hammer can leave the victim very much alive. Margaret McCole discovered this when she called upon an elderly neighbour in Donegal to silence him before word got out that she had stolen his savings. She was very lucky he did survive; otherwise a lengthy prison sentence could have been a life sentence.

All the women in this book have a tale to tell. In an increasingly violent society women are getting in on the act. The days of a drunken man pulling out a knife to end a row are gone. Now that's a unisex crime. Granted, there are only 155 women in prison in Ireland, out of a total prison population of 3,646. But that number will grow.

Women are proving that they are very capable of delivering the cruellest cut.

01 | STABBED BY HER BEST FRIEND
DEBORAH HANNON AND SUZANNE REDDAN

The two girls could have been any two teenagers lounging around outside a shop or waiting for a bus. One was short and pretty, with dark hair and sparkling eyes. The other could have acquitted herself well in a Darryl Hannah lookalike contest. She was tall and slim, with blonde curls cascading down over her shoulders, and a pouty mouth that completed the resemblance to the American actress.

But they weren't lounging outside a shop or waiting for a bus. The two girls were standing in the dock of the modern District Court building in Limerick, grinning at each other. They had both been done for shoplifting, and now they were facing the consequences. But they were young, they were female, and they had a good legal aid lawyer. They would escape with probation, or a community service order.

No one could have guessed that a year later the pretty brunette would be dead, stabbed dozens of times by the pretty blonde, her best friend, in a killing so gruesome it horrified experienced cops in a city that has a reputation for violence.

The slaying of Tracey Butler by Deborah Hannon and Suzanne Reddan is a story of friendship, love and family gone tragically wrong.

Tracey Butler was a Christmas child, born on 14 December 1975, who grew up in Limerick in the eighties. Limerick had always had a reputation as a tough town, and during Tracey's childhood years it earned the nickname Stab City following a brutal incident in which a local criminal, Anthony Kelly, was set upon by members of the McCarthy family. In the ensuing melée he managed to wrest a knife from one of his attackers. Two McCarthy brothers ended up dead, and Anthony Kelly was subsequently tried and acquitted of their murders.

Tracey grew up on Creagh Avenue, Kileely, not half a mile from where that stabbing took place. Kileely is an old part of the city, full of small corporation houses and narrow streets. One of the less gentrified neighbourhoods in Limerick, it lies a few minutes' walk south of the city centre. Five minutes' walk in one direction brings you to the Island Field, while fifteen minutes in the other direction lies Moyross, two of the most notorious spots in the city. Kileely is a different world, where the people hold down jobs, the houses and gardens are well maintained, and crime is something you read about in the local paper, not something you experience every night.

Tracey was one of four children born to Christina and Terence Butler, and everyone described her as bubbly, personable and outgoing. She had an older sister, Sharon, aged twenty-one at the time of the murder, and an older brother, Mark (aged twenty); younger brother Terence (eleven) was the baby of the family. Her parents were separated at the time of her death, and Tracey was living with her mother.

Tracey first met Deborah Hannon, from Cosgrave Park, Moyross, at the local playschool, when they were just toddlers. The two children became inseparable, and remained friends throughout their childhood and teenage years. They began primary school together, played in the yard and fought each other's fights. Both girls made their first Communion together in pretty white dresses, and were still close friends when they left primary school and entered their teens.

'From the time they were in playschool until the death of my husband, those two girls were inseparable. They both left school after primary together, and they looked after each other. They were always fighting on each other's behalf,' said Deborah's mother, Teresa, shortly after Tracey's killing.

Deborah's early years highlight the breakdown of family life that became more common in Ireland in the seventies and eighties. Her mother was just fifteen when she discovered she was pregnant. Her family did not approve, so Teresa ran off to England with her boyfriend, Willie Hannon, also fifteen, and they set up home in London. Deborah was born on her mother's sixteenth birthday. At one point, social services tried to take baby Deborah into care, but when they arrived at the house Willie Hannon refused to open the door and threatened to blow their heads off if they returned. He didn't have a gun, but even then he had attitude.

Needless to say, social services bowed out at that point, and Deborah was left with her teenage parents. They returned to Limerick, where they had two more daughters and a son, and got married. But their relationship had its ups and downs. Teresa wasn't happy in Moyross, because of the violence, joyriding and burglaries. On top of that Willie, who worked as a pub and nightclub bouncer, was a bit of a ladies' man, and throughout his marriage he had a string of girlfriends and a series of affairs—but his blonde daughter adored him, and his wife always took him back.

She didn't seem too bothered by his philandering, saying: 'The first affair was around 1990. She was married. My husband started having an affair with her. He was doing that eventually four nights a week for the next few years. I found out about it after two weeks.

'Her husband came home with him from the pub one night. My husband climbed into the bed beside me and said: "Your man is down there wanting to talk to you." I said I had no man, but I got up and went downstairs, and there was this woman's husband. He said: "Do you know your husband is having sex with my wife?" I said: "What do you want me to do about it? I can't control him. You can control your wife. If you can't control her you're obviously not pleasing her. I don't know why you have to come to me. You should be able to sort her out." That was that and he left.'

It was certainly an unconventional way of taking the news. Teresa was equally unconcerned about the next mistress, a woman

Willie met at a disco. For a while Willie kept both mistresses on the go, and still came home to his wife and children.

Her father's affairs, and her mother's acceptance of them, was the norm in the family as Deborah reached her teenage years. The dysfunctional state of her family, and the constant violence that surrounded her in the troubled Moyross estate, left Deborah with no moral compass. Right and wrong were luxuries for the better parts of town: in her world it was all about survival.

Through those years she and Tracey remained firm friends, but they also began to get on the wrong side of the law. Both unemployed, they turned to shoplifting, and were caught. Tracey ended up with two convictions, and did some time in a juvenile centre, as well as being ordered to do community service: at the time of her death she was doing voluntary work at St Martin's Youth Centre on New Road in the city. Deborah also picked up convictions, and in January 1993 was sentenced to fourteen months in Limerick Prison for larceny.

But the events that led up to the murder began much earlier than that, in December 1992. This was when Willie Hannon met yet another woman, Suzanne Reddan, and began a torrid affair that was to lead to his death. Pretty brunette Suzanne, née Meaney, had married at the age of seventeen, and was a mother of three when she first encountered Willie Hannon. Aged twenty-five, she had taken over a small shop in Moyross, where Willie used to get his paper every morning.

The shop was one of the focal points of the community, and often groups of youths would gather outside it. Sometimes the mood of the mob could turn nasty, and customers would be abused by loutish teens. More than once Suzanne herself took the brunt of the abuse. A few times she called the gardaí, but this could be a double-edged sword. By the time a squad car arrived windows could be broken, goods stolen, and the culprits long gone; and the sight of the flashing blue lights served merely to inflame the louts even further.

There was an instant attraction between Willie Hannon and the new shopkeeper. She fell for him quick and hard. He returned her attentions, and began to fight her corner against the youths gathered outside her house. As the infatuation grew, Suzanne plotted her move.

One evening, according to Teresa Hannon, Suzanne called to her house with her mother. 'She called in for a chat, and I didn't know what was happening. Willie was there that evening. I think she just fancied him,' said Teresa. Then she asked me to go swimming with her the following night. I said I couldn't swim, but Willie said he could, so they arranged to go swimming the following evening. I didn't think anything of it, as her mother was there with her.

'The next thing was they were going swimming three nights a week. Then they were swimming every night for hours. Then they were swimming overnight, and he wasn't coming home at all. I realised that it was happening again, and Willie owned up to it. He said it was just another thing he was doing, and he needed to do it. It wouldn't last.'

But Suzanne had different ideas. She left her husband to be with Willie Hannon, and confided to Teresa that she loved Willie and wanted him to move in with her. By then she was living in a council house in Cosgrave Park, just a few houses away from the Hannons.

'You're dreaming. He says that to all the girls. You want to wise up,' Teresa advised her young rival. Remarkably, the wife and the mistress remained on cordial terms. It was an unusual love triangle, and Suzanne was a regular visitor to the Hannon house. She became very close to Deborah, Willie's daughter.

In February 1993 the first of the incidents that sparked the killing occurred at the Savoy Disco, where Willie Hannon worked on the doors. One night a row broke out in the disco between a number of rival families. There are conflicting accounts of what caused the row. Some people maintain it was over the division of the spoils of an alleged crime; others say that Willie was being taunted about his relationship with Suzanne. Teresa Hannon says the cause was a lot simpler—Willie spilled a drink.

'Suddenly the whole place was fighting, with bottles flying and fists being thrown,' she said. 'The whole house went haywire. I locked myself in the ladies' toilet. I could hear the shouts, screams and noises outside.'

Whatever caused the initial fight, there is no doubt that there was some slagging going on, some of it good-natured but some of it more pointed. It stung Willie. He was the security man, and it was his job to throw himself into the fray, which he did with gusto.

'It started when Willie was going to the toilet and he spilled a drink on a girl. She was with a gang who were slagging him and Suzanne Reddan over their affair,' said Teresa.

The girl's boyfriend sprang up and attacked Willie. Suddenly the place erupted.

'It was like the wild west. I never saw anything like it in my life. At some point three guards burst in to the toilet where I was, and then braced themselves against the closed door, keeping people out. They were terrified. I said, "My husband is out there. Get him or he'll die." They said: "We will in our arses go out there again."

'I learned afterwards that some people had hopped over the bar and were helping themselves to free drink while all this fighting was going on. It lasted for over an hour. Then lorry-loads of cops came, some of them in riot gear. There was also a fleet of ambulances. It all calmed down then and we went down to the hospital.'

While Teresa's account may be exaggerated, Willie did need nine stitches that night. His face, neck and body were covered in bruises, but he was a long way short of being the worst casualty. 'He was swollen and puffy. He had been hit in the face from blows of stools. His friend lost the sight in one of his eyes from a broken bottle.'

One of the people who received minor injuries that night was Tracey Butler, who had suffered cuts and bruises when Willie lashed out at her. The assault let to a rapid cooling off between Tracey and her friend Deborah—Tracey resented Deborah for her father's actions.

There was no time to get the friendship back on track, because shortly after the riot Deborah's past caught up with her. She was convicted of larceny and jailed for fourteen months. She was mouthier than her partner in crime, and had a number of previous convictions, including one for assault, when she had turned on a store security guard after being caught shoplifting.

Around this time Tracey began serving a community service order, also for larceny. She was helping out in St Martin's Youth Centre on the New Road.

Tracey Butler was not the only one who fell out with Willie Hannon following the row in the Savoy. A number of people were out to get the thuggish doorman. Gardaí were well aware that a number of people had vowed to get Willie, but the burly weightlifter was a hard man and not too worried. 'Bullets won't kill me,' he joked. He failed to consider what would happen if his enemies chose weapons other than bullets. That's just what happened a few months later.

In the small hours of 2 July 1993, the Hannons' world came crashing down. On the evening of 1 July, Teresa and Willie went out for a drink. While they were out they bumped into Suzanne Reddan, who joined them. Later in the evening, Willie told Teresa that he would be staying with Suzanne that night.

'I said, "You're not doing that—you've stayed with her twice already this week." He said, "Well, I'll walk her home then."'

The three set out for the walk back to Moyross. It was now past 1 a.m. on 2 July, and Willie Hannon's enemies finally caught up with him. He was on the footpath of the main road near his home when a gang, including a number of youths, surrounded and attacked him.

Moyross is more of a ghetto than an estate. One wide road runs through it, on which stand the church and community centre. Off this main road run smaller roads into the parks, including Cosgrove Park, which were composed entirely of corporation houses, generally poorly maintained. The houses were small, often shabby, graffiti was everywhere, and many of the houses had been boarded up after arson attacks. It was quite common for large groups of youths to gather on the small green areas, drinking and causing havoc. If someone had a grudge against you the group might attack your house, breaking the windows or even firebombing it.

That early July morning a number of people were milling around Cosgrave Park and the surrounding estates. Willie Hannon chose the wrong time to walk home from his night on the town with his two women. 'There were at least eight people who jumped us, all with batons, iron bars and planks,' remembers Teresa.

It is not known what sparked the attack, but it is thought that Willie had words with a group of people he passed, and then struck one of the women. A number of people detached themselves from the group and began to chase him. Some were armed, among them Alan Duggan (aged twenty-two), who had a length of wood, Eric Ryan (nineteen), carrying a sewer rod, and John McGrath (eighteen), who had a sheet of plywood.

'I was held down by the hair by another woman and Suzanne Reddan was grabbed as well, but we weren't touched. It was well planned. It was Willie they were after. He was a weightlifter, thirteen stone and tough, but now they were all battering him.'

Willie suddenly found himself surrounded by a crowd of angry armed people who bore a grudge against him. A group of onlookers watched with interest as the men began to beat him with their sticks, but no one intervened on Willie's behalf. He was not a popular man. As he tried to fight his way through to the safety of his own home, only yards away, the blows rained down on him, he was beaten to the footpath and the attack continued.

Teresa says: 'I was let go and I got up and saw Willie lying on one side of the street with his eyes closed. Blood was coming out of his mouth and out of his ear. I panicked then and ran away. I didn't know it was serious.'

The other woman in his life didn't run. Suzanne ran over to her fallen lover. As she bent over his bloody and battered face she heard laughter from the onlookers. Then a voice said: 'We should pick up his fucking gold watch.'

She believed that the speaker was Sharon Butler, and that Sharon was talking to her younger sister, Tracey. Suzanne looked up. There was no trace of sympathy on either of the girls' faces.

'I saw them walking away. They were smirking and laughing as they walked away. I saw Willie's gold watch on the ground and blood coming from his head, and he was lifeless. I heard Sharon Butler say to Tracey to get the fucking gold watch from the ground. They were laughing at me, and Tracey said to let Willie fucking die,' recalls Suzanne.

The Butler family emphatically deny this version of events. They say that Tracey, who was friendly and good-natured, would not have spoken in that way had she been there: but she wasn't even at the scene. They say that while some of the family—including Tracey—were milling around the area at the time of the attack, none of them was part of the mob that surrounded Willie Hannon. They took no part in the attack, and said nothing to provoke Suzanne Reddan's murderous rage.

Willie Hannon was immediately rushed to Limerick Regional Hospital, where he was diagnosed as suffering serious head injuries. Later that morning the hospital released a statement describing his condition as 'critical'. In fact he had suffered a massive brain haemorrhage and was already brain dead.

A call was made to Limerick Prison and Deborah Hannon was granted temporary release, on compassionate grounds, to be with her family. As they gathered around the bedside of the dying man, Deborah brooded on the loss of the father she worshipped, while Suzanne Reddan became consumed with hatred for the two girls who had joked about his watch as he lay bleeding on the ground. On 4 July Willie Hannon passed away.

'Debbie was very upset when her da was killed. She said she was going to kill them all, every one of them. But I never thought it would come to this,' said Teresa, after events reached their tragic conclusion.

Eventually three men were charged with assault causing actual bodily harm in connection with Willie Hannon's death. Alan Duggan and Eric Ryan were jailed for a year and a half, while John McGrath was sentenced to eleven months.

As the Hannons got on with the task of preparing for Willie's funeral, Deborah and Suzanne were inconsolable. The two women were already close, and Willie's death seemed to strengthen the bond between them.

Deborah's temporary release from prison was extended to allow her to stay at home for a few days after the funeral, to help with the grieving process. But she had other things in mind. Suzanne, meanwhile, was beside herself with grief. She had walked out on her husband for Willie, and now Willie was dead. She wanted to hit back at the world.

Expert forensic psychiatrist Dr Brian McCaffrey says that some sort of trigger is needed to turn a normal person into a murderer. The trigger can be a very strong emotion, or something as minor as a word, a phrase or a look, which snaps someone back to an earlier time of strong negative emotion. (In a later chapter we will see how Galway woman Kathleen Bell turned on her lover when he taunted her about her past sexual abuse.)

In the case of Deborah Hannon and Suzanne Reddan there were two triggers. One was their recollection of the callous behaviour of the Butler sisters as Willie Hannon lay dying, which would have affected Suzanne particularly strongly. The other trigger was grief.

'Grief can be a trigger to let things out,' says Dr McCaffrey. 'You will rarely get someone who goes along and severely injures or kills somebody in a non-emotional situation. The only ones you get doing that are your real hardened criminals, who set out to use someone or kill them. All the rest generally happen at a time of highly charged emotion. That's why it is so difficult for someone like me to do an assessment to decide if a case is murder or manslaughter. Did they have the time to form the intent to kill, or did they act under the influence of the trigger?'

Deborah and Suzanne responded to the trigger, but they had clearly formed the intent to kill.

'We planned it all the time, Suzanne and myself,' said Deborah, in a statement a few days later to gardaí. 'We planned to kill Mark or Sharon or Tracey. I blamed them for killing my father. I kept thinking about my father. We planned it after the funeral. I had the Stanley blade and Suzanne had the knife down at Ballynanty.'

Suzanne said: 'Willie's face kept flashing in front of me and I was in a fit of temper.'

On the evening of 11 July both women dressed in black and went out looking for one of the Butlers. They didn't care which one they found—any of the three older siblings would do. They were dressed in black because, as Deborah later said, that is what they had seen on television. They spent the evening prowling up and down roads, laneways and paths in Ballynanty and Kileely, but to no avail. Although they passed several people, they saw no sign of the Butlers, and they reluctantly abandoned their mission for the night.

The evening of 12 July was a warm, balmy summer's evening. Tracey Butler seemed not to have a care in the world as she sat on the wall of her parents' home. She chatted with her mother, then said she was off to a neighbour's house for tea. Her mother nodded her agreement, and told Tracey not to be out late. Tracey said she'd be back early, then crossed the road to the neighbours'.

As good as her word, she was back early, and she spent the evening in the family home with two friends, Paula and Margaret Woodland, who were from Moyross, a good walk from Kileely. The friends chatted away until about 10.30, when they decided it was getting late and they should head home. As it was a pleasant evening, Tracey decided to walk with them, and the three left Tracey's home on Creagh Avenue as darkness fell.

Unknown to her, two other people had crept out a while earlier. Suzanne Reddan and Deborah Hannon had met for the second night running. They were going to find someone tonight, and any one of the Butlers would do. Deborah's younger sister Julie saw them leave the Hannon house, dressed in black, at 10.30 p.m. They were gone an hour and a half, stalking the shadows.

Oblivious, Tracey strolled to Moyross with Paula and Margaret. The walk took half an hour, and when she left her friends in Moyross she turned and began retracing her steps. On her own now, she decided to take a short-cut through Ballynanty Beg via the Monabroher Road, emerging close to Thomond Park. Thomond Park is the spiritual home of Limerick rugby, and one of the city's landmarks. Now it is a magnificent structure that can hold the largest crowds in a stunning setting, but back then it was just another playing field, though with stands able to accommodate quite a large crowd. It faces a busy and well-lit road, the main artery through the city from Galway to Dublin. From there she went to the bottom of Ballynanty Road, where it curves past a green open space to enter the main Kileely Road, beside St Lelia's Church. Tracey knew these roads well, having spent all her life in the area.

After St Lelia's Church she took a sharp left down a footpath running past some bungalows. Now she was nearly home: all she had to do was reach the Kileely Road end of the path, a distance of some fifty yards. There was a wide pedestrian opening in the concrete wall at the end of the pathway, guarded by a safety rail. Once through the opening she just had to cross the main road and walk the last few yards to her home. She was within a few minutes of safety. But she didn't know she was in any danger.

She passed a local man, Paul Sheehan, and nodded a greeting.

It was now around 11.30 p.m., and the path she was on was not well lit. But there were a few people milling around, and this was her neighbourhood; she had nothing to fear. Suddenly two dark figures detached themselves from the shadows. Both were hooded and dressed head to toe in black, but she knew who they were. The distinctive swagger of one was unmistakable—it was Deborah Hannon. Tracey also recognised Suzanne Reddan.

According to Suzanne, when Tracey recognised the two women she began pulling faces at Deborah. Then she started taunting her, saying they had got Willie and that Teresa would be next. It was too much for the grieving women. They tore into Tracey, unleashing all their pent-up fury.

'You are going down like my father did,' shouted Deborah.

It was a savage attack. Both women attempted to drag Tracey to the ground, so that they could carry out their butchery unhindered. They were armed with knives: Suzanne had a kitchen knife, while Deborah had a sharp-bladed Stanley knife. They began to slash and stab at the teenager as they tried to knock her down. Even in the darkness they could see and feel the gouts of blood.

Tracey fought bravely for her life: she would not make it easy for them. Screaming for help, she pushed Suzanne aside and tried to get free of Deborah. But Suzanne came back at her with the knife, plunging it into her body. At one point Suzanne dropped the knife, but she bent to pick it up and continued to stab at her victim. Squirming and ducking in an attempt to evade some of the blows, Tracey managed to stagger to her feet. Her attackers were so intent on hacking and slashing that they were not holding her down firmly enough, and she took her opportunity to flee.

She began to run across the green area towards the bungalows, only yards away. If only she could reach one, she might save herself.

But Deborah and Suzanne were on her heels, and they were fuelled by hate and rage. And they weren't hampered by gaping wounds and pain.

Tracey did not make the bungalow. She half collapsed and they half dragged her to the ground. Not caring that they could be seen, they continued their nasty work, and began to kick Tracey savagely as she lay prone before them. Then Deborah began to slash at her face with the Stanley knife. Suzanne drove the kitchen knife again and again into her chest. One lung was punctured three times. In all Tracey received forty-nine wounds. Whole chunks of her flesh were hacked off.

The attack was as swift as it was savage. Suddenly both assailants straightened up, turned away, and began to jog off into the darkness. Their work was done.

There were a number of witnesses to the attack, but it all happened so fast that no one could react to save Tracey.

Paul Sheehan was convinced he had seen two men carry out the attack. He said he had passed Tracey a few minutes earlier on the path and a few minutes later had heard screams. When he turned at the sound, he saw what he took to be two men attacking the girl. The men were dressed in black from head to toe, and they seemed to be dragging Tracey by the arms. He saw only one of the assailants stabbing her. This was presumably Suzanne, as she had the carving knife: you don't stab with a Stanley blade, you slash— and in the darkness, from a distance, a slashing movement could look like a slap or a punch.

They seemed to be trying to drag Tracey towards a house, he thought. Tracey pushed one of the people aside, but the person she pushed came back and started sticking a knife into her.

She shouted: 'Help! Help!' and then: 'Stop!'

Edward McCarthy was also in the area. He heard someone shouting for help, and saw two people with that person. The two were dressed in black and he could not make them out. One of the two had Tracey by the hair, and the other was coming behind her. 'The one behind her dropped something, then picked it up again. I saw that it was a knife. The person started stabbing the girl, and stabbed her about five or six times,' he said.

He saw Tracey fall to the ground and her two attackers run off. 'I could not say if they were men or women, but when they ran away they jogged like girls,' he said.

Tracey managed to pull herself up and stagger towards one of the cottages. Phyllis Dumas was in bed at the time. She heard someone knocking on her window, and then heard her brother, who shared the house on Ballynanty Road with her, going to the door. A girl fell in. 'She was covered in blood and asked for an ambulance to be called. She said: "I can't breathe,"' said Ms Dumas. Her brother, John Brommell, said that he had also heard the knocking on the window, and a voice calling, 'Somebody help me.'

'I opened the front door and she stumbled into the hallway and fell on the floor. Her face was cut and covered with blood,' he remembered. He phoned for an ambulance immediately, while doing his best to make the girl comfortable. She was complaining that she couldn't breathe, and asked for water.

The ambulance arrived speedily, getting to the bungalow at 11.34 p.m. At 11.40 p.m. Tracey's mother, who lived only a hundred and fifty yards away, was told that her daughter lay bleeding in a nearby house. Tracey was speedily removed to Limerick Regional Hospital. She was still conscious and able to talk a little, despite the punctured lung. But by one o'clock the following morning, less than two hours after the attack, Tracey was dead.

The autopsy revealed that her right lung had been punctured once, and her left lung three times. There were fourteen stab wounds to her neck, back, chest and arms, and thirty-five other injuries, including several cuts to her face and arms. The cause of death was shock and haemorrhage due to collapsed lungs.

She did manage to make a brief statement to gardaí before she slipped away, but this statement was to prove a major red herring in the early hours of the investigation. She said that she had been attacked by two men. Clearly she recognised both of her attackers. Why, in her dying moments, did she conceal their identity? There are a couple of possible explanations: perhaps she was confused and delirious with pain and blood loss; or perhaps she kept their identity secret as a last act of friendship to Deborah. Or perhaps she did not believe she was about to die—she was, after all, in hospital with experienced medics on hand—and she kept silent because she wanted to deal with this situation herself, as soon as she was out of hospital. The code of 'omertà', or silence, is as strong in Limerick as it ever was in the Mafia's Sicilian stronghold: people do not grass on each other in the city, which is why feuds have festered so long there, and claimed so many lives.

Whatever Tracey's reasons, the gardaí did initially work on the assumption that they were looking for two male attackers, and toyed with the idea that Tracey's death was perhaps connected with one of the ongoing feuds.

Meanwhile, Deborah and Suzanne had run from the scene to Deborah's house in Cosgrove Park, quite a distance away. Deborah's sister Julie remembers them arriving home. 'They just ran past me. I followed them into the kitchen and asked them what had happened. They said they had stabbed Tracey Butler,' she said.

They quickly changed out of their bloody clothes, putting them into a plastic bag for disposal. Then they cleaned themselves off. Several members of the household saw them.

Teresa Hannon remembered her daughter and Suzanne leaving the house a few hours earlier, both dressed in dark clothes. It was around midnight when they returned. She heard a knock on the door, then went into the kitchen, where she saw both women taking off their clothes. Their hands were stained scarlet with blood. She saw them put the clothes into a plastic bag, then one of them produced a bloody knife, which also went into a bag. Realising the enormity of what she believed had happened, Teresa became weak and fainted.

Cooler heads in the house took over the clean-up. Suzanne's young brother, Christopher Meaney, was in the house. He had been babysitting for his sister. He took the clothes in the plastic bag, tore them up and burned them; then he took the kitchen knife, snapped it in half, and burned that, obviously in an attempt to burn away the forensic evidence. He then disposed of the knife and the Stanley knife. Detective Con Daly recovered the broken knife in the green on Moyross about six days later. The following day he recovered the Stanley knife in Kinsella's Field, Moyross.

The day following the killing, Limerick woke up to the shocking news that a teenager had been savagely butchered within walking distance of the city centre. Gardaí were looking for two men dressed in black, and were appealing for witnesses.

One who came forward immediately was Deborah Hannon. The brazen killer decided the best way to throw the gardaí off the scent was to come forward openly. She knew that investigators were looking to talk to anyone who knew Tracey, so she went to the Garda station and made a statement, saying that she was a very close friend of the deceased, but had no idea who would want her dead. She did not wait long to make her statement—she was up at the station first thing in the morning after the killing.

She was brazening it out, and so was Suzanne; but right from the beginning the strain began to tell on the older woman. While Deborah had a history with the law, Suzanne had never been in trouble before, and she began taking Valium to calm herself down.

Unknown to either of the two, Deborah's mother was still reeling from the shock of what her daughter had done. Teresa Hannon needed to talk to someone. The day after the killing she approached Detective PJ Barry, a cheerful veteran of the force whom she knew slightly. She told PJ what she had seen the previous evening.

Within twenty-four hours the investigation turned around completely, and detectives were now seeking to build a case against the two women. They worked diligently, recovering the murder weapons and interviewing every possible potential witness.

Tracey's funeral Mass was held on 15 July, two days after her death. The church was packed to the rafters, but one person was noticeable by her absence. Tracey's friend Deborah didn't have the neck to show up at the church, or at the burial afterwards at Mount St Lawrence Cemetery.

After the service, Tracey's devastated mother, Christina, appealed to the general public for help. 'Please, I am begging with you to come to get these that did that,' she said to reporters (including myself) at the funeral.

The gardaí had issued a description of the killers: they were aged between nineteen and twenty-five, dressed in black, and around

5'4" and 5'6" in height. The gardaí said they were keeping an open mind as to whether they were men or women, but local journalists knew they were looking for two women. Within a few days the whole community knew who was behind the savage slaying, and were clearly not happy to have two killers in their midst; so Deborah and Suzanne left Limerick and went to Tipperary, where they stayed with one of Deborah's nine uncles who lived in the county.

But the net was closing, and closing fast. On the morning of 17 July there was a knock on the door of the house in Tipperary. There was a squad car parked outside. Deborah and Suzanne were arrested by Detective Sergeant Daniel Haugh and brought to Henry Street Garda Station in Limerick, where they were questioned for several hours before making statements. Then, at a special evening sitting of the District Court before Judge Michael Reilly, they were charged with murder. The judge knew Deborah well: he had sentenced her for larceny, and now he saw her charged with murder. He remanded both women in custody to await trial.

While they were in custody the two women fared differently. Suzanne was deeply depressed and suicidal, making at least one attempt on her life, and was moved to the Central Mental Hospital for treatment. She was very worried about the future of her children, and concerned for their safety. Threats had been made against her young daughter.

Deborah got on better, quickly settling into prison life. That Christmas she was granted temporary release to spend time with her family over the festive season, on condition that she stay in Tipperary with one of her uncles. It was feared that if she was seen in Limerick she could be killed in a reprisal for Tracey's murder. But Deborah ignored the condition, and spent Christmas in Moyross.

The trial lasted a month, but several days of it were taken up in legal argument in the absence of the jury. The defence wanted certain statements made by both women in interviews with the gardaí excluded from the trial, but they lost this application.

Both women pleaded not guilty to murder. A number of witnesses gave evidence, but neither woman was called into the box. However, the statements they made to the gardaí were read out. These were frighteningly graphic.

Deborah's statement said that after she met Tracey, 'I told her you are going down like my father did. We were holding on to her and I was thinking about my father. She said something about getting my mother next. We grabbed her and were stabbing her. I think I used the Stanley knife on her face.

'Suzanne Reddan and I decided to kill one of the Butlers. I got a Stanley knife from my father's tool box. We were dressed in black, because that is what we see them wearing on television. I was not nervous as I was thinking of my father. We were looking for any one of them to kill them. I didn't care if they died because they did not care if my father died.

'At 11.30 p.m. we met Tracey Butler coming out onto the road. We grabbed her by the arms and pushed her into a wall. She managed to get halfway across the road towards the houses. I kept thinking about my father. I was hitting her with the knife. She kept saying to fuck away, that Mark and Sharon would get my mother. She was crouching. I didn't care if she was dead because we had gone out to kill her.'

Suzanne's statement was also read out. She said that she had been there when Willie Hannon was killed. 'They were laughing at me and Tracey said to let Willie fucking die. I took this very hard. I have been missing Willie and have very bitter feelings towards those involved in killing him.

'Before we left the house I put a knife up my sleeve in case we met anyone. We met Tracey Butler. As we were coming close to one another Tracey began making faces at Deborah. We grabbed her on each side and started fighting with her. She fell on the grass, and I fell too. Then she got up and started running towards the bungalows. She fell and we both started kicking her. I got the knife out of my sleeve and stabbed her in the chest at least once. When I stabbed Tracey I kept thinking about Willie and the night he was attacked, and his face kept flashing before me.'

It was pretty explosive stuff, and it fairly much sealed the fate of the two women. At the end of the prosecution's case, Suzanne's barrister stood up to present his case. Limerick solicitor Shaun Elder had hired a heavyweight: Patrick McEntee was one of the most experienced and wily criminal defenders in the State. He informed the court that he had just three witnesses, including consultant psychologist Dr Art O'Connor, all medical experts who were there to testify as to the psychological condition of Suzanne Reddan at the time of the killing. But the State objected to these witnesses. The jury was sent out, and both sides got down to some intensive legal argument. Mr McEntee argued that grief had thrown Suzanne into a psychological state that mitigated the murder: after her arrest she had suffered depression, had attempted suicide, and had been treated at the Central Mental Hospital. But this was not considered a defence. After hearing both sides Mr Justice Richard Johnston ruled that the medical evidence was inadmissible.

After two hours the jury was called back and the trial resumed. Mr McEntee announced that he had no witnesses to call, and the defence rested. Deborah Hannon was represented by barrister Michael Feehan, instructed by Limerick solicitor Ted McCarthy. He stood and announced that he too had no witnesses. Neither woman offered a defence.

Under the circumstances the verdict was almost a formality, but a formality the jury had to go through. The judge gave them their final instructions, telling them that they had three options: guilty of murder; not guilty of murder; or not guilty of murder but guilty of manslaughter.

'A verdict of not guilty is unlikely in view of the statements we have heard, but it is still open. There is no concept of diminished responsibility in Irish law,' said Judge Johnston.

The jury of six men and six women took six hours to deliberate. When they returned the court was packed to await their verdict, despite the fact that it was almost 9 p.m. The foreman of the jury passed the verdict over to the judge, who read it out. Both women had been found guilty of murder, by a majority verdict.

Suzanne, twenty-six, broke down and fell from her chair in the dock to the floor. She was clearly near the end of her tether, and she had to be assisted from the court. Friends and family were in the courtroom, but there was nothing they could do for her.

The judge said that he was aware that Suzanne had been ill and he would like to ensure that she was looked after and received

proper treatment. He said that Suzanne should remain in the
Central Mental Hospital, where she was receiving treatment, until
she was deemed fit to serve her sentence.

Deborah was alone in the court. Teresa Hannon had attended
some of the earlier days of the trial (she was a witness against her
daughter), but by the end she had stopped coming to the court.
Under the intense strain of the whole experience she had decided
she had to leave Limerick, so she moved her entire family to
England, where she remained for several years. 'Limerick will
always be Stab City to me. I can never go back there,' she said.

Clutching three packs of Benson and Hedges cigarettes, Deborah
was led from the court to begin her life sentence.

But the nastiness was not over. As Suzanne was leaving the court
she heard vicious whisperings. Then someone screamed at her:
'I'm going to get Nicole and I'm going to cut her up.' It was Mark
Butler, and his words chilled Suzanne. Nicole was her daughter,
and not ten years old. Then another voice joined in: 'You whore!
You whore! Nicole's next!' It was Sharon Butler.

The judge, when he heard about the incident, was incensed. He
issued a warrant, and as Sharon and Mark Butler and their aunt
Deirdre Mulqueen stepped off the train in Limerick the following
morning (they had spent the night in Dublin) gardaí were waiting
for them. They were immediately arrested and brought back to
Dublin, where they faced an irate judge.

Suzanne and others told him what had been shouted at her in
the courtroom. Superintendent Liam Quinn, in charge of the
Limerick division, said that there had been continuous threats
made since the murder, and that there had been a very difficult
atmosphere for the past five or six months.

The judge ordered all three to sign a bond to keep the peace for
three years, or face an enquiry 'which could lead to a contempt of
court hearing and jail'. All three agreed to sign the bond, which
ordered them to stay away from the Meaney and Reddan families.

But back in Limerick the bitterness lived on. In the immediate
aftermath of the murder there was remorse and recriminations.

Christine Butler, Tracey's mother, said she wished she had kept
her daughter away from the girl she called a devil. 'She's a devil

from hell, and my Tracey is an angel,' she cried. 'The two will only serve eight years. Is that justice? Pigs in the slaughterhouse don't get a death like they gave my daughter.'

A few miles away, in a quiet neighbourhood, Suzanne Reddan's parents were confused about how their lovely daughter had gone so badly wrong, and, just like Christine Butler, they were eager to push the blame onto Deborah Hannon. 'We still can't understand what happened,' said Rose Meaney, Suzanne's mother. 'All we know for sure is that our daughter is not a murderer. That's a gut feeling we both have. We believe she was set up, probably as revenge for her affair with Willie Hannon.'

Her father, Christy, an electronics engineer on disability following an accident, said: 'I said to her: "Suzanne, tell me if you did it, because we'd rather know." She said: "I was there, but I didn't put a knife into that girl. I swear." We think she's holding something back, there's something she's not telling us. She's obviously terrified of Deborah Hannon. You could see her shaking every time she had to pass her in the court.'

In their first few months in custody the two women reacted differently to their situation. Suzanne Reddan gradually became well enough to be moved from the hospital to the prison, where she gradually adapted well, taking part in drama activities, and getting good reviews for a play she acted in. In letters to her mother and her mother-in-law she expressed her regret at what she had done. In contrast, Deborah Hannon seemed unconcerned about it all and showed no remorse. Deborah also tried her hand at prison drama, and developed an interest in martial arts.

Both women lodged appeals against their convictions, but these were rejected. They served their full time, and are now quietly trying to rebuild their lives.

02 | ALL FOR A DOG
UNA BLACK

Having a baby should be one of the most wonderful experiences in a woman's life. The final months, when the morning sickness is done with and the bundle of joy within you is kicking like a young hopeful auditioning for a role in *Riverdance*, should be a time of hope and contentment. For many women the nesting instinct kicks in as they get ready for the new arrival. The baby room is done up, shops are scoured for pretty pink or blue booties, and lists of names are pored over assiduously.

Una Black missed out on all this. Over eight months pregnant, she stood in the dock on a hot summer day at the end of July 2008. The court had accepted her plea of guilty to the charge of manslaughter, rather than trying her on the more serious charge of murder. The judge's response to her plea would shape her life over the next number of years far more than the growing life within her.

Una Black was accused of killing a man in a senseless act of rage over a provocation so slight you wouldn't raise your voice over it. Murder is normally a male crime—men tend to get drunk and get into fights, and in these days of increasing violence they think nothing of running home and returning with a knife or using a broken bottle or glass to slash at their victim. What was shocking about the Una Black case was that it was a woman who had resorted to these bloody tactics.

John Malone, originally from Tullamore, County Offaly, was a quiet man who lived alone in the Walter Macken flats in Mervue, a working-class area of Galway city. Unemployed, he had lived in the ground floor apartment for ten years. It would be fair to say that John was a troubled individual: he suffered from depression and also battled an alcohol addiction. He was living off disability benefit. To top it all he was estranged from his family—he had not been back to Tullamore in several years, and they had not been to Galway to see him. But they still retained some affection for him. As his sister, Josephine, said: 'He was very bubbly, a good lad. He had his problems too, like us all, but he was a nice chap.'

John had a sixteen-year-old son, but it was several years since he had been with his son's mother, and contact was limited. In many ways it was a lonely existence, living on his own in a small flat in a strange city, but he wasn't a recluse. His flat was on the ground floor of one of the four blocks of towers that make up the Walter Macken complex, situated close to Mervue church.

Una Black also had a troubled background. Now aged twenty-four, she had been sexually abused as a girl; she had a history of psychiatric problems; and, like John Malone, she was an alcohol abuser. There had also been some episodes of depression and self-harm.

For about three years before his death, Una and John had been friends and drinking buddies. They often drank together, and she was a regular visitor to his flat. They were near neighbours; she had grown up on Bishop O'Donnell Road in Galway, and she lived in an apartment in the Walter Macken complex with her boyfriend, Thomas Donohue.

For some reason Una had got it into her head that she was unable to conceive a child, believing that she had a medical condition that rendered her infertile. Although she was only in her early twenties this upset her greatly. She bought a puppy, to which she became very attached, lavishing her love on the animal. But there was a problem: her boyfriend had a daughter from a previous relationship, and she was allergic to the hairs from the dog. The couple could not keep the dog in their flat.

Rather than give up her puppy, Una persuaded her friend and neighbour John Malone to take the animal in. The arrangement was that he would mind the dog, but she would take him out regularly for exercise, and help look after him. That worked, for a while. But in November 2006 Una Black got a dose of the flu. For several days she did not come near John's flat, and she did not take the puppy out for exercise. This began to annoy John Malone.

On the evening of Saturday 2 December, John Malone called in on Una and Thomas. Although there was some tension over the dog, they got on well initially. John stayed for quite a while, and a good deal of alcohol was consumed. During the course of the evening the topic of the dog came up, and John Malone dropped a bombshell. He told Una, to her fury, that he had got fed up with minding the animal, and had sold it for €135. John Malone then returned to his flat.

Una was very upset—perhaps the anti-depressants she was taking reacted with the alcohol, heightening her emotions—and some time later that evening she decided to tackle John about the dog. She believed he still had the dog in his apartment, and she wanted it back.

She left her own apartment and called on her neighbour. It was very late at night, and a lot of alcohol had been drunk. Things got heated, and they fought. Una retreated, but it was only a tactical withdrawal. She returned to her own apartment and got a sharp kitchen knife, then went back to John Malone's flat, determined that she was going to come home with her dog. It was now close to 5.30 a.m. on the morning of 3 December.

She pounded on the door and John came out into the corridor to confront her. But this time Una was ready. She took out the knife and stabbed viciously at John's chest.

The medical evidence later revealed no defensive wounds on John's arms, indicating that he was caught completely unawares. The knife entered deeply, puncturing a lung. John collapsed to the floor, gurgling.

Perhaps belatedly realising the enormity of what she had done, Una Black rang the emergency services. She told the 999 operator that two men had been fighting outside the Walter Macken flats, and one of them had drawn a knife and stabbed the other. An ambulance was quickly on the scene. They found Mr Malone lying face down in a pool of blood. He was taken immediately to Galway University Hospital, where he was pronounced dead at 6.43 a.m. Doctors determined that he had suffered a punctured lung.

The Garda investigation was swift. Una Black's story about seeing two men fight was quickly dismissed, and within hours Una and her boyfriend Thomas Donohue were arrested and brought to Mill Street Garda Station for questioning. Una Black had a scrape to her forearm and her clothes were badly stained, which gardaí thought were consistent with her having been involved in a struggle.

Neighbours were shocked when they woke up on Sunday morning to the news. They all remembered John Malone as a quiet man, but friendly and well-liked. One, Margaret Doyle, complained that when her flat had been broken into while she was ill she had asked for CCTV cameras to be put up in the flats; but the cameras had not appeared.

On Sunday evening the gardaí released Thomas Donohue, but extended Una Black's period of detention. They were not satisfied with her story. Late that evening Garda Paudie O'Shea formally charged Una with assault causing serious harm, to which she made no reply. No charges were ever brought against Thomas Donohue: gardaí were satisfied he had nothing to do with the attack.

The following morning Ms Black appeared before the District Court. She was released on bail, on her own bond of €600 and an independent bond of €3,000. Judge Mary Fahy said that she must live with her mother at Bishop O'Donnell Road, must not interfere in any way with witnesses, and must stay away from the Walter Macken flats.

Later the charge was changed to one of murder. Ms Black's defence team fought hard to have the trial heard in Galway rather than Dublin. The vast majority of serious criminal trials, and all murder trials, were traditionally heard in the Four Courts in Dublin, but there was a huge backlog in the system, and some cases took years to come to trial. In the late nineties, in an effort to alleviate the backlog, the Central Criminal Court began hearing cases outside Dublin. The system was tried on an experimental basis in Limerick, a city which was battling a murderous drugs war, and the experiment worked. Cases came to trial far quicker, and justice was seen to be done swiftly.

However, the system of a mobile Central Criminal Court did get off to a rocky start in Limerick. In January 2003 drug gang boss Kieran Keane and his nephew Owen Tracy were abducted and taken from the city. Keane had his hands tied behind his back, he was tortured, then shot in the back of the head. The gun jammed when it came to Tracy's turn, so his would-be killers took out a knife and stabbed him seventeen times. Miraculously, he survived.

Under the old system it could have taken three or four years for a trial that significant to reach the courts. However, it was decided to move the Central Criminal Court to Limerick to speed up the process, and on 21 October the trial opened—and closed! It proved impossible to swear in a jury in a city where people were terrified of the gangs and their vengeance. But the groundwork for a swift trial had been put in place, and a month later, at Cloverhill Court in Dublin, the five killers were convicted and sentenced to life imprisonment. It was the first time in the history of the State that the Central Criminal Court had sat in a Dublin venue other than the Four Courts.

Now Una Black's legal team were petitioning for the Central Criminal Court to come to Galway. They succeeded in their aim. For only the second time in the history of the State, Galway was going to see a high-profile murder trial.

Just like the Limerick experiment it got off to a difficult start. This time the problem was not with the jury: enough people from the panel showed up to enable the court to pick a jury easily. The problem was that Una Black did not show up.

Ms Black had panicked and run. It turned out that she did not have a medical condition which rendered her infertile: in fact, when the day of her trial loomed she was seven months pregnant, and sporting a very prominent bump. Feeling unable to face the trial in her condition, she did a runner.

On Tuesday 8 April 2008, the Central Criminal Court arrived in the City of the Tribes in all its pomp and splendour. The barristers in their flowing gowns and horsehair wigs, the solicitors in their shiny suits and garish ties, the stern judge, and the panel of people too silly or too curious to evade jury duty, were all gathered in Galway's historic old courthouse. Mr Justice Paul Carney called proceedings to order.

The first business of the day was to empanel a jury. This process is nothing like what you see in American movies. Solicitors have the right to object to potential jurors—and in some cases to object without reason—but in practice they rarely do. It's a relatively easy task to find twelve people willing to give up a week of their time to hear a case.

Once the jury was sworn in, the court hit a snag: Una Black was not in the building. The members of the jury were swiftly removed to a private room in the court building, where they could be kept isolated from what was going on. Mr Justice Carney was being scrupulously fair: he did not want them to know that Ms Black had done a runner, in case it prejudiced them against her.

Once the jury was removed, Detective Superintendent PJ Durkan explained that Ms Black was on bail, and that she had left the jurisdiction. His information was that she had boarded the 9.15 p.m. Rosslare to Fishguard ferry the previous evening. During the next few hours frantic efforts were made to locate Ms Black. Finally, in the afternoon, prosecuting barrister Aileen Donnelly told the court that she had been speaking to Ms Black's legal team, and was assured that Ms Black would return to Ireland by ferry the following day, Wednesday. Mr Justice Carney agreed to put the case back until Thursday morning.

But on Thursday morning Ms Black was still missing. The judge was told that a ticket had been bought in her name, but she had not boarded the ferry. Superintendent Durkan said that he believed she was still in Wales.

At that point Ms Black's mother, Geraldine, interrupted the proceedings. Standing up in the body of the court, she apologised to the judge for her daughter's absence. The judge did not appreciate the interruption. He said that the court had put in place elaborate measures to ensure that jurors would not know what was going on, to avoid prejudicing the trial, and now Ms Black's mother was 'busily feeding them information'. He said that when he had come to Galway everyone had made assumptions about what he was going to do. 'And I do not like that!' he thundered.

He explained to the jury that details had been kept from them and the public so that when Ms Black did return she would receive a fair trial. 'But her mother prejudiced all of that by telling everyone what was going on. We were told she was going to take a boat back but she didn't. She is still in Wales. The Gardaí know where she is.

'I know that the European arrest warrants have been extremely effective in the experience of this court, and this court has had people back within a matter of days on European arrest warrants. Ms Black should be notified that it is known where she is, and that I will entertain a European arrest warrant for her in the morning.'

Looking at Ms Black's mother, he added: 'Her mother frustrated the arrangements put in place by this court, and it is a matter for the Director of Public Prosecutions whether or not any action should be taken against her.' (In the end no action was taken against Geraldine Black.) The jury was discharged. The trial would not be heard in Galway.

Justice Carney decided to give Ms Black one final chance; her defence team were told that if she was not present in court on Friday morning at 11 a.m., he would issue the European arrest warrant. 'Strong representations were made to the court to hold this trial in Galway and the court agreed to that. But now the trial will have to take place in Dublin,' he said.

The following day Ms Black did board the Fishguard ferry, but not in time to make Galway by 11 a.m. Now heavily pregnant, she was arrested and taken into custody when she disembarked at Rosslare, and brought directly before the High Court in Dublin, where she was remanded in custody until her new trial date. Una Black's days at liberty were over.

Her new trial was set for May 26; because of the advanced state of her pregnancy Mr Justice Carney refused to consider a later date.

When the case was called in the Four Courts on Monday 26 May, Una Black pleaded not guilty to the murder of John Malone, but guilty of manslaughter. Prosecuting barrister Aileen Donnelly told the court that this plea was acceptable and Mr Justice Carney put the case back until 28 July for sentencing.

On that morning Ms Black appeared a lonely figure in the dock. Dressed in a white blouse and black trousers, she occasionally patted her stomach almost absent-mindedly. At one point she glanced in the direction of John Malone's sisters, who were in court for the sentencing, and quickly looked away again.

The court was told that while Ms Black had initially denied any involvement in the stabbing, she later told gardaí that she had inflicted the fatal wound during a row, but she did not know how it had happened, and did not intend to kill Mr Malone. She had been drinking alcohol and taking anti-depressants on the night in question.

She initially told gardaí that Mr Malone had pulled out a knife, but later agreed that it was she who had taken a knife to the scene during her second attempt to get her dog. 'I knew he would come at me, and I wanted him to keep away and to scare him. We struggled and I stabbed him. I can't understand how it happened,' she said.

Defence barrister Diarmaid McGuinness said that Ms Black deeply regretted her actions. He read a letter from her in which she said she was truly sorry and ashamed, and 'wished to God she could take it back'.

She had no previous convictions and had never been in trouble before, though she had a history of psychological problems.

A plea was made for lenience because of Ms Black's pregnancy, but the judge was having none of it. 'I have to have regard to the senseless reason for which Mr Malone died. This crime is at the top end of the scale of gravity, because Ms Black had equipped herself with a knife before she visited Mr Malone,' he said, adding that the voluntary consumption of alcohol and drugs does not diminish criminal responsibility, nor does it mitigate a defendant's responsibility to society. He also said that the dysfunctional nature of Ms Black's background was of 'minimal importance' in this case.

Ms Black showed no reaction when he said that the case merited a twelve-year sentence, but he reduced this to nine years because of the guilty plea, and because Ms Black had never been in trouble before.

Mr Malone's family welcomed the sentence. His sister Josephine said it had been a difficult time for the family. 'I suppose we have been offered a sentence, but at the end of the day it won't bring our brother back.' She said that the family had not seen John for a few years before his death, 'And we didn't think when we did see him we'd be bringing him home in a coffin, so it's sad.' John's eighteen-year-old son Jonathan said that he felt 'destroyed' by the killing of his father. 'He didn't deserve to get what he did. He was a loving person and he'd do anything for you.'

Ms Black was removed from the court to begin her sentence in the Dochas Centre, the women's unit at Mountjoy Prison, where, in contrast to the men's prison, the prisoners live in relative comfort. They are housed in apartment-like settings rather than cells, and have washing and cooking facilities. There are nurses and a qualified midwife at the centre, so they were well prepared to cater for a heavily pregnant prisoner.

Within days of her incarceration Ms Black's mother spoke on the radio, denying claims that her daughter had got pregnant to gain sympathy during her trial. If that had been the plan, it had misfired spectacularly.

On Monday 1 September Una Black went into labour, and was removed to the Rotunda Hospital, where she gave birth to a healthy girl, whom she named Nicole. A few days later she was back in the Dochas unit. The centre has a fully equipped crèche, and Ms Black is not the only mother there. In fact, two other convicts had given birth inside the prison that year: in June a Venezuelan woman had given birth to a girl; and six months previously a Cork woman had had a baby daughter. The most famous prison mum was Charlotte Mulhall, the 'Scissors Sister', who had briefly taken care of her infant boy there when she began her life sentence for the murder of Farah Swaleh Noor.

Under prison rules Ms Black will be allowed to look after her baby for only twelve months, after which time the child will be removed from the prison, to be cared for by a family member. Her mother Geraldine has said that she will care for her granddaughter when the time comes to separate her from her mother. 'When the child is taken from Una she knows that I'll be there with her every day. And Una knows I will bring Nicole up to the prison every day,' Geraldine Black said. 'At the end of the day she is still her mother, and that's the way I look at it.'

Looking at Una Black's wasted life, and the tragic death of John Malone, it all seems such a high price to pay for something as trivial as a row over a puppy. Geraldine Black had a terrible burden to bear. It is tragic for a mother to see a daughter jailed, but Geraldine was living through the nightmare for the second time that year. Geraldine's other daughter, Nicola, aged twenty-three, had been convicted in April 2008 of trying to smuggle two kilos of cocaine from South America to Amsterdam. She is currently doing two years in a tough high-security prison in Suriname.

03 | LIKE MOTHER, LIKE DAUGHTER

KELLY NOBLE

The Spanish philosopher George Santayana warned us that those of us who cannot remember the past are condemned to repeat it. American industrialist Henry Ford, equally famously, said that history is bunk. When we look at the tragic case of teen killer Kelly Noble we have to concede that while Ford was a dab hand at making money, he knew damn all about history and its implications.

In many ways the story of Kelly is one of the saddest in this book. Her background was as dysfunctional as they come. She was the daughter of two heroin abusers, and her father was a monster who had his daughter smoking cannabis when she was still in primary school. Her mother killed her father in a vicious attack, and was then jailed, leaving young Kelly on her own.

She tried to make a new life for herself, but became a mother when she was still in her teens. Then she drew the attention of the town bully. On the day she finally snapped and drove a kitchen knife into the chest of her tormentor she hadn't set out to do harm to anyone: she was doing her shopping, accompanied by her two toddlers. She was attacked, but went a giant step too far in defending herself.

Everything about Kelly Noble screams tragedy. But to tell her story properly we must tell the story of her mother, Jacqui Noble, and of Kelly's upbringing.

Kelly Noble's parents were both heroin abusers, and her father, Derek Benson, was a career criminal and drug dealer. They had Kelly when they were both just twenty-one and living in a flat in Sandyhill Avenue, Ballymun. In the eighties and early nineties Ballymun was a hellhole, with rampant vandalism, violence and drug abuse. The Dunne family made Ballymun the centre of their heroin empire before the gardaí cracked down on them. The flats, now gone, were among the worst slums in Ireland.

Derek Benson was the sort of man who gave Ballymun its reputation. He was extremely violent and abusive, and made life for his young family a living hell. A neighbour, Ms Claire Keely, remembered Jacqui telling her that Benson had hit her with a plank because she had not cooked him his breakfast. 'The first time I met Jacqui her hand was badly swollen. She said she did not get up to make Derek's breakfast that morning, and he hit her with a plank.' Assaults were commonplace. 'One day she ran into my flat, followed by Derek. He ran after her into my bedroom. He was killing her. He was beating her and kicking her while she was on the ground,' said Ms Keely. Like all the neighbours, she knew that Derek was dealing drugs. She was not surprised when Jacqui got a barring order against him.

Jacqui had met Benson when she was just sixteen, and they began going out, though even then his violence was a problem. Within six months Benson was beating his young girlfriend. 'I was sixteen when he gave me a kick into the face at Hallowe'en. He busted my eye,' said Jacqui.

Shortly afterwards she became pregnant, but her mother persuaded her to have an abortion. Her parents wanted her to keep away from her increasingly violent and unhinged boyfriend, but the couple stayed together. Jacqui became pregnant again, and had a daughter, Kelly, when she was twenty-one. At the christening Benson became very drunk, and went berserk. He smashed windows in her parents' house, then attacked Jacqui's father, biting him viciously on the back. 'To the day he died he had two bite marks on his back,' Jacqui said. He also attacked the family dog, cruelly kicking the defenceless animal. On another occasion Benson 'split my eye open because his stew was not right on the plate'.

Benson, like many violent men, knew how to inflict a beating without leaving obvious marks. He was a master of the body punch, often hitting or kicking Jacqui in the ribs or on the back, where the marks would not show. He also took great pleasure in acting out his sadistic sexual fantasies on the mother of his young child. Jacqui was frequently tied to the chair or bed and forced to engage in oral or anal sex.

Over the next number of years Jacqui got pregnant three more times, but each time had an abortion: she did not want to have another child with Benson because of his violence. She frequently sought refuge with family or friends when the beatings became too much for her, but fear of Benson always brought her back.

Benson's violent attacks were not restricted to his wife; he also beat his young daughter. Kelly grew up in a house where violence was the norm. She saw her mother being beaten regularly, yet she still idolised her father—even when he turned on her, she was devoted to him. But her crazy home life was affecting her developing personality. She was just six when her school principal contacted Jacqui about her behaviour.

Kelly was brought to St Claire's Unit at Temple Street Hospital in 1993 for assessment, and evidence was found that she was being sexually abused. A complaint was made to the gardaí, but the young child withdrew her complaint, allegedly after Benson 'got at her'.

By the time she was eight she was smoking cannabis, under his direction. He had also trained her to inject him with heroin. Occasionally, as she got older, he made her take part in his dealing activities. He also beat her. Jacqui caught him once, when Kelly was only seven or eight, kicking and punching his daughter in her bedroom. The gardaí were called and he was removed, but he was back in the flat the following morning, and life resumed as if nothing had happened.

Jacqui received hospital treatment more than once for injuries consistent with beatings, including fractured ribs and extensive bruising. In 1997, when Kelly was nine, her mum secured a barring order against Benson, but he breached it. As he entered Jacqui's flat, shouting abuse at her, he was arrested by Garda Sinead Magee, who brought him before the district court. He was released on bail. As he was being brought to the custody office of the court to sign the bail bond he turned to the garda and said: 'I guarantee you I'll be in Jacqui Noble's flat tonight and she won't be making a complaint.'

He was immediately returned to the court, where bail was revoked. Reacting with fury, Benson 'swung around and hit me in an effort to knock me down the stairs,' said Garda Magee.

For this assault he received a six-month sentence, but on his release he was back to torment his family. It is no wonder that Kelly Noble's life was a mess. By the age of thirteen, according to her mother, she was well under the control of her domineering father. As Kelly entered her teenage years, Jacqui began to suspect that Benson was sexually abusing her again. She claimed that Kelly 'often slept in the same bed as her father'. Around this time Kelly was diagnosed with attention deficit disorder.

'Derek allowed Kelly to drink alcohol and smoke hash, and also showed her how to inject heroin. He had her going out selling rips,' said Jacqui. 'I tried to leave him lots of times, but he always told me that if I left he'd find me anywhere and he'd cut Kelly up in front of me, and he'd cut me up,' she added.

Over the course of her relationship with Benson, Jacqui had been beaten regularly, raped, and was hospitalised at least twice. Now she could see the same fate in store for her daughter. She had had enough, and when her parents, who had been her refuge during the worst times of her life, died, she was cast even further adrift. But they did leave her their house at Knowth Court, Ballymun. It was a small inheritance, but enough to give Jacqui the breathing space she needed. She moved out of the flat she shared with Benson, and she and Kelly began planning their new life together. Kelly was still seeing her father, but at least they had escaped from the family home.

But it was not so easy to get away from the violent drug dealer. Benson felt that part of Jacqui's inheritance was due to him, as

Jacqui's partner, and he demanded his share, so that he could buy a flat and get a motorbike. Matters were coming to a head, and his insistence on a portion of the inheritance was driving his former partner to distraction. She could see only one way out; so she approached a man she knew.

Paul Hopkins was a twenty-one-year-old doorman in a Drumcondra pub. He had a reputation locally as a hard man, and he had reason to dislike Derek Benson—over the previous four years Benson had threatened, bullied and assaulted him on a number of occasions. When Benson threatened Hopkins's girlfriend and baby daughter that he would burn them after he was 'finished with them', Hopkins took this as a threat. He believed that Benson intended to rape his girlfriend.

When Jacqui Noble approached him on Thursday 11 May 2000, he was ripe for action. She knew him well, and thought he was the man for the job. She asked him to kill Derek, for a fee of between £3,000 and £5,000, and gave him a deposit of £200.

Hopkins used £50 to purchase a sword from his brother, and he bought some sleeping pills and a mobile phone. He had a simple plan in mind. Jacqui would visit Benson in his flat, and slip him the sleeping pills. She would wait until they took effect, then phone Hopkins, who would come in with his sword and finish off the sleeping man.

The following evening they put the plan into operation. Jacqui went to Benson's flat, and during the course of the evening she slipped him the sleeping pills. Her task was made easier by the fact that Benson had undergone dental surgery that day, after which he had taken painkillers, and followed them with cannabis. The combination of the three drugs knocked him out. Sometime before 3 a.m. on Saturday 13 May, she used the new phone to contact Hopkins. He arrived carrying a bag containing the sword. She let him in, then slipped away. Hopkins approached the sleeping figure on the bed, quietly removed the sword, and raised it over his head . . .

The murder was brutal. Benson woke and put up a savage struggle for his life, fighting tooth and nail against his sword-wielding attacker. The extensive defensive wounds on his forearms and hands showed the extent of the struggle: they were deep wounds, deep enough to sever multiple muscle tendons. But it was a losing battle. He fell under a number of stabbing and hacking wounds to his body.

State Pathologist Dr Marie Cassidy later testified that Benson had been the victim of a 'sustained and vicious' assault in which he was stabbed twenty-five times. Some of the wounds went right through his body, entering the stomach or chest and exiting through the back, and a number of times he was literally impaled on the sword. In addition, he sustained sixty cutting or incised wounds in the frenzied attack. 'These wounds extended from his head to his toes,' Dr Cassidy said. Seventeen of the wounds were to the head and neck alone. One, particularly horrific, was a gaping wound to the neck which went through to the cervical spine. Dr Cassidy thought this 'slicing or hacking injury' was an attempt to decapitate the victim. The direction of some of the thrusts indicated that Benson was on the ground at one stage of the assault, with his attacker raining down blow after blow with the sword. 'The cause of death was multiple stab, incised and cutting injuries to the head, trunk and limbs,' she said.

When he was satisfied with his bloody work Hopkins tried to set fire to the apartment, then ran from the scene of carnage. He must have been exhausted from his efforts. At one point he staggered and put his hands on the wall of the flat complex stairwell as he ran from the scene. Investigators found the bloody handprint later that day.

The attack had not gone according to plan. Benson should have been quietly dispatched in his sleep, but the struggle he had put up had alerted neighbours. One, Claire Keely, said she heard screams coming from her neighbours' flat at 3 a.m. 'I heard someone— I think it was Derek Benson—say "For God's sake", or "For fuck's sake". I saw smoke and fire coming from the flat.' She immediately dialled the emergency services and asked for the fire brigade. She also rang Jacqui Noble to tell her that the flat she shared with Benson was on fire. It was news that did not surprise Ms Noble.

When the fire brigade arrived Derek Benson was, miraculously, still alive. Despite being stabbed clean through a number of times, and having his head almost severed, he was still breathing when the firefighters broke into the flat; but he died on the way to hospital.

Gardaí initially concluded from the savagery of the attack and the attempt to destroy evidence by fire that this was a gangland hit. Only a short time previously three Ennis men had been tortured and shot in an apartment in Scheveningen, Holland, and the apartment doused in petrol and torched. That attack was over a drug deal that had gone wrong, and gardaí wondered if the Ballymun incident was something similar. They were unsure if the setting of fires in the apartment was an attempt to destroy forensic evidence, or if it was an act of premeditated violence aimed at sending out a threatening message to rival criminals.

The newspapers accepted the gangland hit theory. Benson was a known drug dealer who also had convictions for burglary. The *Irish Times* reported: 'The murder of Mr Benson brings the number of unsolved gangland murders in Dublin during the past twenty months to eighteen. Most of these were as a result of inter-gang rivalry, but at least two are believed to have been carried out by the IRA.'

A sixty-strong team of investigators was put in place, and there were door-to-door interviews and a frantic search for the murder weapon, which was initially believed to be a twelve-inch knife. Swords are almost unheard of as murder weapons. But it didn't take long for gardaí to realise this was a far simpler case, and within a week Paul Hopkins, aged twenty-one, of Sillogue Road, Ballymun, was in custody. The murder weapon had been recovered and was in the hands of the Garda Technical Bureau. A few days later Jacqui Noble was arrested and charged with murder.

It took nearly four years for the case to come to trial. Jacqui and Kelly moved to a council house in Laytown, County Meath, a small seaside village about two miles off the main Dublin to Belfast road and a few miles north of Balbriggan—a far cry from the flats at Ballymun.

The trial opened in January 2004, and both Jacqui Noble and Paul Hopkins pleaded not guilty. Jacqui said that she had not hired Hopkins to kill her partner, while Hopkins claimed that he had only intended to frighten Benson, but that his victim had woken up and was killed in the ensuing struggle.

'I intended to scare him. I poked him and he jumped up from the bed. As we struggled the sword fell on the floor. He picked it up and swung it at me. My fingers got cut, and I lost control. I think I went into like a frenzied attack. I just started swinging. Afterwards I felt sick and scared,' said Hopkins.

On the witness stand Jacqui denied giving Hopkins money to carry out the killing. She said she gave him £200 because he wanted to buy a bike to get to work.

'Did you want to see Derek Benson dead?' she was asked.

'Yeah and no.'

'Did you see any other way of living with your daughter?'

'No,' she replied.

Closing the case, the prosecuting barrister, Tom O'Connell, said that Jacqui's inheritance, which Benson wanted to get his hands on, precipitated the killing, 'although she had contemplated killing him for some time,' he pointed out. 'There is no defence in this case. Evidence that Ms Noble had a dog's life at the hands of Derek Benson is no justification for getting him killed.' He also said that self-defence was not an issue: 'On this night there was no attack on Ms Noble. The killing was coldly planned two days beforehand.'

Barrister Isobel Kennedy, representing Paul Hopkins, disagreed. 'That is absolutely absurd. The defence of self-defence is clearly open to Mr Hopkins. He did not go to the flat with the intention of killing the deceased, but to frighten him. You have heard that the accused was afraid of Mr Benson. The deceased had threatened to burn his girlfriend and baby daughter.'

She said that Benson should not have been killed, but she reminded the jury to look at the character of Benson and that of Hopkins, who until now had never been in trouble with the gardaí, who described him as a 'decent fellow from a decent family'.

Jacqui Kelly's defence team, led by barrister Mary Ellen Ring, tried to have the evidence about her fourteen years of abuse at the hands of Benson taken into account, but the judge, Mr Justice Henry Abbott, would not allow this. At the time he was acting within the law. There was at that time no defence of diminished responsibility available under Irish law because the law relating to diminished responsibility had not been updated since before the formation of the State.

For many years the law relating to insanity in Ireland was a bit of a jumble, and the relevant law was the quaintly named Trial of Lunatics Act 1883. Back then, Sigmund Freud was still a student, and Carl Jung was still in short pants. While some sympathy was shown to those suffering mental defects, it was sympathy of a Victorian nature, rather than the gentler approach of more modern times. For instance, an 'insane' person could still be found guilty as charged—the official verdict was 'guilty but insane'. This changed in 2006, with the passing of the Criminal Justice (Insanity) Act, and now the relevant verdict is 'not guilty by reason of insanity'. It might appear to be a small change, but it indicates a vast shift in perception. However, the end result is the same: detention in the Central Mental Hospital in Dundrum, Dublin.

But there is one other significant change; the mental state of the accused prior to a crime can now be taken into account. It is open to a jury to find that a person is guilty of a killing, but that their state of mind somewhat mitigates that guilt. Under those circumstances the charge is reduced to manslaughter, in which case the mandatory life sentence for murder no longer applies, and a judge may impose a lesser sentence.

Under the new legislation Jacqui might well have been convicted of manslaughter: but the trial was conducted under the old legislation, and the judge ruled that psychiatric and psychological evidence was inadmissible. He also ruled out the defence of provocation.

The jury of seven men and five women took seven hours to return a verdict, finding both Noble and Hopkins guilty of murder. Judge Abbott sentenced them both to life imprisonment. There were tearful scenes as he passed sentence: two women jurors cried openly, while two of the men were visibly upset as the verdict was read out. Jacqui also cried, while her relations, neighbours, and Hopkins's family sobbed at the back of the court.

Meanwhile Jacqui's daughter, Kelly, did her best to get on with her life. Her abusive father was gone from her life, but so was her mother, her rock of support, and she was in foster care in a strange town. Although she had been devoted to her dad, she came to terms with what had happened, revealing on RTÉ radio's popular *Liveline* phone-in show, 'My mother got done for murder, life without bail. My father that she killed, Derek Benson, he was an animal basically. He didn't treat either of us with respect. He basically made our lives hell. He had me selling drugs when I was thirteen, and he had me smoking hash when I was eight and nine. She killed him for me, basically. She was serving life with him, and now she's serving life without him.'

Kelly confirmed the account her mother had given to the court of the abuse Benson had put her through. 'He bashed me loads of times as well. Like, I was eight years of age and I was slagging this girl over something, and he gave me three minutes to get home. Then he broke a tennis racket over my chin, and I had to go to hospital and get eight stitches in my chin. I could hear him killing my ma all the time in the next bedroom and I'd lie there with my hands over my ears praying to God that he'd stop.

'If he was still alive now I'd probably be out selling drugs. I'd probably be a prostitute. God only knows what I would be. I'm actually glad my father is dead. My mother looks ten years younger behind bars, because she's free of him.'

By the time she was nineteen Kelly had managed to establish some sort of a life for herself. She was living in a council house in Seaview, Laytown, a single mother of two toddlers, Jasmine and Leon, and she seemed to be successfully battling a four-year drug addiction. But it was hard to leave her troubled life behind her, and she did have a cavalier attitude to the law, as well as a propensity for attracting trouble.

For instance, on 12 March 2006, Kelly needed to get into nearby Dublin. Her own car had been seized by the gardaí and was being held in Dublin, so Kelly stole a car from a house at the Rise, Inse Bay, Laytown. She was stopped and found to have no licence and no insurance.

But she wasn't the only troubled young woman in Laytown. Emma McLoughlin was also nineteen, and also a mother of two young children. And she had taken a violent dislike to Kelly, which, it is fair to say, was entirely mutual. Whatever sparked it, the two had clashed on a number of occasions, and since Laytown is a small place with a small teenage population, it was inevitable that they could not avoid each other.

Emma McLoughlin was a local girl, and while she did not have the chaotic background of her nemesis, she was every bit as difficult and trouble-prone. She suffered from attention deficit hyperactivity disorder and even in primary school she was a handful. She went to the local schools, entering Scoil an Spioraid Naoimh in Laytown in third class, but by the time she was eleven, the school had had enough of her. The previous year, when she was ten, the school had requested an assessment of the troubled girl, but this did not happen for a further three years.

School principal Maurice Daly, an experienced educator, said that in October 1998, not long into that school year, he wrote a letter to the school's board of management which stated that the safety of pupils and staff in the school could not be guaranteed as long as Emma McLoughlin remained a pupil. The letter was sent after one complaint too many, when Emma was just eleven. She then wrote to the school asking for another chance and apologising for her behaviour, saying that every time she got into trouble she did not 'feel the pain that you do'. Mr Daly said that she had also written to the mother of a child in the school to apologise for hitting him in the PE hall. She had asked to meet face to face to offer the apology in person.

That's a lot of trouble for a primary school kid to be in, and things only became worse as Emma got older. She hung out with other teens, drinking and smoking, ignored her studies, was pregnant at sixteen, had two children while still in her teens, and was often in trouble with the law. To top it all, she had violent tendencies.

After her death her family tried to downplay her troubled history, but the facts speak for themselves. In June 2005 Emma's young sister Shona, two years her junior, made a statement to the gardaí describing how her sister had broken her jaw and knocked her unconscious in a row over a mobile phone. Shona said that she had feared that her sister, who had been kicking her in the face, would kill her. When she regained consciousness she was in hospital and was told her brain was swollen and her jaw broken. She subsequently withdrew her complaint.

But Emma was well known to the gardaí. They were aware that she had once tried to attack Kelly Noble with a hammer. She had accused the Dublin girl of kicking her when she was pregnant at sixteen. There was also an allegation of an assault on a twelve-year-old neighbour, and a seven-year-old child. At the time of her death, charges against Emma were going through the courts, and she had been ordered to attend an anger management course.

However, the teenager was trying to fight her demons. She had begun an early school leavers' programme, and was also attending counselling. But as the events of 2 June 2006 would prove, she had not managed to bring her temper under control. As school principal Maurice Daly explained, her attention deficit hyperactivity disorder meant that she was prone to explode like a volcano one moment, then be perfectly calm the next.

What happened that warm, sunny June evening would throw a shocking light on the secret world of teenagers. The evidence to emerge would 'paint a picture of teenage lives out of control in a sea of drink, drugs and violence, of a world where binge drinking in a field seemed the pleasant option on a sunny summer's afternoon, and of a child predestined to self-destruct where early intervention might have saved her,' as the *Irish Times* put it.

That evening, 2 June 2006, was a normal enough evening in the pleasant seaside village. Kelly was at home with her two children and a friend, Niamh Cullen, who often lent a hand with the children, minding them if Kelly needed to go out. A little before 9 p.m. Kelly asked her friend to look after her elder child, Jasmine, who was then four, while she went to the shop. She put little Leon in his buggy and walked out to Pat's supermarket, at Ninch in the village. Pat's is a substantial supermarket, where you can pick up most of what you need. Kelly just wanted a few odds and ends: milk for the kids and cigarettes for herself. She entered the shop and began walking the aisles, picking out the few things she needed. But she had been spotted going in. Emma McLoughlin had been hanging around outside, and followed Kelly into the shop. She confronted the young mother and began shouting loudly at her. There were three assistants working in the shop that evening, and they all saw Emma approach Kelly and shout at her.

Loren Boshell said that he had seen Kelly come into the shop at around ten past nine, with her young son in a buggy. A few minutes later he saw Emma come into the shop, and an argument seemed to flare up between the two women. 'Emma was saying to Kelly: "Why did you kick me in the stomach when I was pregnant?"' he said, adding that it was a one-line argument, and that Emma kept repeating the same allegation.

His brother, William Boshell, tried to intervene between the two women. Kelly seemed quite calm, but Emma was 'irritable' and he thought she had been drinking. As William separated the two women Emma suddenly swung her arm out and lashed out at Kelly, catching her cleanly in the face with the punch. To the staff in the shop it was obvious which of the two young women was the aggressor.

'Kelly was just like any other mother with a buggy, getting her groceries and going about her business, when she came under a sustained verbal onslaught from Emma McLoughlin,' said Mr Boshell. He added that the shop staff asked Emma to leave.

William Boshell said that Emma appeared to be 'on a bit of a high' when she confronted Kelly in the shop. 'She wanted an answer, and she was hell-bent on getting it,' as he put it. Separating the two, he told them to forget about what had happened in the past—any alleged kicking had been three years previously.

His shift was nearly over, and after asking Emma to leave, he got ready to go himself. He thought the situation had calmed down, but as he drove away from the shop he could see that the row had flared up again on the street outside, he told the court.

Nineteen-year-old Deborah Cantwell, who was working in Pat's supermarket on the night, also observed the row: 'Emma just kept saying: "Why did you kick me when I was pregnant?"' She noticed at one point that Kelly's lip was bleeding, but she did not see the punch that caused it. She and her boss asked Emma to leave. Kelly was dabbing her lip with a tissue, and Deborah overheard her talking on her mobile phone. 'I heard her asking for a blade or something,' she said. Kelly was in a bad mood after the confrontation, and she told the young shop assistant that she was 'going to slice her up'.

A few minutes later Niamh Cullen arrived, accompanied by Kelly's daughter, Jasmine. Niamh had been in Kelly's house minding the child when she got the call from her friend. Although the line was bad, she could make out that Kelly was telling her that Emma had attacked her, and that she was afraid she was going to get a beating if she left the shop.

'She asked me to bring a knife down to Pat's shop and to come down and collect the children. I grabbed a knife, put it into a small school bag, and hurried down to the shop,' she said. It didn't take her long; the shop was just around the corner from where Kelly lived.

When she got there a group of children were gathered outside. They told her not to go in because there had been a fight and Kelly had been punched in the face. Niamh entered the shop, carrying the school bag, and found Kelly by the counter, holding a tissue to her face, which was bleeding. Kelly asked had she brought the knife and Niamh opened the school bag, showing her a sharp kitchen knife. Kelly took the knife, shoved it up her sleeve, and put the bag on the back of the buggy. Niamh assumed she was just going to use the knife to frighten off Emma and her friends. At that point that was probably Kelly's intention.

A young boy who had spent the day drinking in the sandy dunes was in the shop that evening and he saw the fight between the two women. After Emma had left he saw Niamh arrive and hand something over to Kelly. 'I heard Kelly say to the woman: "Give me the knife." They were just inside the door of the shop at the time,' he said. Hearing this troubled him, and he left the shop to find Emma. He went up the road to where she was standing, and the young woman told him that she had just 'boxed Kelly on the nose'. He told her that Kelly had asked for a knife, and advised her to 'leave it out'. He knew Emma was a headstrong person and not the type to listen to advice, so he wasn't surprised a few minutes later to see her squaring up to Kelly outside the shop.

Emma was waiting for Kelly when she left the supermarket with her friend Niamh. 'We left the shop and turned left, but Emma approached us. She had Kelly, not pinned, but was in front of her stopping her from moving away from the window. Kelly and Emma started shouting at each other, and the children started to cry,' Niamh said.

Kelly herself said that Emma was shouting at her, saying: 'Fight me now. Now I'm not pregnant.'

Fearing that she was about to 'have the head kicked off me', she allowed the knife to slip from her sleeve into her hand.

Emma's younger sister Shona came over to Niamh and said that she was not going to get involved. (At that point she had not noticed the knife.) Niamh said that neither was she. She said that Shona was trying to comfort Kelly's son, but little Leon did not like strangers and was becoming more upset. 'I was trying to get the children to calm down and not be looking at the two women,' she said.

The next thing she was aware of was a loud thud, then Kelly pushed past her, taking the buggy with her. Niamh grabbed four-year-old Jasmine and followed. 'I turned around to see if anyone was following us, and I saw Emma lying on the ground,' she said.

Kelly's account of those fatal few seconds is that she had the knife up her sleeve and her hands behind her back. 'Emma went for me. She was saying: "Fight me. Now I'm not pregnant." I heard Shona telling her that I had a knife and to get away, but she just went for me. Emma said: "Do you think I'm scared of a knife, do you?" and came at me and said: "What the fuck, are you afraid of me?" I said "Keep away from me," but she just lunged at me, and the knife stuck in her. I didn't want to kill her. I just wanted her to run away. It was self-defence, big time.' Kelly added that her daughter was terrified of Emma because she had seen her coming at her mother with a hammer in the past.

Shona's account of the altercation is slightly different. She had been drinking with Emma that evening, and they had gone to the shop to get more drink, and to buy crisps. She saw the two women arguing. 'They were rowing for a while, and Emma was saying: "Why did you hit me in the train station?" Then Emma hit Kelly, and Kelly pushed her,' she said.

The row continued when Kelly came out of the shop. 'She was saying to Emma: "Hit me!" but she said no, she didn't want to fight any more. She rang my da and said we were going home. But then I seen Emma get stabbed. I seen Kelly stabbing Emma. When she took the knife out it was full of blood and I knew she was after stabbing Emma.'

As Emma hit the ground Kelly pulled out the blade, glowing crimson in the late evening sun, and ran from the scene.

The accounts of the eyewitnesses vary slightly, but one thing is consistent. Emma was stabbed once in the chest by Kelly. It was a deep wound; the blade sank eight inches into Emma's chest, puncturing a lung. She collapsed onto her stomach on the ground.

Not far up the road Kelly saw a car. Her second cousin's partner Miriam Phelan was at the wheel; she was leaving the Seaview Estate on her way to work. Kelly stepped in front of her and flagged her down. 'She said, "I've done something terrible,"' said Ms Phelan. 'I asked her what, and she said she had stabbed Emma McLoughlin. She said that she thought she had killed her or something like that. She was very shaken by it. She looked very distressed.' Ms Phelan asked Kelly where she had got the knife: 'She said she sent her friend to get the knife for her.'

Later that night, around an hour after the incident, Edel McLoughlin, another sister of the victim, rang Kelly on her mobile. 'I asked her why she had stabbed my sister. She said that she had sorted it out. I said my sister was lying dead in hospital, and she said "She deserved it,"' said the tearful teenager.

It was a simple open and shut case for the gardaí: there were several eyewitnesses; and Kelly did not deny that she had struck the fatal blow. Initially she maintained that Emma had produced the knife, but she later came clean, admitting that she had asked Niamh Cullen to bring the knife for her. But she maintained from the beginning that it was self-defence.

When the case came for trial Kelly pleaded not guilty to murder, but guilty to manslaughter. The court did not accept this plea, so the trial went ahead. Kelly cut a lonely figure in court. Her father was dead, her mother was in jail, and she had no one with her. In contrast, the McLoughlins showed up in force every day. The family were devastated at the loss of their daughter, describing her death as leaving a hole that could not be filled. The victim's mother did not attend the court; she had been too ill since the murder. Emma's two young children had been taken into care, as had Kelly's children, though she had regular contact with them.

Kelly told the court that she regretted the killing, and that she wished she could turn back the clock. 'I very much regret it—I did not mean to kill her. No way. I just went to the shop to get milk for my kids,' she said. 'I have more than remorse. If I could turn back the clock I wouldn't have gone to the shop.'

After hearing several days of evidence the jury retired to consider their verdict. Mr Justice Barry White told them that in order to convict Ms Noble of murder they must be satisfied beyond all reasonable doubt that the issue of self-defence did not arise. If they felt that self-defence was a significant factor, or if they thought Ms Noble was provoked to such an extent as to have lost self-control and to no longer have been master of her own mind, they had the option of convicting her of manslaughter instead.

After over four hours of debate, spread over two days, the jury returned with a unanimous verdict of guilty on the charge of possession of a knife with intent to intimidate or cause harm, but they told the judge that they could not reach agreement on the main charge. Justice White told them that he would accept a majority verdict. A few minutes later the jury returned to the court.

Kelly held her head in her hands, but showed little emotion as the verdict was read out. The jury had found her not guilty of murder, but guilty of manslaughter. They believed that she had been acting in self-defence.

Passing sentence, Justice White said that the killing had been at the upper end of the scale of seriousness, but he was obliged to accept the jury's verdict that Ms Kelly had acted in self-defence. He accepted that she did not seek or start the fight with Ms McLoughlin, but she did phone a friend to get a knife for her. After Ms McLoughlin was asked to leave the shop, Ms Noble chose to ask for a knife rather than phone the gardaí for help. For this reason he was going to impose a substantial sentence.

'I do not accept that the knife was not intended as a weapon, and that you did not intend to use it,' he said, sentencing Ms Kelly to ten years in prison, with the last two years suspended.

Niamh Cullen, the friend who brought her the knife, was tried separately on the charge of possession of a knife contrary to the Firearms and Offensive Weapons Act. In court she apologised to the McLoughlin family, saying that she had acted out of fear for her friend and had no idea of the consequences that would follow. She thought the knife would just be waved around to allow Kelly get away from Emma. She was given a twelve-month suspended sentence.

An appeal court later reduced Kelly Noble's sentence to six years, declaring that her crime fell in the middle of the severity scale for manslaughter, and that she had shown considerable remorse. The appeal judges noted that Kelly had battled a heroin addiction and horrendous family circumstances, and had made serious and meaningful efforts to grapple with her difficulties and turn her life around. She had no previous convictions, and was unlikely to reoffend. Reports from the prison indicated she was getting on well in the Dochas unit of Mountjoy. She was studying fabric and fashion, and was very helpful to other inmates.

In a way the conviction of Kelly Noble brought a sort of ghastly completion to her story. She was reunited with the mother who had killed for her sake. They are both in the same prison, the only mother and daughter pair to have been convicted of killing in the history of the State.

But it is a reunion they would both have wished not to have.

04 A GIRL OF AN UNNATURAL KIND

MARY COLE

The Four Courts was packed. There was standing room only in the courtroom itself, and every time someone squeezed out of the room someone else wedged themselves in to take their place. The corridor outside was equally busy, and people thronged the rotunda at the heart of the court building, hoping for some news to filter through from those closer to the action.

Outside it was raining heavily, and a bitter wind blew down the Liffey. But the bleak March weather did nothing to deter the eager spectators. As the four days of the trial wore on the crowd outside grew until by the end of the trial there were several hundred people milling around the streets waiting for news.

Back in 1928 there was no television, and radio was primitive. There might be one crystal set in the parish, and everyone would gather around for important matches, not crowding too much in case they put off the players, so the only way to get news from Dublin was to go there yourself, or wait for the following morning's newspaper.

As the *Irish Times* remarked: 'The court was packed for four days. The passages and staircases were full, and in the street outside hundreds remained out of curiosity all day in the rain. It must be a quarter of a century since so much general public interest was shown in a murder trial in Dublin.'

The reason for the interest was simple: the accused was a child; and she was accused of killing two children—children she was supposed to be minding.

Statistics show that women rarely kill, but killings carried out by children are even rarer; which is why these cases exert such a horrified fascination. The murder in Peckham, London of ten-year-old Damilola Taylor by two young bullies, Ricky and Danny Preddie, aged just eleven and twelve, on 27 November 2000 horrified not only Britain but the world. Damilola had been captured on CCTV just a few minutes before his death as he cheerfully returned home from the library.

Seven years before, two ten-year-olds, Jon Venables and Robert Thompson, had caused even more revulsion when they snatched two-year-old James Bulger from a shopping centre in Bootle, near Liverpool. They took the terrified toddler to a railway embankment, stoned him and beat him to death with an iron bar. Then they placed his body on the rail line, where it was severed by the next train. Apart from the age of the killers, what most horrified people was the callousness with which they carried out their crime. The two boys, both well-known tearaways, spent the day truanting from school, hanging around the shopping mall looking for a child to snatch. They had planned that their afternoon jaunt would end in murder. This was not horseplay that got out of control. This was pure evil.

But as far back as 1968 an eleven-year-old girl was making headlines worldwide. Mary Bell was convicted of strangling to death two children, one aged three and the other four. A victim of sexual abuse herself (though this did not come out in the trial), she was convicted of manslaughter due to diminished responsibility, and served twelve years. Some authorities consider her to be the world's youngest female serial killer.

Of course all those cases have one thing in common: they took place in England. Such a thing wouldn't happen here. But it did, and more than once. In one famous missing child case in Ireland the chief suspects are children who went to school with the missing child. And teens dying in fights with other teens outside nightclubs have become a staple of our summer newspapers.

The autumn of 2000 was no different; in many ways it started the trend. Leaving Cert and post-Leaving Cert students got into a fight outside Annabel's nightclub at the Burlington Hotel, Dublin. One student, Brian Murphy, seems to have started the ruckus, which turned into a free-for-all involving several former Blackrock College students. During the course of the fight Brian Murphy ended up on the ground and was kicked savagely in the head. He died of his injuries. Four boys—Andrew Frame (Donnybrook), Sean Mackey (Foxrock), Desmond Ryan (Dalkey), and Andrew Laide (Castleblaney)—were found not guilty of manslaughter, but some were convicted of lesser charges. All were in their late teens, and none had yet joined the workforce.

Not all late-night killings are confined to kids from good schools and the nicer parts of the country. As society has grown more desensitised to violence the incidents have become worse and worse. No longer is a row sorted out in a fair fight between two men using their fists, with a circle of referees on hand to stop the action before someone gets seriously hurt. Now someone will draw a knife, or a broken bottle will be used. Being knocked down no longer stops an attack; it is quite common for assault victims to be kicked viciously in the head, or struck with sticks, as they lie on the ground.

A row that broke out in Supermac's fast food outlet in Ennis on 23 June 2007 spilled over into the street and a young child, fourteen-year-old Michael Doherty, was stabbed through the heart by a garda's son, John McGovern. McGovern was just seventeen at the time of the fatal assault. Tragically, Michael Doherty, a Traveller, was on his way home from spending the day at the Spancil Hill horse fair, and had just stopped for a bag of chips. Afterwards McGovern was heard to remark: 'He was a knacker. He deserved it.' McGovern was convicted of manslaughter, and in March 2009 was sentenced to six years in prison.

Young people have been killed over things as trivial as the jacket they were wearing, the phone they were using, or just because they got on the wrong side of someone who, for whatever reason, no longer knew or cared about the value of life.

Typical of this was the killing of Ben Smith in Tallaght one afternoon in late August 1998. Ben was sitting on the wall outside his house, with his brother David, when a bunch of youths—all well known to the gardaí—asked him for a cigarette. The fourteen-year-old replied that he had none. With that someone slashed his brother in the face, then turned on Ben and drove a screwdriver into his eye, killing him.

The sixteen-year-old who was convicted of Ben's murder was a well-known thug and a joy-rider. When a protest group in the area approached his home to ask his parents to bring the boy under control, the boy's father drove a car into the crowd, scattering them.

But Ireland's most infamous child killers were not youths caught up in an increasingly frenetic and violent world. Our two most notorious underage killers set out deliberately to take a life. And, rather remarkably, both were girls.

A girl of fifteen, who has never been named for legal reasons, gunned down chip shop owner Franco Sacco in his bed in Rathfarnham, Dublin in 1997. Her story is told in the next chapter.

But the most notorious child killer in Irish legal history is probably fourteen-year-old Mary Cole, convicted in 1928 of drowning two children in her care. The case horrified a nation that thought it was inured to horror after the excesses of the civil war. A number of factors make the case stand out: the accused was a young girl; she killed not once, but twice; and she maintained a cool and unconcerned demeanour throughout the trial.

Her case bears remarkable similarities to that of Mary Bell, the eleven-year-old Scottish girl convicted of double murder forty years later, who we mentioned briefly earlier in this chapter. That case, in 1968, made waves worldwide, highlighting the dark side of the swinging sixties. It is worth recalling briefly.

Mary Bell was the daughter of an Edinburgh prostitute. Throughout her early life she was repeatedly abandoned then reclaimed by her mother, and on one occasion she was hospitalised after swallowing an overdose of pills she found in the house. As she grew older she was occasionally sold to clients by her uncaring mother, and by the age of five had been raped both anally and orally. By any standards her childhood was horrendous.

Mary was a bright and intelligent child, but cold and withdrawn, and prone to violent outbursts. At kindergarten she had been caught choking another child, and on being stopped she said: 'Why? Can it kill him?'

By the time she was ten she was living with her mother in Scotswood, an economically depressed community 275 miles north of London. She was avoided by most of her schoolmates, but an older girl, Norma Bell (no relation) followed her slavishly. Norma was a dull girl, and had fallen under the spell of her younger, brighter and more attractive companion.

Mary was one day shy of her eleventh birthday when she killed for the first time, strangling four-year-old Martin Browne on 25 May 1968. Her behaviour afterwards should have raised the alarm; she tried to show her friend Norma the body, and she called to the house of the grieving mother and asked to see Martin.

'Martin is dead,' replied Mrs Brown.

'I know. I want to see him in his coffin,' grinned the girl.

Over the next few weeks a number of incidents occurred, including the local nursery school being broken into and vandalised. Mary was again prevented from choking a young child. Then, on 31 July, she struck again. This time the victim was three-year-old Brian Howe. A crude 'M' had been carved on his stomach, and some of his hair had been cut off. His body had been abandoned in a field and covered in flowers. This time Mary had not acted alone—she had brought her friend Norma with her.

Mary Bell was fingered because of her unnatural behaviour around the time. In court she appeared bright and unrepentant. Convicted of manslaughter (due to diminished responsibility) she served twelve years before being released to begin a new life under a different name.

Psychologist Dr Robert Orten said: 'I think this girl must be regarded as suffering from psychopathic personality, demonstrated by a lack of feeling quality to other humans, and a liability to act on impulse and without forethought. She showed no remorse whatsoever, no tears and no anxiety. She was completely unemotional about the whole affair and merely resentful at her detention.'

Those words could have perfectly described Mary Cole.

Mary, who was born in Laois in November 1912, was the eldest of seven children. Her father was a labourer, and her parents lived in Camross, a tiny village near Rathdowney. Mary grew up in the small local community, and went to the national school, which was run by a husband and wife, Michael and Anastasia Flynn, from the age of seven until she was thirteen. The Flynns were well off by the standards of the day; they both held solid state jobs as national school teachers, and they had a farm, as well as a comfortable two-storey house. As their family grew they were in a position to be able to afford servants. They took on local girl Kate Murray, but when Anastasia fell pregnant again they decided they needed a second servant.

Mary Cole had by then left Camross with her parents, who had relocated to Mountrath, near Portlaoise. She had been a bit of a handful as a child, but had matured. The thirteen-year-old seemed a perfect candidate to the Flynns. She was bright and mature beyond her years, and she was used to country living. In addition to housework and childminding, she would be able to help out on the farm with tasks such as feeding and milking the cows. The position was what was then called a maid of all work. When the Flynns interviewed her in August 1926 Mary seemed full of enthusiasm, and the following month she moved in with them. She had a small room of her own in an extension to the main house.

The arrangement worked out well. Mary got on well with the older children, Maureen and Patricia (Pat), and also seemed to bond with the toddlers and the new baby. It was a busy household; with Anastasia out teaching, Mary ended up minding five children in addition to her other duties. Her working day began at seven, when she cooked breakfast for the family. At eight she cooked breakfast for a workman; then, when the children had gone to school, she had to clean up and take care of the baby, tidy the bedrooms, clean the parlour and do all the housework. The baby was left in her care all through the last months of 1926 and into the following spring. In the evenings Mary often had to feed the calves, and bring a cow to the nearby outhouse for milking. Nothing seemed out of the ordinary, but the other servant, Kate Murray, did notice that the eldest child, Maureen, seemed a lot fonder of Mary than Mary was of her.

Anastasia Flynn came to rely on her new young servant, and apparently regarded her with some affection, taking on the role of surrogate mother to the teenager. On one occasion she bought her a stylish dark blue gaberdine suit, a fancy jumper, and stockings; but she noticed that the stylish new threads seemed to make her young charge 'giddy'.

In the spring of 1927, when Mary had just turned fourteen, Michael Flynn began to hear disturbing reports in the schoolyard. Mary Cole was the subject of schoolboy gossip, and when Michael confronted his pupils they reluctantly told him that Mary was known to 'entertain' boys after the household had gone to sleep for the night. She would leave her lights on and would come to the window and talk to boys hanging around outside. Michael was horrified. The Ireland of eighty years ago was a more innocent place than it is now, and coming to the window and talking to strange boys in the middle of the night was a serious infraction of the moral code.

He and his wife confronted Mary on 27 March, but the servant vehemently denied any wrongdoing, claiming that she was completely innocent. They let the matter rest, with a severe warning to the girl that she needed to be a lot more prudent and circumspect in her conduct. Mrs Flynn also threatened to speak to Mary's mother about the matter if there were any recurrence.

A few months later, in June, the rumours began again. This time there was a disturbing new element: Michael Flynn heard that one boy had not only spoken to Mary through the window, but had climbed through the window and joined her in the bedroom. This could not be ignored. Mary was confronted again, and again denied any wrongdoing. At their wits' end, the couple turned for help to the only man they could think of, the local parish priest, Fr Walshe.

Later that week Fr Walshe rounded up three of the boys who were said to hang around outside Mary's window, and marched them to the Flynn house. The confrontation was fruitless; Mary would not back down. She was innocent. Unbowed, Fr Walshe left, vowing to return. The next night Anastasia Flynn let Mary know that the priest was coming back, this time with another boy—the boy who had allegedly climbed through her window. Realising that the game was up, Mary reluctantly told Mrs Flynn that the allegations were true. When the priest arrived she would not meet him, but she did add to her confession. She said she had climbed out of the window herself one night, and foolishly spent the night in the company of the boy, but it was his fault. She had been with him from four to six in the morning, 'but we had no improper relations with each other that morning'.

This was obviously difficult to accept. The two had hardly met in the darkness of the night to go bird watching. At fourteen Mary was mature beyond her years, and looked like a young woman. Her budding sexuality and her precociousness were causing concern.

Forty years later, the Mary Bell case would show similar features. Mature beyond her years, Bell was sexualised early by her prostitute mother. Although there is no evidence of a sexual element in the murders she committed or in her episodes of violence, as a teenager Bell managed to escape from prison for three days, and during that brief spell of freedom, while she was desperately trying to evade being caught, she managed to lose her virginity, as she gleefully told the tabloid press on her recapture.

The horrified Mrs Flynn wanted to fire Mary Cole on the spot, but the priest intervened, asking her to give the girl another chance. Mary herself went down on her knees and begged forgiveness. 'The poor magdalen. Keep her on and be a mother to her,' the priest advised.

Mrs Flynn was reluctant, but eventually agreed. However, she said that she would speak to Mary's mother about the matter. The following Saturday she visited Mrs Cole, along with Mary, and laid the whole situation before her. Mary's father was not present. Mrs Flynn said that if Mary sought another position, she would have to tell any prospective new employer about the incident.

Mrs Cole was shocked at her daughter's behaviour, and both women agreed that the best thing was to stop spoiling Mary and clip her wings a bit. Anastasia Flynn decided that a good first move would be to take back the navy gaberdine suit and the jumper. Little did she know how big a mistake she was making with that simple decision.

Mary Cole felt that her private life was her own. She deeply resented the priest being called in to 'take her character', and she was incensed at losing her fashionable clothes.

For the next fortnight the atmosphere in the Flynn household was tense. Mrs Flynn found it difficult to be at ease with her wayward servant, and Mary Cole was seething with resentment. Mrs Flynn said that she was a bit cool with Mary for the next few weeks, and the girl was silent and sullen: but Mary said that this was not the case; she continued to do her best to please Mrs Flynn in every way. In any case, both agree that by the end of two weeks relations had returned to an even keel.

On 27 July Mrs Flynn returned from school at 3.30 p.m. and ate the dinner that Mary Cole had prepared for her. All the children were in the house. Philomena, a year and a half old, fell out of her pram and started crying, so Mrs Flynn picked her up and cuddled her on her knee by the fire until she fell asleep. She put the sleeping child into the cot, and told Mary to feed her when she woke up. It was now 4.30 p.m. Feeling tired, Mrs Flynn decided to slip upstairs and snooze for a while. 'That was the last time I saw Philomena alive,' she said.

When the child woke, Mary fed her, then allowed her to toddle out into the yard to play with the other children. Then Mary tidied up the dinner things, and began doing the weekly clothes wash. It was after five when she was finished. Calling the children into the house, she set out to bring in the cow. Her instructions were clear on one point—her primary duty was to care for the children, and she was not to leave them unless there was an adult supervising them. But Mary went out for the cow anyway. She said that although Michael Flynn was away that day at an agricultural show, Mrs Flynn was upstairs, so she felt she could go out. She said she did not realise that Mrs Flynn was asleep.

She came back with the cow a while later, and Mrs Flynn, woken by the Angelus bells, came down the stairs. Mary complained that there was no feed for the calf, so Mrs Flynn gave her money and she set off for Phelan's shop, a short distance down the road. At the time, according to Mary, all the children were in the house.

Here accounts differ. Mary said that she went to the shop, made her purchases, and came back to the Flynn house. She was alone at the time. But two witnesses, John Hennessy and Mary Bastic, had seen Mary with a young child. Significantly, they said that the child was wearing a red coat. Little Philomena did have a red coat, but later that evening the coat was found back in the house.

When Mary returned from the shop she saw a child waving at her from an upstairs window, and she waved back. Entering the kitchen, Mrs Flynn asked her had she seen Philomena. 'She's upstairs—she just waved to me,' said Mary.

Mrs Flynn went upstairs, but found that the waver was another child, Patricia. Philomena was missing. Not yet two, she couldn't have gone far. Mrs Flynn immediately went out looking for her. Mary joined in the search, as did a few neighbours.

John Gorman recalled walking along the bank of the small river that ran through the farm. He saw Mary Cole on the other side of the river, and called to her. She shouted back: 'It would be an awful thing if the child was drowned.'

At that point the child had been missing only a very short while, and there was no suspicion that she could have made her way as far as the river. That would have required her, at under two years old, to climb over a high ditch and through a two-strand barbed wire fence, then cross over a field of oats that was a good foot taller than her. Alternatively, she could have forced her way through piles of thick furze, an equally unlikely scenario.

'I asked her had the child ever been down to the river before, and she said something I couldn't catch,' he said.

However, Mary Cole's words proved prophetic. She walked along one side of the bank, while John Gorman walked along the other. She was a little ahead of him and they had gone about a hundred yards when she suddenly screamed: 'The child is here.'

John Gorman didn't believe her at first, since he could not himself see anything. But he crossed the river, and then spotted the white clothes in the water. The child was lying face down in about sixteen inches of water, her head towards the bank. Gorman scooped the little bundle into his arms and shouted at Mary to help him, but she seemed frozen. She didn't come towards him.

'I called Mary back to assist me in trying to restore the child's life. She stood where she was. I saw that the child was dead, and I carried her to the house,' he said.

Quickly he brought Philomena home and laid her on the kitchen table before a shocked Anastasia Flynn. All efforts to revive her proved fruitless, and the doctor arrived to formally pronounce the child dead. During all this time Mary did not cry or seem unduly upset. When Michael Flynn arrived home from the Rathdowney show a little after nine o'clock it was to a house of despair and a wife in hysterics.

The inquest was held the following day, as was the norm in those days. The coroner returned a verdict of accidental death. The local GP, Dr Phelan, had noticed a discoloration on Philomena's forehead, but nothing to raise his suspicions. No one commented on the discrepancies between Mary's story and the testimony of the two witnesses who had seen the child in the red coat with her minutes before the fatal incident.

In the days following the drowning, Mary reminded her employers that Philomena had wandered off once before, about two weeks previously. On that occasion Mary had found her in the field leading to the river and had brought her back to the house. At the time she had told Mrs Flynn that she had found Philomena in a field, but now she changed her story, claiming that she had caught the child heading towards the river.

'Oh my God, why didn't you tell me that at first, and I could have gone down there?' said the grief-stricken woman. She was torturing herself with the thought that if she had known earlier that the child had once headed for the river, she could have gone straight there, and perhaps got to her child in time.

A week later, partly to get away and partly because it had already been planned, Anastasia Flynn and the older children went to Tramore in Waterford, a beach resort just a few miles from Waterford city, and a popular summer destination, for a short holiday. Mary Cole remained at the Flynn home in Camross with Michael Flynn, the baby, and the other servant, Kate Murray. Kate Murray said that while Mrs Flynn was away Mary confided to her that she still deeply resented the priest being called in over her behaviour, and the fact that her lovely outfit had been taken from her.

When Mrs Flynn returned from Tramore there was more drama. On the afternoon of 12 August, Mary was minding the children in the yard. Kate Murray was on her day off. Mrs Flynn went down to the local shop. When she came back she smelled smoke coming from the parlour. The sofa was smouldering, and about to burst into flames. There was a box of matches on the floor, and spent matches littering the room. Screaming for Mary, she managed to quench the fire before it ignited into a fireball. Another few minutes and she might not have been able to save the house.

Mary had her excuse to hand: six-year-old Maureen loved playing with matches, and although she had scolded her about this, the child continued to play with matches when her back was turned. Reluctantly Mrs Flynn accepted this story, relieved that no real damage had been done.

A characteristic of psychopathic serial killers—a category into which Mary Cole almost certainly falls—is a fascination with fire. Many psychopaths have a history of starting fires in childhood.

Ten days later disaster struck again—and this time there was no averting it. Maureen, Mary's 'fire-starter', drowned in circumstances eerily similar to those of her younger sister's death, at around the same time of the evening on Monday 22 August. It was a wet day, and the children had been cooped up inside. Michael Flynn, their father, was reading in the parlour.

Housekeeper Kate Murray was in the kitchen with the baby. Mary Cole washed up the dinner things, then went to her room, Maureen following her. Some time later Mary got ready to feed the calf, and Maureen wanted to go with her. Kate saw the child fetch a kettle and put it on the fire to boil water for the feed, then follow Mary from the house. Her mother watched her go. 'And I never saw her alive again,' she said.

Michael Flynn looked up from his book and saw Mary Cole head out to feed the calf, though he didn't spot his daughter with her; but a neighbour, John Tynan, was cycling past the house and saw the young girl skip out of the door, with Mary following her, holding a bucket. When Mary returned twenty minutes later, Maureen was nowhere to be seen.

Michael Flynn didn't panic—he wasn't aware that his daughter was missing until the housekeeper told him. Then he quickly organised a search, sending people off in different directions. Perhaps because of what had happened to his other daughter he was very quick to respond to the new emergency.

A few minutes later he came across a sight no father should ever have to see; his daughter lying face down on the stony river bed, in about eight or nine inches of water. 'Her face was red, there was froth in her mouth, and she appeared to be dead. When I carried her home I could see a black bruise on her forehead,' he said.

Dr McCarthy, who came to the house immediately and tried artificial respiration, also noticed the bruise, which he believed had been caused while the child was still alive. He thought it was the result of external violence of some sort, or contact with a blunt object. But no alarm bells rang.

In the recriminations that followed, Mary Cole stuck to her story that Maureen had not accompanied her that evening. 'She wanted to accompany me when I went to fetch the cow, but I would not take her because she was too fond of telling tales,' Mary told her friend Kate Tobin. 'When I came back she was missing.'

This version of events was accepted by everyone, and the inquest, again held speedily, proclaimed that this second drowning was also accidental.

A few days after the inquest there was another fire in the Flynn household: this time the curtains were found blazing brightly. The fire was quickly brought under control, but it seemed as if the family had no luck. Their servant didn't seem overly sympathetic.

'If Mrs Flynn brought the priest down on me twice, she had two inquests in the house,' she told a shocked Kate Tobin.

With two children dead, the Flynns no longer needed a second servant, so they gave Mary notice. She left their service on 31 August, with not the slightest stain on her character. Mrs Flynn even gave her a present when she returned to her home. Mary's mother told Mrs Flynn that her sister-in-law in England could get work for Mary in a department store, to which Mrs Flynn replied that she hoped that the tragic events of the summer had not caused Mary to want to leave Ireland. Mrs Cole assured her that this was not the case.

Mary planned to spend some weeks at home in Mountrath before emigrating. It looked as if she had got away with murder.

But unknown to her, the local gardaí were not satisfied that two children drowning in such similar circumstances was a coincidence, and they were worried about the suspicious bruises on both girls' foreheads.

They began interviewing witnesses and collecting statements, and they soon began to home in on the servant who bore a grudge about a blue suit that had been taken from her. Her comment about the two inquests in the house was particularly damning, and too many witnesses had placed her in the company of the children shortly before their deaths.

In October they alerted their colleagues in Mountrath, who interviewed Mary and found her sullen. She admitted nothing. They told her mother to forget about getting Mary to England: she wasn't to leave the country until 'certain matters' were cleared up.

In November Mary Cole was brought in for further questioning. She made a detailed and lengthy statement, in which she denied any involvement in the drowning, and claimed that while she was not happy with her treatment at the hands of Mrs Flynn, she accepted it and knew that it was deserved. She insisted she had nothing to hide. The investigators thought otherwise, and on Thursday 1 December she was arrested.

Her trial the following March was sensational. Mary played her part. She was dressed smartly and was very self-possessed, looking a fully developed young woman rather than a girl of fifteen. She followed the proceedings closely, but rarely betrayed any emotion.

Opening the prosecution, barrister William Corrigan said, 'This is the most extraordinary of extraordinary cases that could be submitted to a court of justice. So extraordinary is the case that even the parents of the dead children did not suspect that they had been murdered until long after the girl had left their employment, nineteen days after the death of the second child.

'In dealing with this case the jury will have to put from your minds all that you have experienced or heard or read of juvenile crime, because no standard of conduct would lead you to think that the girl charged in this case could have successfully destroyed two children without raising some suspicion in the minds of their parents.

'You are dealing with a girl who looks considerably older than her less than sixteen years. She is a girl of an unnatural kind. She has an intellect developed in a manner that is disordered but it is a powerful intellect, as you will see. Up to October neither the local police nor the doctors who attended the inquests ever for a moment suspected that the children had met their ends other than by the merest accident.

'That is one proof of this girl's skill and unnatural ingenuity. In an ordinary case all those extraordinary facts would be adduced in proof of the innocence of this girl, but when you come to appreciate her nature you will, I think, see that they become evidence of her guilt, and that she possessed and exercised an extraordinary skill in deluding everyone, including the police and doctors.

'This girl, young as she is by years, must have the mind not only of an adult, but an adult of strange experience; because in conversations with people after the tragedies she made use of some very gruesome expressions. She ascribed the misfortunes that had befallen the Flynn family as a judgement on Mrs Flynn for having brought charges against her before the priest, and she said that if she had been exposed and her character taken away, the Flynns had had two inquests.

'That was a strange thought in the mind of a girl of less than sixteen—the balancing of good for evil in the fortunes of the Flynns. They had wronged her, and because of that, they had had two inquests. These two deaths were brought about by her wicked deeds, concealing her malice against those people in a way that can only fittingly be described as infernal. It is not human.'

The court heard medical evidence that the bruises on the foreheads of both victims were probably caused by their heads being pressed into the stony bank of the river. Immersion lasting between thirty seconds and a minute was probably sufficient to drown such small children.

Counsel for the defence James Walsh must have sensed that things were not going well for his client, because he took the extraordinary decision to attack the character and circumstances of Mrs Flynn, the grieving mother.

'The prosecution has painted a picture of a sorrowing mother,' he told a disbelieving jury on the fourth and final day of the trial. 'Well, while my sympathies go out to every father and mother who loses their children in any circumstances, where two little girls were brought in dead from the river very little of my sympathy goes out to Mrs Flynn.

'Mr Corrigan, in order to attract your sympathy, told you how the sorrowing mother took her other children and left the scene of her grief for a time. He tells you that poor people like the Flynns have to push and strive. But what are the real facts? Mrs Flynn and her husband were in receipt of five hundred and fifty pounds a year between them as national teachers. They had in addition a farm of thirty acres, and stock. They also have a motor car. These are the poor people, according to Mr Corrigan, who can afford only one servant, Mary Cole, who was the absolute slave in this household.

'I put Mary Cole in the witness box and she has not wavered in her story or been caught out at all. She could not vary her story, because she was telling the simple truth.

'This girl, whose future is in your hands, does not fully realise the effect of an adverse verdict. Sorrow came into the home of Mr and Mrs Flynn when their children were taken from them, but the parting of a mother from her convict daughter, her first born child, is a greater sorrow. In death there is no dishonour. Before you come to the conclusion to part this mother and daughter in the disgrace of a conviction, you must be satisfied that the State has established their case. The facts allow for only one conclusion— not guilty.'

After four days in the dock Mary Cole finally showed some emotion. When her barrister spoke about her mother, the teenager cried.

William Corrigan showed no sympathy. 'This phenomenal juvenile criminal, untaught and without experience, presents to you the case of a girl who looks a woman in appearance, and has a mind more powerful and more agile an imagination than any of you could come across in the experience of a lifetime.

'You will have noticed she gave her evidence with a cleverness and coolness that was unnatural. One who has little or no education, without having ever, perhaps, even seen a cinema show, faced a lengthy cross-examination with almost miraculous equanimity. We are dealing with a portentous case of juvenile monstrosity; for if you hold that drowning has been done, then there is no one who could be charged with it but the girl in the dock, and she did it with supernatural cleverness and ingenuity.'

After the closing speeches the court broke for lunch. Mrs Flynn was naturally incensed at the attack on her and the way her grief had been belittled in the court. She sought out James Walsh and gave him a piece of her mind. Things became heated and she had to be pulled away from him.

After lunch Mr Justice Byrne had strong words to say about the incident. Calling Mrs Flynn forward, he said: 'An incident of a very unpleasant nature has been mentioned to me. It appears that during the luncheon interval you met counsel for the defence outside this court and made an observation to him which he reported to me. I have taken into account the very natural strain under which you must be labouring, and on account of that I pass over the incident. Were it not for that I would have taken a very drastic course.'

He then gave the jury their final instructions, and sent them off to deliberate. The huge crowds in the court complex and on the streets outside did not have long to wait. After only forty minutes the jury returned and the foreman handed their verdict to the court clerk. Mary Cole watched closely but dispassionately as the judge received the judgement. He looked up at the court and pronounced the verdict—guilty on both charges of murder.

Mary Cole held her composure. She knew that she had little to fear: her age meant that she could not be given the death penalty.

A relatively recent change in the law ruled that defendants had to be sixteen or over to swing for murder.

The judge looked at her. 'You have been convicted of the murder of two little children, one of them under two years and the other under seven. The murder of children of that age is, under any circumstances, so utterly abhorrent to every natural instinct that it is difficult to imagine how such a crime could be committed. But it is all the more abhorrent when, as in this case, the children who were murdered were children to whom, for a period, you had been attending day after day, seeing after their wants, nursing them, feeding them and caring for them,' he said. 'If you had been a few months older these crimes would have entailed a sentence of death. By reason of your age the law has mercifully enacted that you will not suffer such a sentence.'

Mr Justice Byrne sentenced Mary Cole to life imprisonment. Coolly, she turned to her mother, who was in tears, then left the dock without any sign of emotion.

The devastated Flynns were left to rebuild their shattered lives. Unable to stay in the house where a trusted servant had drowned two of their children, they gave up their teaching posts in Camross. With their four surviving children—and Mary Cole's confidante Kate Tobin as a servant—they moved to Tipperary to begin the slow task of rebuilding their lives.

05 | DIVORCE, IRISH STYLE
ANNA MARIA SACCO AND FRIEND

K illers, like comedians, normally work alone, but you occasionally find a double act. People who chose to kill in pairs are understandably rare. The ultimate taboo within society is killing. With the possible exception of raping a child, there are few things more depraved than taking another person's life, which is why killers tend to operate alone and keep their activities hidden under a veil of secrecy.

But sometimes a killing is carried out by two accomplices. Often the reason is pragmatic—the killing may have been part of another crime, such as a burglary—or a number of people got drunk and a fight broke out.

It is very rarely that a killing is carried out by two people who planned it carefully well in advance. The psychology of such cases is interesting.

Zoologists maintain that within any animal population there is a dominant five per cent at the top of the group. These are the lions who lead a pride, the mature bull elephants, the leader of a dog pack and so on. One in twenty of a population has that indefinable leadership quality: the rest are followers.

This holds true in human societies. Only some people are born with natural leadership instincts, and psychologists put the number at one in twenty. This accords with the experiences of many of our top leaders. Ernest Shackleton, the famous Antarctic explorer, famously said that one man in twenty was a leader, and that the secret on a long expedition was to identify those few people, and put them in charge of something. Others would follow them, which would prevent the non-leaders sulking and causing mutiny. He also claimed that there was one troublemaker in each group of twenty, and if you identified the troublemaker you should keep them close to you. He applied these insights well during his year-long retreat from Antarctica in 1916. After his ship sank in ice he left most of his men on Elephant Island while he crossed the treacherous seas to South Georgia to raise a rescue mission. He brought the troublemakers with him, and left the leaders on Elephant Island, and everyone was saved.

Leadership is closely allied to dominance. Psychologists tell us that people have high, medium or low dominance. People with high dominance tend to be the go-getters. They have high energy and a strong sex drive. They lead lives of excitement and get things done. People with medium dominance have these qualities but to a much lesser extent. Those with low dominance are the drifters: they take what life throws at them, are relatively unemotional, and are generally happy with their lot.

A problem arises when there are too many dominant people, too many natural leaders, in a group. For instance, in a school with four hundred pupils there will be twenty natural leaders fighting for dominance. Dominance is not related to talent. Some of those twenty will be talented athletes, good debaters, academically gifted; others will have no discernible talents; and the occasional one will be downright stupid. Those who are talented in some field can excel in their chosen area, and this fulfils their dominance needs, but those without talent are left with a problem. They see themselves as the top dogs, but no one else agrees, so they occasionally resort to short-cuts to get to the top. They cheat and lie. This short-cut mentality can lead to a criminal mind-set.

John George Haigh, the acid-bath murderer of the 1940s, was a typical example. A bright, intelligent man, he wanted to be a success. In early life he won academic scholarships, so he was well educated, but in the class-conscious Britain of the time he was going to find it difficult to rise above middle-class mediocrity. In addition, he decided he didn't want to put in the work; so he would take short-cuts. He was fired from a job at the age of twenty-one for dipping into the till. The short-cut mentality wasn't working out too well.

Over the next number of years he made his living as a conman, and did a couple of stints in prison. While he was serving a four-year sentence he came up with what he thought was the perfect con. If he did someone out of their life savings they might come after him; but if he killed them there was one problem less. However, that would risk a murder charge. Then he got the big idea: if there was no body, there could be no murder charge. He began experimenting in prison, and discovered that strong sulphuric acid would dissolve a mouse completely in thirty minutes, leaving no evidence of its existence.

Released from prison in 1944, he was ready to put his plan into action. Over the next four years Haigh killed between six and nine people, and disposed of their bodies in large vats of acid. Once they were sludge he was able to pour them down manholes and get rid of them forever. One of his operations netted him the equivalent, in today's money, of €240,000.

Then his last victim was reported missing. Police traced a link between her and Haigh, and visited his workshop. They found several suspicious items, including a receipt for the dry-cleaning of his victim's fur coat (which he planned to sell). But there was no sign of her body—all they found was a large drum full of sludge—and Haigh thought he was home and dry. Unfortunately for him, a forensic examination of the sludge uncovered three gallstones and a denture, which was identified as belonging to his victim. And a couple of months later Haigh had an urgent appointment with the hangman.

Haigh's story shows how in his case the short-cut mentality led to a life of crime and murder. Murder is often a short-cut solution to a problem. This can be particularly true in the domestic setting in which women often kill, or try to kill.

The 'Black Widow', Catherine Nevin, had her husband killed in Jack White's Pub, Wicklow because it was simpler than divorcing him, and it would leave her with all his money, not just half of it. It was a short-cut. She was unhappy in the marriage and had a string of lovers: but she liked the perks of being the wife of a rich publican. Jack White's in Brittas Bay was a very successful pub, and gave her an enviable lifestyle.

She decided on a divorce Irish style. She arranged for two men to break into the pub on the night of 19 March 1996. The takings from a busy St Patrick's weekend would be substantial. The deal was that they would gun down her husband, and their fee for the job would be the weekend takings—which ran to over €50,000. It was a great plan, but it hit one snag: she was caught. Now she is serving life in Mountjoy.

Another woman with aspirations to be a black widow is Ennis native Sharon Collins. She famously used the internet to try and find someone to help her with her problem. Her rich boyfriend, businessman PJ Howard, was not willing to marry her, and he planned to leave his substantial wealth, based on property and some successful businesses, to his two sons. So she Googled 'hitman', and found a website called hitmanforhire.com. This put her in contact with Essam Eid.

Eid was a poker dealer from Las Vegas and about as much of a hitman as Mickey Mouse. His con was simple; he would take a substantial down payment on a hit, then ask the intended victim for a similar down payment to cancel the hit. It had worked in America. He arrived in Ennis and contacted the Howards, telling them that he had been hired to kill them, but for a fee he would go home instead. They agreed on a fee, but when he arrived to collect it the gardaí were waiting for him.

Sharon Collins was convicted of attempted murder, and is now enjoying the hospitality of the State in Mountjoy. Fellow inmates in the Dochas Centre at the prison describe her as 'highly manipulative'. Like Catherine Nevin, she has the reputation of seeing herself as the queen bee.

What Catherine Nevin and Sharon Collins have in common is that they are both highly dominant women, and this became evident during the court cases. Nevin had a voracious appetite for lovers, and Collins had a similar colourful history, though she claimed in court that this was due to the influence of her boyfriend. Both had high expectations about how they should live and how they should be treated. Both decided to use criminal short-cuts rather than more conventional channels to solve their problems. Nevin could have got a divorce; Collins could have worked to make her relationship what she wanted it to be.

The annals of crime are full of such stories. Many Irish women have chosen to kill a husband—or to get someone else to kill their husband for them—to escape abuse, to gain an inheritance, or simply to move on to a new man. It's a crime that often arises when a dominant person looks for a short-cut to get what they feel is rightly theirs.

A highly dominant person tends to form relationships with people of slightly lower dominance, which means that he or she will get their way, and be the leader in the relationship. This applies not only to romantic relationships but also to friendships and business relationships; and it quite clearly applies to criminal relationships.

However, psychiatrist Dr Brian McCaffrey warns that the influence of one partner over another is not a simple matter of a bad person influencing a good, or normal, person.

'In most of the big murders by a couple they are both bad,' he says. 'Killing is such an horrific thing to do that it is going beyond the bounds of credibility that you could be so influenced that you would go and participate in a killing unless you have something within you which is not healthy.'

Ian Brady, the Moors murderer, was a highly dominant man. When he joined Millwell Merchandising, a chemical supply company in Manchester, he met Myra Hindley, a woman with a reputation of being the office bitch. She was a highly dominant woman, who was looking for an even higher-dominance man. When they met, it was a union made in hell. They began to explore the pleasures of violence, living the creed of the Marquis de Sade: 'Rape is not a crime; it is a state of mind. Murder is a hobby and a supreme pleasure.'

They killed a number of children before they were eventually caught. At their trial in 1966 they were both sentenced to life. Myra Hindley died in prison in 2002, and Ian Brady was eventually transferred to a hospital for the criminally insane, where he will end his days. Psychologists agree that while Brady and Hindley are among the worst serial killers in Britain, neither would have killed had they not met. Their psychological profiles merged to produce a murderous result.

One of Ireland's most notorious underage killers might never have bloodied her hands if she had not fallen under the spell of an older girl. The murder of Franco Sacco was unusual for a number of reasons, but one of the most notable was because no one did any significant time for the killing. The other reason this case stands out is that Franco was gunned down by a fifteen-year-old girl. She was very much under the spell of her older friend when she pulled the trigger, but her friend played no active part in the killing.

The Italian community in Ireland is a strong one, and one that has retained its distinctiveness throughout the years. Some non-Irish nationals, such as the British, Germans and Americans, tend to integrate seamlessly into Irish society. Others, notably the Chinese and Italian communities, remain within their own cultural enclaves.

A huge number of the Italians in Ireland originated from the same part of Italy, a rural region centred on the village of Cassino, not far south of Rome. Although it is close to one of the most cosmopolitan cities in the world, in the 1980s Cassino and the surrounding Frosinone region was a throwback to an earlier age. People still followed their traditional way of life and the Church had great influence. Chauvinism was strongly evident, and men ruled the roost. Family was important. You married whom you were expected to marry, and you devoted yourself to family—not just your own immediate family, but the whole extended family. You were part of the clan, and there was no walking away from your obligations to it.

When Luigi Sacco came to Ireland this is the world he left, though he never left it entirely; he had a property in his village in Italy, to which he hoped to retire. But in Ireland, Luigi thrived. Like many of his compatriots who came to Ireland he went into the fast food industry. He set up a chipper in the centre of Dublin, which did very well, and lived above the premises on Parnell Street.

Although Italians abroad tend to stick together, Luigi did go outside the community for a wife. He married a Donegal woman, Lorna, and they had four daughters—Caterina, Anna Maria, Giovanna and Louisa. In addition he had a stepson, Danny. Life was good for the Saccos. Luigi had chosen a secure business and he was good at it.

Gradually he expanded, opening new branches throughout the city and in 1986 he decided he needed to recruit new staff, people he could trust completely; his own people. Where better to seek them than in his own village? That summer he returned to Italy for a few weeks on a visit that was part holiday, part recruitment drive. During the holiday he called, as usual, on his uncle Pasquale in the nearby town of Casa Lattico. Pasquale said that his young son Franco, then eighteen, would be an ideal candidate. Not afraid of hard work, Franco was ambitious to get on in the world, and that wasn't going to happen in rural Italy.

So Franco went to Ireland, began working in the growing chipper empire and moved in with his benefactor. Luigi's pretty young daughter Anna Maria was then just ten, but she grew attached to her second cousin once removed. Franco did stand out; he was what every hack fortune teller predicts for young women— a tall, dark, handsome stranger.

On his twenty-first birthday, when Anna Maria was thirteen, they kissed for the first time. Her infatuation grew into something more, and the young girl gradually fell in love with Franco. By now the family had moved from Parnell Street to a house in Kimmage, and Franco had gone with them. Luigi had opened new shops in Ranelagh, Rathfarnham and Crumlin. As the affair developed Anna Maria lost her virginity to her Italian lover. She thought they were made for one another, despite the warning signs of his temper and occasional violent outbursts. Little did she realise that these were to grow with the relationship.

Luigi did not approve of his daughter's liaison, but it is likely he did not take it too seriously—she was still young—but in 1994 he took the opportunity to separate the two lovers. He went on an extended holiday back to his homeland, taking the family with him for the summer months, and leaving Franco in charge of the chippers back in Ireland.

Anna Maria was now eighteen, and had grown into a beautiful young woman. She appeared more mature than many of the girls back in her father's village, and she thrived on the attention she received there. She spoke fluent Italian, and she loved the summer. For a while it looked as if she was interested in a 'respectable' young man Luigi had invited over for coffee one morning. But the summer romance didn't blossom, and the summer didn't last forever. Eventually the family returned to Kimmage, and Anna Maria returned to her true love.

By now the relationship was a serious and acknowledged one, and the warning bells were beginning to ring. Family and friends warned the young girl that Franco was a tyrant, an old-fashioned chauvinist with a violent temper and a tendency to lash out. He was not suitable husband material, and if she did not back off now, she could be condemning herself to a lifetime of misery. Already his violent streak was in evidence: he had beaten her on a number of occasions, when he felt her behaviour fell short of what he expected.

But Anna Maria defied the warning signs. She announced that the couple were to get married on 25 May 1995, her nineteenth birthday. By now they had been going out for six years. Although it took her months to pluck up the courage to tell her parents (which should have been a warning sign in itself), she was firmly committed to her man.

Meanwhile, another relationship was also blossoming. A pretty young teenager with a reputation as a bit of a wild child had begun hanging around one of the chippers. A regular school drop-out— who had finally been expelled from school—and a bit of a trouble-maker, the young girl was already dabbling with drink and drugs in her early teens. She and Anna Maria got on very well together, and they were soon inseparable friends. They went swimming together, drinking together, and dancing together. Franco was not happy—he didn't like Anna Maria's new friend at all. But what could he do? The young girl, who was from an Italian-Irish background, would become central to the unfolding tragedy. For legal reasons her name has never been revealed to the public.

Anna Maria confided in her new friend that Franco could be a bit of a handful. From the age of sixteen she had been living half in fear of him. He had his rules, and if she didn't conform he was not afraid to enforce his will with a few slaps, she told her young companion. 'If I didn't obey him I got an odd punch or a kick in the legs,' she said.

A few weeks before the wedding Anna Maria got a bad attack of cold feet. She and her young friend boarded a plane for Edinburgh. This was partly a last fling before her marriage; but it also had a more serious aim. Anna Maria hoped that her trip would serve as a warning to Franco that he could not take his young fiancée for granted, and that he would have to re-evaluate his violent behaviour. 'I wanted to give him a fright and get him to stop hitting me,' she said.

Eventually her father tracked the girls down, and he and Franco persuaded Anna Maria to return for the wedding. Franco turned on all his Latin charm. The wedding was on again.

On Thursday 25 May 1995, Anna Maria walked down the aisle with her Italian lover. Afterwards there was an elaborate reception at the Victor Hotel in Dun Laoghaire, attended by family and friends and many of the extensive Italian community in Dublin. It was a joyous occasion, and the couple looked to have a secure future as they jetted off to Italy (where else?) for their honeymoon.

Luigi was renting them one of his chip shops, Luigi's in Rathfarnham, which gave Franco a steady and profitable business to run. He was giving them a good deal on the rent, to give them a leg-up in their first years together. The couple bought a house in The Glen, off Boden Park in Rathfarnham, close to the chipper, and after a while they moved into a new house, which cost them £125,000, quite a sum in those days, in Castleamber Park in Templeogue.

But the marriage was a failure, almost from the start. Anna Maria was a lively young woman, eager for fun, who enjoyed socialising. Her new husband was older than her, and came from a very traditional background in which women were not encouraged to have a life outside their marriage. He wanted her to work in the chipper, keep the house, and be available to fulfil his conjugal rights. She wanted a life.

Whatever hope the marriage had, it was doomed by two factors. The first was Franco's propensity for violence. The second was Anna Maria's friendship with her teenage companion. In fact, shortly after the marriage, the young girl moved into the new house in Castleamber Park, much to Franco's annoyance. It is surprising that Franco let the girl stay. He disliked her intensely, was jealous of her relationship with his wife, and he openly referred to her as 'that *putana*'—the Italian word for prostitute.

During the early months of the marriage Franco tried to make it work. He curbed his temper, and the beatings stopped. He managed the chipper with Anna Maria, and her young friend helped out there, but running his own business, and making sure he made Luigi's rent every month, involved hard work and long hours, and Franco was often exhausted when he returned home.

Both partners found that being married was completely different from fooling around in the first flush of love. Anna Maria discovered that their passionate early relationship did not necessarily make Franco suitable husband material. In fact they weren't long married when Franco's eyes began to wander, and there is some suggestion that he embarked on extra-marital affairs. But his young wife also had a roving eye. When her husband was toiling late at the chipper she began going out with her young friend. One of their haunts was Club 2000, a nightclub in the Spawell complex in nearby Tallaght, and only a few months after her marriage she met a handsome barman, Peter Gifford.

Their relationship began as friendship, but quickly developed. It became a Tuesday night ritual: Anna Maria and some of the chipper staff would go out clubbing, and Peter and some friends would join them. Talk often turned to her violent husband. She told Peter about the beatings, and about how her husband had once used a baseball bat on her. She showed up for one date with her arm in a sling. Their affair started less than a year after Anna Maria's wedding, and continued into the summer of 1996. Even after the affair ended she remained in contact with Peter.

While the stories she told her lover may have been exaggerated for effect, Peter seemed to take them seriously. He told Anna Maria that he had 'friends' who could get rid of Franco. As they lay in bed together, her blonde head on his shoulder, she would sob to him about her unhappiness, and he would reassure her that he was trying to contact his 'friend', but the man was on the run. It should have been obvious that he had no 'friend', and that he was not going to help her get rid of her abusive husband. As he admitted in court afterwards, he pretended he could help Anna Maria because he was stupid—he didn't believe that she was serious, and if he said no, she would find someone else. But Anna Maria was very serious about getting someone to kill her husband.

Peter Gifford wasn't the only person in whom Anna Maria confided. One night she bumped into the brother of a friend of hers, a young man on the fringes of the Dublin underworld. She asked him how much it would cost to have someone killed. 'A thousand pounds gets a man killed,' he replied with confidence. She got the money together and handed it over, but he disappeared and did nothing for her.

The marriage was not a year old, and she was already desperately looking for a way out—a violent and bloody way out. Then, just after Christmas, disaster struck. In January 1997 the chipper in Rathfarnham went up in flames. Extensive damage was caused, and the chipper was closed for several weeks while it was being rebuilt. Investigators had discovered the mysterious blaze was caused by someone deliberately tampering with the gas pipe. It had been an attempt on Franco's life—he was the man who always lit the ovens at the start of the day.

It is doubtful that Franco ever realised that an attempt had been made to kill him, and no suspect for the blaze was ever identified. Franco remained in Dublin, overseeing the rebuilding work, while his wife and her young friend took off for a holiday in the sun. When she returned home she confronted her husband about an affair he was having with a young Italian woman who had been brought over to work in another of Luigi's chippers. During the confrontation she also admitted to having an affair herself.

The couple made up and decided to give their marriage one last try, but it was a doomed effort. Franco had always been a violent man who insisted on his rights, and he was not about to change. In early March he returned from the chipper one night, and demanded sex. When Anna Maria refused (she had a medical condition at the time) he took off his belt and beat her with it. 'Lie down and take it, or I'll kill you,' he screamed as he raped his wife. Afterwards they argued loudly, Anna Maria threatening to take out a barring order against Franco.

'If you go to the police I'll kill you for sure. I don't care about the law in this country. The most I'd get for killing you would be seven years. You know what your problem is? You're Irish. You have no Italian blood in you,' he sneered.

Over the next few days it became obvious to everyone how deeply flawed the marriage was. Anna Maria usually wore her blonde hair in a ponytail, but she let it loose to try and conceal the black eye her husband had given her: however, her mother spotted it when they met in the Ranelagh chipper the following day.

'What happened?' asked her mother. But before she could reply Anna Maria blacked out, collapsing onto the tiled floor. An ambulance was called and she was taken to St Vincent's Hospital. She was four months pregnant, and being abused by her husband, but she would not make a complaint. She was released from hospital and went home. Then she was confronted by even more horror: her young friend confided that Franco had started molesting her. A bad situation was getting worse by the day.

On 18 March Franco celebrated his twenty-ninth birthday. He went out with a bunch of male friends to Little Caesar's, an Italian restaurant off Grafton Street. Anna Maria was not celebrating with her husband—she was behind the counter at the chipper.

The following evening Franco also took time off, leaving Anna Maria in charge. He just put on his leather jacket and headed out of the door. He went to visit a friend, Gioacchino Dinardi, at his house, where they watched football together, then he went home, picking up a video on the way.

Meanwhile Anna Maria, her sister Caterina and her young friend ran the chipper for the night. At some point Peter Gifford arrived.

He knew Franco was out, and talk inevitably turned to the birthday boy. They all agreed it would be great if he was dead. But how would they get rid of the body?

'We'll chop him up and stick him in the oven,' joked Caterina.

Anna Maria asked Peter if he had managed to track down his friend, but he said the man was still on the run. Then Anna Maria's fifteen-year-old friend piped up. 'I'll do it,' she announced. Franco's fate was sealed, though no one in the chipper, bar Anna Maria and her young friend, realised it.

Franco came home ahead of his wife, and settled down to watch *Heat*, a crime thriller starring Robert de Niro and Al Pacino. Shortly afterwards Anna Maria and her friend arrived. They had got a lift from Peter Gifford, but he had dropped them off around the corner because he didn't want Franco to see him.

The two girls sat down to watch the film with Franco. In one scene in the film de Niro loads a shotgun. Franco, a keen hunter, kept a shotgun under the stairs, which he used to shoot birds, and had over four hundred cartridges in the shed.

'You couldn't kill someone with your gun,' the young girl said.

'Fucking sure you could,' he answered. His reply sealed his fate.

After the movie ended Franco went to bed.

'Are you coming?' he asked his wife. It was his not so subtle way of telling her that he expected sex before he went to sleep.

'I'll be up in a few minutes,' she said.

The two girls, one fifteen and the other just nineteen, poured brandy into two glasses and knocked them back. The younger of the two fetched the shotgun and loaded it.

'Are you going to do it now?' Anna Maria asked.

'Yes.'

Anna Maria went upstairs to see if her husband was asleep yet, but he was still awake. She came downstairs to tell her companion that it would have to wait. Both girls went back upstairs and the fifteen-year-old went into her room, bringing the shotgun with her. Anna Maria joined her husband and meekly let him have his way with her, before they rolled away from each other and went to sleep.

The following morning the alarm clock woke Anna Maria at 11 a.m. Her husband turned over and told her to make sure to open the chipper on time, then went back to sleep, clutching the pillow to his face. Anna Maria went into the next door bedroom and woke her young friend. Then she went downstairs to put on the coffee.

A few minutes later a single shot rang out. It was over. Moments later the young girl came running down the stairs. 'I'm after killing him,' she cried.

Anna Maria went upstairs. Although the curtains were drawn, she could see the figure of her husband on the bed, a gaping wound in his head. Blood was oozing in a big pool around him. Trying to appear calm, both girls left the house and climbed into the car. As Anna Maria reversed out of the house, she nearly ran into a Garda squad car.

Their first stop was the chipper, where they attempted to fire up the fryers. But they couldn't light them, so they hung the 'closed' sign on the shop door. Then they drove to Anna Maria's sister. Caterina was horrified, though perhaps not surprised, at their news. The three women agreed they would have to return to the house and clean up the mess. They also contacted Peter Gifford and asked for his help to dispose of the body, but he made his excuses and didn't get involved.

The clean-up was gruesome. Initially Anna Maria wouldn't go up to the bedroom, and left the dirty work to her two companions. Armed with buckets of warm water and containers of Flash, they rolled up their sleeves and got stuck in. The first thing was to get the body off the bed and wrapped up for disposal. As one Garda witness, Detective William Brennan of the ballistics section of the Garda Technical Bureau, later described it: 'Eight bed sheets of various colours, five padded quilts and duvet covers, an electric blanket and two hand towels were wrapped around the body.'

From the patterns of blood in the room gardaí determined that Franco's body had been dragged from the bed to be wrapped, either for disposal or to make the scene less gruesome. He was clutching a pillow to his head. Evidently he had been hugging the pillow when he was shot in his sleep, and it had stuck to him as the blood congealed. The clean-up was not very efficient; fragments of skull were subsequently found, and there was pink staining around the toilet.

Although it was grim work, there were moments of dark humour. At one point Caterina came down the stairs with something jellyish and gooey in a yellow cloth, with which she chased the screaming Anna Maria around the kitchen. The substance was part of Franco's brain.

Anna Maria left the house while her sister and friend continued to clean up, flushing pellets and bits of brain matter down the toilet. After a while they tired of the job, and went to the chipper in Ranelagh, returning to the house a little later. Anna Maria seemed not to have grasped just how much trouble they were in. 'I kept thinking; no, he's asleep. Everything's okay,' she later revealed. As her two companions continued to clean up, she was downstairs, vomiting.

They left the house again and went their separate ways, still unsure about how to handle the situation. Perhaps seeking to establish that she knew nothing about the murder, Anna Maria rang Franco's friend Gioacchino Dinardi, some time between 8 p.m. and 8.45 p.m. Anna Maria asked him was Franco with him, or had he seen him, to which he replied that he had not seen him since the night before. 'Then the phone went dead,' he said.

But unknown to the new widow, events had taken a dramatic turn. Shortly before 8 p.m. her teenage friend, with a companion, had run into the public office of Rathfarnham Garda Station and blurted out that she had shot Franco Sacco.

'I shot Franco,' she told the startled officer in charge, Garda Ronan Walden. She was hysterical, and he had the sense to realise this was something that needed checking out, so he sent men around to the Sacco residence. Sirens blazing, the squad cars pulled into Castleamber. Within minutes the gardaí had found the body, and sealed off the house.

Happy that her phone call would establish that she knew nothing about Franco's death, Anna Maria drove up to her home, with her sister, shortly before 9 p.m. As she got out of the car Garda Patrick Norville approached her and broke the bad news; her husband was dead inside the house, murdered by a shot to the head.

'There was no easy way to do it. I told her her husband was dead. She got very upset and hysterical,' he said. Anna Maria began screaming and kicking and banging her head on the door. 'No, no, no!' she wailed, playing the part of a shocked and grieving widow to perfection. But the gardaí already had the admission of the fifteen-year-old shooter, and the net was closing in on Anna Maria. Four days after Franco's death she went into the garda station and made a statement denying any involvement in the shooting but admitting she had been in the house at the time. She claimed that she panicked when she realised Franco was dead, and all she had been involved in was the subsequent brief cover-up.

Investigators didn't buy it. They charged both Anna Maria and her young accomplice with murder.

The case against the young girl was easy to make; they had a confession and she pleaded guilty when the case came to trial. She did try to mitigate her guilt by claiming that she never intended Franco to die. She just wanted to give him a scare with the gun. 'I wanted to frighten him. I heard a bang and then there was blood all over the place. I didn't think it was loaded,' she claimed. 'I didn't know how to put the bullets in.' She was sentenced to seven years.

In May 1998 it was Anna Maria's turn. She pleaded not guilty. It was a sensational trial that attracted huge media attention. The victim was a 'hot Latin lover'; his alleged killers a young girl and a glamorous blonde widow. The widow had a six-month-old baby; and she said in court that though she had had an extramarital affair, of which she was not proud, the baby girl was her husband's. She had been named Francesca in his honour.

The trial was a difficult one for the prosecution. They had to prove beyond a reasonable doubt that Anna Maria had pushed her young friend into firing the fatal shot. It was not good enough to prove that the pair had discussed the matter in a haphazard fashion, or that Anna Maria was aware of the shooting—she had to have ordered and directed it. A complication was that, because of her age and other legal reasons, the younger woman was not called upon to testify.

Then the defence went on the attack, accusing the investigating gardaí of putting pressure on Anna Maria to make a statement which implicated her in the killing. They also accused the gardaí of rough-house tactics in their interrogation.

In her evidence, Anna Maria's mother said she had noticed red marks on her daughter's neck after she was questioned. 'The only think I could think of was that they're fairly big men and she's only a little small skinny thing,' she tearfully told the court. One allegation, that a named detective garda had grabbed her by the neck and pushed her against a wall during the questioning, was enough to muddy the waters. The jury was unable to reach a verdict, and Anna Maria was released on bail to await a retrial.

The second trial, held in March of the following year, lasted fifteen days. A critical factor in this new trial was a ruling by the judge on the reliability of the evidence given by the young girl who had pulled the trigger. He decided that he did not believe her story about Franco Sacco having molested her. He made it clear to the jury that this was a tissue of lies, and if she had lied about that, what else was she lying about? She was an unreliable witness and anything she said that tended to implicate Mrs Sacco in her husband's murder was to be ignored.

With this clear instruction to the jury the result was in no doubt. They decided that there was no evidence to tie Anna Maria into the plot to kill her husband, and she was acquitted. She walked from the Four Courts a free woman. Smiling and carrying her two-year-old daughter, she was ready to get on with the rest of her life.

And what became of the teenage gunwoman? After her conviction there was the inevitable appeal, but her defence did not appeal the decision, just the sentence. The appeal court ruled that because of her age the girl was not ready for an adult prison. Since there was no suitable juvenile facility to hold her she was released on probation, after serving just a few months. In November 1999 the courts ruled that she was obeying the conditions of her probation, and she was effectively granted her freedom.

After coming out of detention she trained as a hairdresser. Because of her short detention she was no older than the other trainee hairdressers, and blended in perfectly. She now works in that industry.

To this day her identity has never been revealed by the media, though her affairs are still occasionally documented for a fascinated public. She last came to public attention almost a decade ago. The Sunday papers were keeping tabs on her love life. *Coronation Street* star Chris Bisson had a whirlwind romance with the teenage girl who blasted chip shop owner Franco Sacco to death with a shotgun, the *Irish Sunday Mirror* revealed to its titillated readers on 21 April 2002.

The paper went on to reveal that the self-confessed killer, who could not be named for legal reasons, had a number of dates with the actor who played cabbie Vikram Desai in the television soap. Bisson (then twenty-seven) was unaware that the woman he was kissing and cuddling in a Dublin pub had killed a man when she was just fifteen.

The girl, who had matured into a pretty young woman, had met the actor when she was eighteen, and she confirmed to reporters that two years later they were still 'good friends'. She added, 'He is a lovely guy and I kissed him once or twice when we were out together. But I don't want to talk about it too much because he hates girls who kiss and tell—and I don't want to be one of those girls.'

She first met Bisson while out for a drink in the Capitol Bar on Dublin's Aungier Street. 'The first time I met him, he was over in Dublin for the weekend with friends,' she said. 'He loves it over in Ireland and comes over about twice a year. He thinks the pubs and clubs are great and the people are really nice. I just happened to be out in the same pub and bumped into him. He was surrounded by women and was getting loads of attention.

'But he wasn't bothered with the girls who were crawling all over him. Myself and my friend were just standing there talking to each other and being cool,' said the hairdresser.

Bisson was smitten. And when he returned to England, he did not forget about the girl he had met in Ireland. He kept in contact, regularly calling and texting her. 'We got on really well and he kept in touch even after he went home, which was nice,' she said. 'At one point he called me up and asked me to come over and visit him, but I couldn't at the time. After that meeting in Dublin we got to know each other very well.'

When he returned to Ireland the following year, to take part in a celebrity football match, he looked her up again. 'He asked me if I'd like to go out for the night with him and we went to the Kitchen nightclub in the Clarence Hotel and then on to Renards nightclub.'

The couple spent the night smooching—much to the surprise of one onlooker in the Kitchen who knew about the girl's murder conviction, and who had spotted Chris straight away: 'All the celebs went into the VIP area, but he stayed out at the bar to talk to this girl. They were sitting very close and seemed very intimate together—they were looking into each other's eyes and enjoying the company. A short while later I met her in the toilet and I asked: "What's the story with you and that fella?" and she grinned and said: "Well, we'll have to wait and see." She and Chris were there for about two hours and then left together. They looked just like any other couple, kissing away in the corner.'

Little did the *Corrie* star realise he was getting intimate with a cold-blooded killer. A killer who, because of the lack of a suitable detention centre, got away with murder.

06 | THE SMILING FACE OF THE DEPRESSIVE

MARY KEEGAN

I n the first six years of this new century 336 people were murdered in Ireland, twenty-six of whom were children. Most
murdered children are killed by their mother or father, but
what drives a loving parent to kill? 'Usually insanity,' says Dr Brian
McCaffrey. This is not a glib dismissal of these tragic cases. He has
worked on several cases of this nature, and bases his opinion on
solid facts. He is often called upon to assist a court in deciding
whether someone is fit to plea, or whether they were not legally
sane at the time of a killing.

'All mine were insane,' he says. 'In cases of women killing
children, it is not necessarily a psychiatric condition from childhood. Some of them can be quite normal. There are two broad
types of conditions that might lead a mother to kill. There are the
schizophrenic cases and the depressive cases.

'When a woman kills her child you are going to get very few, if
any, cases that are not psychiatric in origin. Post-natal depression
is very serious, both from a suicide point of view, and from a
danger of killing children. The sad thing is that it can be very
treatable.'

Dr McCaffrey confirmed that in the majority of cases in which a
woman kills her children she will also attempt to take her own life.

'If a woman kills the child because of a depressive illness there is a high risk of suicide.' The matter is less clear if the psychiatric condition is schizophrenic rather than depressive.

The list of children killed by their mothers over the past few years makes depressing reading. In July 2007 the bodies of Nollaig Owen (aged thirty-three) and her son Tadhg were recovered from the River Araglin in County Cork. In January of the same year Eileen Murphy threw herself from the Cliffs of Moher, taking her four-year-old son Evan to his death with her. Incredibly Evan survived the seven hundred-foot fall, but died later of the injuries he received.

In May 2007 a particularly tragic case occurred in Letterkenny, County Donegal. Young mother Caitriona Innes (twenty-six) hung herself after suffocating her seven-year-old daughter Caitlin at their home. The tragedy happened following the little girl's first Holy Communion celebrations.

In May 2006 psychiatrist Dr Lynn Gibbs drowned her teenage daughter. That case is covered in Chapter 9 of this book.

Sharon Grace (twenty-eight) drowned herself and her two young daughters Mikayla (four) and Abbey (three) at Kaats Strand, Wexford, in April 2005. She spared her son. A short time earlier she had tried to speak to a social worker at a Wexford hospital, but was told that none was available.

There have been other cases—too many of them. Not all make a big splash, and some turn out better than others. A Clare woman who set fire to her home in September 2005—when her husband and three children were inside—was given a suspended sentence because of her psychiatric condition. Luckily no one was injured in the arson attack.

Dr John Connolly, an expert in suicide, says: 'It is very difficult to know why some parents feel the need to take the life of a child with them. Some people who are very depressed can see things in a very black-and-white fashion and feel the only way to end their pain is to end their life, and they don't want to leave their children behind. Other people have the idea that they don't want their children to grow up in a world they perceive to be terrible.'

It would make depressing reading to examine each case in detail, but this chapter will focus on one such case which illustrates how depression can quietly eat away at a woman until she cannot take any more. In the next chapter we will see how a schizophrenic condition can also lead to murder.

The Keegans, who lived in the south Dublin suburb of Firhouse, seemed to be a very happy family. Brian Keegan worked as an engineer with the technical support unit of a Dun Laoghaire lawnmower business. His wife Mary, forty-one, was a part-time beautician who also worked in a bank. She was on a job-share at GE Money, just behind Dublin Castle in the centre of the city, where she worked as an administrator. She got on well with her colleagues, and had framed photos of her sons on her desk in the large open-plan office.

The couple had met when they were both in their early twenties. Mary grew up on Anne Devlin Road, in nearby Rathfarnham. People remember her as a carefree young girl who looked after her appearance and always dressed well. She met Brian, who was a mechanic from the area, and they fell in love. They moved into a pleasant home in Firhouse, in the shadow of the Dublin Mountains, and had two lovely children. Things were going well.

A neighbour, Peter Hale, said they were a lovely family with no problems that he could see. They had two active young boys, who were full of fun and life and very well looked after. Glenn was the older of the two, a sports-mad ten-year-old who loved playing hurling. He was in fourth class in the nearby Scoil Treasa on Ballycullan Avenue. But he threw himself into other activities as well—he was involved in a school production of *Snow White and the Seven Dwarfs*, in which he was going to be singing on stage.

Andrew, just a month short of his seventh birthday, was quieter. He was in first class at Scoil Carmel, a sister school to Scoil Treasa for the lower age groups. His brother had gone to the school a few years earlier, and their mother had also attended there.

The two boys were close and often played outside on the road. The Keegans lived in a pleasant semi-detached house on a quiet cul-de-sac at Killakee Walk, Firhouse. Mary was always careful to leave the door open when the boys were outside.

In early February 2006, Brian Keegan was sent by his employers on a week-long trip to a trade fair in the United States. He had no worries about going. His wife had been feeling a bit down of late, but nothing to be unduly worried about. She was a happy woman, known for her smile. All her neighbours commented on her cheerfulness.

Before he left for America the family went to the Scholars pub in Firhouse for lunch. It was their favourite bar, and they often went there as a family. They were the picture of happiness, joking and laughing over the meal, the boys running around the feet of the staff as little boys do.

'You couldn't meet a nicer bunch of people. Mary was quite simply an amazing person,' remembers one waiter. 'There are couples who come in here and you get rumblings that all is not right,' said another. 'You can't help wondering what goes on when they go home at night. But Brian and Mary were not like that. They weren't the sort you worried about,' said another waiter.

Mary coped well in the absence of her husband. He would only be gone for a week, and she didn't seem bothered. She was keeping a lid on her depression, and very few people knew anything about it. 'Mary had up days and down days just like everyone else. But she was such a caring person and had such a great sense of humour that it is hard to imagine her ever getting cross,' said one friend.

On Thursday 10 February 2006 Mary left GE Money as usual, saying a cheery goodbye to her colleagues. None of them suspected they would never see her again.

On Friday Mary went about her day as usual. The bubbly brunette dropped in on her boys' childminder, Mary Russell. Mrs Russell's daughter had recently got married, and Mary left off a present for her. 'She was happy and laughing. I never noticed anything wrong,' said Mrs Russell. 'The Mary that did this is not the Mary I know and love.'

That evening Mary dropped in on a neighbour to pick up her younger son, Andrew. Andrew often went to play at the house of his best friend Evan Tobin. She needed to pick him up before six to take him to GAA training: both boys had to be at the Sancta Maria all-weather pitch for six. Glenn was training that night; Andrew didn't train, but he often went up with his mother to watch. As it was usually their father, Brian, who brought the two boys to training, Brian was a familiar figure in the club.

Noel Sheridan, manager of Ballyboden St Enda's, said: 'Glenn was an all-rounder in sports. He wanted to play everything.'

The training session that night was important, because Glenn had a game the following morning. After the session the two boys went home with their mother.

The following morning nothing looked amiss. Mary brought Glenn to the Ballyboden St Enda's grounds, where he lined out for his underage team as usual, and enjoyed the game. His mother and little brother watched and cheered from the sidelines. Mary chatted to other young mothers about the next week's games, and seemed to be in good form. When Glenn's team won she whooped with joy.

Mary brought the children home after the game, and there was still no evidence that anything was amiss. Nothing is known of her movements once they got home, but it appears, from forensic evidence, that nothing notable happened that evening. The boys went to bed as normal.

But at some point during that lonely night, with her husband thousands of miles away, the depression that was eating at the soul of Mary Keegan finally won. She got up and locked the doors of the house. Then she woke her two startled sons and marched them down to the kitchen, closing the door behind them. They must have been surprised, as it was the early hours of Sunday morning. However, they were probably too groggy with sleep to know what was happening.

What came next was mercifully swift. Mary picked up a sharp carving knife and drove it into the back of one of her sons. She then turned on the other quickly and drove the knife into his stomach. Both boys would have died almost instantly, indicated by the fact that neither had any defensive wounds. Even at that tender age they would have fought valiantly for their lives had they had the chance—they would at least have got a hand in the way of the knife—and the fact that no such wounds were found suggests a swift death.

Both boys suffered multiple stab wounds—at least twenty. It is probable that she killed each boy quickly then went back to the bodies and continued her frenzied attack, driving the knife repeatedly into each body.

After killing both her sons, Mary turned the knife on herself. She slashed at her neck, then drove the knife into her left wrist a number of times, severing an artery and bleeding out within minutes.

A cut to the side of the neck or the inside of the thigh will bleed in rapid powerful gushes, causing death very quickly. A slit wrist takes longer to lead to death, as the artery is far thinner and carries far less blood than the leg or neck arteries. It may have taken a few minutes before Mary Keegan lost consciousness, and death would have followed swiftly.

Meanwhile, Brian Keegan, oblivious to the tragedy, was, with some difficulty, making his way home from the trade fair. Winter flying is often hampered by the weather conditions, and Brian's flight had been delayed by snowstorms in New York. When he finally got home on Monday morning he rang the house to see if Mary was there. He had not brought his house keys with him on the trip, assuming that she would be at home to let him in. There was no answer. He was slightly surprised because it was mid-term break and he thought Mary would be there with the kids: she wasn't due to go to work that day. But perhaps she had gone on an errand? He rang the childminder, Mrs Russell, to see had she left the two boys with her. But she hadn't.

Not knowing what to think, Brian rang a neighbour. The man was a garda, but he was off duty and Brian caught him at home. He explained his predicament—he had no key and he couldn't contact Mary. He might need help to break into his house. The neighbour said he would go up the road and try to get into the house before Brian got home from Dublin Airport. Not waiting for Brian meant that he unknowingly spared him a haunting sight.

The off-duty garda managed to get into the house, and made the grim discovery in the kitchen. Both boys were dead. Mary Keegan was sitting in a pool of blood, also dead. The room was covered in blood, like a scene from a nightmare.

Retreating, he rang the gardaí. The house was quickly sealed off. Forensic scientists, anxious to preserve the scene, took the precaution of getting a ladder and climbing in over the back wall to enter the house. This was the scene Brian Keegan returned to. Mercifully his neighbour was able to shield him from the bloody horror in his kitchen.

'It was quite a sight,' said one garda.

'It was a terrible scene for any guard to have to come across, really awful,' said another, senior, officer. 'Obviously there was a lot of blood. We'll now begin trying to determine exactly what went wrong.'

Mr Keegan was instantly taken from the scene to be comforted by relations. It would be two days before he could make a proper statement to the gardaí, and it didn't throw much light on what could turn a loving, happy mother into a killer.

The autopsy report shed no light: it showed the boys had suffered multiple stab wounds to their backs, faces and necks, and that their mother had bled to death after stabbing herself and cutting her wrists. There was no suicide note.

There was a great deal of speculation that Mary Keegan was suffering from depression, but little evidence to back this up. She had been to see her doctor on a few occasions, but these visits were for minor matters unrelated to depression. Some people thought she might have been worried about money, but her husband had a job, she had a job, and they had no financial difficulties.

There was also a suggestion that she may have suffered a psychotic reaction to a new skin treatment she was using, a proposition that is highly unlikely but not completely impossible. During the early nineties an acne cure had to be severely restricted when it was discovered that long-term use caused depression in a small number of people, some of whom had taken their own lives.

Dr McCaffrey says that murder–suicide cases are frequently linked to depression. Depression is a hidden illness—people often don't talk about it, going to great lengths to keep up a cheerful appearance. It can be treated quite easily, generally with a course of anti-depressants and some talking therapy. But if untreated it festers, and can cause major problems. Mary Keegan didn't look depressed to anyone on her final weekend, but appearances can be deceptive.

It is well known that suicides often happen when people are coming out of a depression. In the depths of despair they do not have the energy to kill themselves, but when they are emerging from a depressed state, their energy returns before the black mood has lifted fully, and that is the danger time.

'Energy levels can improve before the thought processes improve. In other words, they can have the physical energy without the mental energy. So they can actually kill themselves or their child before they are out of the real depression,' says Dr McCaffrey.

This may have been the case with Mary Keegan. She was coping as best she could while her husband was away, but the depression was building. She took her sons home from the football game around lunchtime on Saturday, and she was alone in the house all night, with worries and fears preying on her mind. Then perhaps she thought about her husband, on his way home and due back on Sunday. Mary didn't know about the delay to his flight. Perhaps her mood began to lift; but her physical energy peaked before she had lifted out of the depression—and then her mind flipped.

No one knows. Neighbours felt guilty afterwards. It is a small, quiet estate—why didn't they hear the boys screaming? Why didn't they notice that the family were not seen all day on Sunday? The truth is that the boys probably didn't scream: it would all have happened too quickly.

The community rallied around Brian, in shocked disbelief at the tragedy that had engulfed his life, and the one thing that he kept hearing was that Mary had been a happy woman. Before the funeral, Brian released a statement saying that he was 'devastated and in shock' over the loss of his wife and children, and appealing for privacy to allow him time to grieve.

At the inquest eight months later a little light was shed on why the tragedy had occurred. The inquest heard evidence that Mrs Keegan was suffering from delusions of poverty and became psychotic as a result. Had she survived her suicide attempt and been tried for the murder of her sons, she would have been found insane, as she was incapable of fully understanding what she was doing when she killed the boys.

Brian Keegan spoke movingly about the love he felt for his wife, despite his grief at the loss of his entire family. 'I would like to state clearly that I am proud to have known and married Mary. She was the most loving and generous person I ever met and was an inspiration to me and our beautiful children Glenn and Andrew,' Mr Keegan said in a statement released by his solicitor. 'Unbeknownst to myself and those close to her, Mary became over a short period of time engulfed in depression. This led to Mary's actions on that fateful day.

'There is, however, no anger in my heart towards her as her actions were borne out of a will to protect our children from the harshness she perceived in this world, however inconceivable or incomprehensible this may appear to us.'

The jury returned a verdict of death by suicide in relation to Mrs Keegan's death and an open verdict on the deaths of Andrew and Glenn.

One elderly neighbour summed up the tragedy: 'There was nothing we could have done. We didn't know about Mary's depression. She hid it very well, because she always seemed to be smiling. Depression is a black hole that can lead people to do things few of us can understand. Something flipped in her brain that day. Maybe it was a moment of insanity.

'No one knows the truth of what goes on behind closed doors. Would any of us willingly open our doors and claim we have nothing to hide? And nowadays people think you're being nosy if you ask questions about their private lives. In the past we knew everything about everyone. Maybe that was a better way to be. There will be no answers here. Mary has taken her story to the grave.'

07 | MUMMY, PLEASE! I WANT TO LIVE

JACQUELINE COSTELLO

'Mummy, please! I want to live,' screamed the eight-year-old boy, staring in horror at his mother, who had always loved him, always been a rock. 'I don't want to die.' But her hands tightened around his neck, and she kept squeezing, until the light went out in his eyes, and his head lolled to the side, and he was dead.

When children are killed there are many possible motives. In the case of a seriously ill child it may be a mercy killing. It might be the result of a psychotic episode in which the parent believes they are being commanded to kill the child, or an altruistic belief that the murder is in some way saving the child from a greater hurt. Sometimes a child dies an accidental death from maltreatment; sometimes killing a child is revenge against a partner or spouse.

While the examples of child murders in the preceding chapter may give the impression that killing your child, or filicide, is a peculiarly female crime, this is not the case. The number of mothers who kill their children is roughly the same as the number of fathers who do so. For every one of the children listed in the last chapter who was killed by their mother, another child was killed by their father.

Six-year-old Deirdre Crowley was kidnapped by her father and shot when the gardaí moved in on him; George McGloin stabbed his two-year-old daughter in the neck; in Westmeath, Greg Fox killed his wife Debbie and their two young sons. Arthur McElhill set his house in Omagh on fire, killing himself, his wife and their five children. Adrian Dunne went out and bought coffins for everyone, then came home and killed his wife and two girls before taking his own life.

While more or less the same number of fathers and mothers kill their children, there tend to be differences in motivation. Fathers are less likely to kill for altruistic motives, and more likely to kill during abusive emotional outbursts. Killings are often triggered by the breakdown of a relationship. Men are more likely to take their own lives after the event (suicide is in any case more prevalent among men than among women); and they also have a greater tendency towards familicide, the killing of the entire family.

Women, according to international studies, are more likely to use a hands-on approach to killing, favouring methods such as drowning, suffocation or strangulation, while men are more likely to use a weapon. (Sometimes women do use weapons, however, as we saw in the last chapter.) Mothers seem more likely than fathers to kill younger children. The killing of teenage children is extremely rare all over the world, which is why the case of Dr Lynn Gibbs (described in Chapter 9) is so unusual.

In most cases of murder–suicide there is a history of mental illness. Sometimes a parent can become so depressed that they believe life is hopeless, and because they see their child as an extension of themselves, of course life seems hopeless for the child as well.

'If someone is in such a severe depressive state that they have a feeling their circumstances are hopeless, the suicidal motivation can extend to significant others,' according to Dr John Bogue, a forensic psychologist at NUI Galway.

Many people think filicide is a recent phenomenon. There was a series of cases in which parents killed their children around the summer of 2001, with six children losing their lives. Was this another sign of the breakdown of society in the modern world? It seems not—if anything, it's a rarer occurrence now than it ever was. 'In the 1950s one in six homicides involved the killing of a baby. In 1952, for example, the majority of recorded homicides involved babies. People have short memories,' says Dr Ian O'Donnell of UCD's Institute of Criminology.

Sifting through all the theories, three strands emerge: killers can be sad, mad or bad. Dr Brian McCaffrey distinguishes between women who kill their children when they are suffering from depressive illnesses (and these women are likely to attempt to take their own lives afterwards), and those who kill because of a schizophrenic condition. In layman's terms these are the sad and the mad. There is another category: some people are just appalling parents, with no normal maternal or paternal feelings for their children, and no care for their welfare. They are the bad—the people who abuse and neglect children until they die—and they are the subject of the next chapter. This chapter focuses on the mad.

'The Costello case was very sad. That poor girl went in to the psychiatric unit in Waterford and was walking along when she got this awful smell. It was actually a schizophrenic perception. In schizophrenia sensations can be magnified a thousand times. The girl thought the smell was so bad it was like rotting corpses in the unit, so she was terrified of going in. She went home and an hour later killed an eight-year-old boy. It was an awfully sad case,' said Dr McCaffrey.

Jacqueline Costello was originally from Waterford. She met and fell in love with Stephen O'Keeffe, and they moved in together. They shared a house in Woodlawn Grove, and over the next few years they had three children. The first, Robert, was a bright, intelligent boy who was eight in 2000. He was followed five years later by Martin. Then came the third son, Stephen, who was twenty-two months old in the autumn of that year.

Stephen O'Keeffe remembers the good times with Jacqueline. In the earlier years of the relationship, he said, 'I couldn't have been happier; she was fine and we were thrilled. We had three children and one was as beautiful as the other. Jackie was a mother who was second to none. They were really good kids, she'd do anything for them.'

They had a 'good family life', but Jacqueline suffered from bouts of depression and the 'baby blues', which began to spoil a situation which had once been 'absolutely perfect'. The time came when Jacqueline's character 'changed totally'. 'She began drinking very heavily, she wasn't listening to me, and she became abusive.'

She had some history of psychiatric problems, and it appears that she was beginning to suffer from the same problems again.

In 1995 she had begun seeing Dr Derek O'Sullivan, a consultant psychiatrist, who diagnosed depression and began treating her with a range of anti-depressants. None of them seemed to have much of an effect, so he briefly switched her medication, putting her on something normally prescribed to schizophrenics. She responded well to the new drugs, but for some reason the regime was discontinued, and she was put back on the anti-depressants and mood stabilisers, which did not have a huge impact on her condition.

Giving evidence at the trial, Dr Brian McCaffrey said that he did not believe that Jacqueline was suffering from depression. He said that the onset of her problems was over a year after the birth of Robert, so this was not a case of baby blues. 'I believe she was a misdiagnosed schizophrenic,' he said. The clue, he said, lay in how well she responded when her medication was switched. 'To me that was a clue to the diagnosis. It was not for the treatment of depression, but she responded.'

When her schizophrenia went untreated her mental problems grew. Jacqueline began to drink and she also became addicted to drugs. Her personality was changing and the people around her found it difficult to cope with her behaviour and mood swings. Her parents found it particularly difficult.

Thomas and Irene Costello helped her through one crisis after another: in 1995, when she overdosed in an apparent suicide attempt; and on another occasion, when she tried to cut herself. But they were both, especially Irene, finding it more and more difficult. Jacqueline began having problems again in September 2000 and on one occasion arrived at her parents' house in an agitated state. 'We were wrecked from it all. We couldn't go through it again,' said Thomas Costello. Applying the principle of 'tough love', and feeling that his wife could not cope with the demands of their daughter, he turned Jacqueline away from the house. He would later describe that as 'the biggest mistake of my life'. Jacqueline was under a great deal of strain and the schizophrenia was again taking a grip on her mind. But no one knew what was happening to her, because her condition remained undiagnosed.

A few weeks later thirty-year-old Jacqueline separated from her partner of ten years, and moved out of the city. She found a bungalow in the pretty village of Mullinavat, and moved in, taking the three children with her. Mullinavat, in south Kilkenny, is a little village on the main Waterford to Dublin road, about eight miles north of Waterford city.

Although they were no longer living together, Jacqueline remained close to Stephen O'Keeffe, and he regularly visited his three children. He wasn't the only visitor from her past life. An elderly couple, who were Jehovah's Witnesses, had befriended Jacqueline, and on Saturday 21 October they decided to drop in on her to see how she was settling in. John and Maria Ramshaw were disturbed by what they saw that day: Jacqueline was clearly stressed, and was behaving strangely. 'She heard voices and thought it was God talking to her,' said Maria.

During that visit John had been less concerned: he thought Jacqueline and her three children were a normal family; but he did say that Jacqueline was 'very emotionally volatile' and 'emotionally in turmoil'. The couple arranged to call in on Jacqueline a week later, then returned to Waterford.

Unfortunately, the voices in Jacqueline's head were becoming stronger, and her schizophrenia was growing. During the week after the Ramshaws' visit, Stephen O'Keeffe called out to see the kids. They were delighted to see him, but he was very concerned when he saw his partner. She didn't appear well, and he was not happy with the upkeep of the house. Alarm bells began to ring.

He was concerned enough to ring Jacqueline's GP when he returned to Waterford, and to contact a social worker to express his concern. The social worker rang him back and said she thought Jacqueline was okay, but he wasn't convinced.

During that week, Jacqueline made several phone calls to her brother, Patrick Costello, in which she seemed very agitated, which is one reason Patrick had decided to drive down from Dublin that weekend to stay in the family home in Waterford. 'I travelled down because of the phone calls,' he said.

The final call came on the morning of 28 October, a Saturday. This time Jacqueline was highly agitated, and kept passing the phone to her eldest son. 'She kept handing the phone to Robert. I told him not to worry and that I'd be down that night.' But Robert was worried: he had seen the signs that his mother's mental problems were growing, but there was nothing he could do to help her.

That morning Stephen O'Keeffe arrived at the house. The children were delighted to see him, and Robert in particular was beaming at his father. It would be one of the last memories Stephen had of his son.

Stephen managed to persuade Jacqueline to come with him to the hospital. She needed to be checked out, and perhaps put on appropriate medication. She was reluctant, but eventually got into the car and they drove to Waterford; however, when they arrived she became very upset and was reluctant to go in. When she did eventually get into the hospital she was seen by a doctor and a nurse, but her agitation grew. She panicked and ran from the hospital.

'She suffered an olfactory hallucination,' said Dr McCaffrey. 'It was actually a schizophrenic perception. In schizophrenia sensations can be magnified a thousand times. For example, a person can be walking along and see just a crack on the pavement. But for that person it seems a major crevice that they can't step over.

'The smell—Jacqueline thought the smell was so bad it was like rotting corpses, and she ran away from there, she was so terrified of going in.'

Dr McCaffrey said that Jacqueline should not have been allowed to leave Waterford Regional Hospital that day. 'She should have been admitted. She should have been detained as an involuntary patient and committed,' he said. Unfortunately, that did not happen, and Stephen reluctantly drove his ex-partner back to Mullinavat, leaving her there with the children.

He later recalled how 'thrilled' Robert was to see him on that last morning. 'A smile came on his face, his eyes lit up, like: "Daddy's here, it's going to be all right."' As Stephen drove back into Waterford he had no idea how far from all right it was. Now Jacqueline was on her own. Her brother was not due for hours, and the Ramshaws were not expected until later in the afternoon. She was on her own, and the voices in her head were getting louder. They were telling her that Robert was possessed.

She walked into the house and began to do some housework, but the children seemed to be everywhere, constantly under her feet. As she told gardaí later, she was cleaning the house and the children were laughing at her. 'They were running around me. I had no rest at all. I just wanted to clean up and be normal,' she said.

In her first statement she said she wanted Robert to take some tablets. 'I just wanted him to take the sleeping tablets. He said: "No fucking way." So I caught him by the throat and killed him.'

Later she expanded on that. 'I don't know what happened. I said to Robert: "You know what has to be done, take some sleeping tablets." He said: "I don't want them. I want to live. I want to live." "You'll be grand and you'll be doing us all a favour," I told him.'

The delusional mother tried to force-feed her son the sleeping tablets. She had bottles of Seven-Up out on the table to help him swallow them, but he resisted. So she tried something else. 'I don't know what happened. I don't know where I got the strength. I put my hand around his throat. I just made sure he died. I couldn't look. I felt so sick. I just couldn't believe what happened to me.'

Questioned about whether she had blocked his mouth as well as strangling him, she replied: 'No, I don't remember putting my hand over his mouth at any stage.'

To strangle a full-grown man with a thick neck takes some strength. To strangle a young boy takes very little pressure or effort. Because of the relative size of an adult's hands and a child's neck, strangulation does two things: the air supply is cut off, making breathing impossible; and the carotid artery to the brain, which runs up the side of the neck, is blocked. Unconsciousness follows within half a minute, even less if the strangulation cuts off the blood supply efficiently. Death follows soon after.

The autopsy later revealed that Robert had died as a result of asphyxiation, partial suffocation, and compression of the neck, as well as inhalation of gastric contents. It sounds horrible but at least it would have been quick.

Less than an hour later a car pulled up outside the house. It was the two Jehovah's Witnesses who had befriended Jacqueline. They were shocked when they came into the front garden of the house. Maria Ramshaw said that she and her husband found Jacqueline in the garden, shouting and crying loudly.

'I saw her standing in the garden. She was shouting and blaspheming. She was really very, very upset and was waving her arms around. She seemed very distressed and upset.'

When Jacqueline became aware of her visitors she seemed to calm down. She invited them in and said: 'Come in, then, you might as well see the evidence.'

The Ramshaws went into the kitchen and looked around. There were bottles of Seven-Up strewn all around, and an awful lot of tablets. Jacqueline told her visitors not to drink the Seven-Up as it was poisoned. But it was not the bottles that drew their attention. Straight away Maria saw a small body slumped in the sitting room. At this stage Jacqueline seemed calm, and said to them: 'Don't let the three-year-old see.' Then she left the house and went into the garage, attempting to lock herself in.

The couple rushed into the sitting room and found the little boy lying on his back. There was a small kitten sitting on his chest. 'It made me feel terrible. He was lying very still, his legs spread out and his arms up, with bubbles of froth coming out of his mouth,' said Mrs Ramshaw. She immediately got down on the carpet and tried to revive the young boy. She could see no signs of life, and she failed to find a pulse. Her husband ran next door to ring for the emergency services. After a while, Jacqueline came back into the house in a distressed state. She said she was going to kill herself. 'She kept repeating: "I'm only twenty-seven years old,"' said Maria Ramshaw.

The neighbours were shocked when Garda cars and an ambulance showed up in the quiet village. Eileen Lannon said: 'They appeared to be a normal, quiet family. I only saw her once. She was walking with the children, and had one of them in a buggy and was holding one by the hand. You'd see the children playing outside the house.'

'It's the last thing you would expect in a place like this,' said her husband John. 'It's a terrible thing to happen on your doorstep and everyone is very upset.'

Jacqueline's brother Patrick was also shocked when a squad car pulled up outside the family home in Waterford city. 'My first thought was that my sister had harmed herself, but they were looking for someone to identify the body,' he said. 'When they told me Jackie was implicated I was stunned.'

On Sunday afternoon Jacqueline was charged with murder before a special sitting of Waterford District Court.

Two days later a large crowd turned out for the removal of Robert's remains. St Paul's Church in Lisduggan, Waterford, was full for the short ceremony, and Robert's father was one of the men carrying the small white coffin. The look in his son's eyes the last time they had met must have haunted him.

At the funeral Mass the following day, Fr Paul Waldron said that only a few months ago many of the same people had gathered around the same altar to see Robert celebrate his first Communion. 'It seems to make no sense that we are gathered here this morning for his funeral.'

Jacqueline's trial was held in April 2002. She pleaded not guilty to murder. Prosecuting barrister Miriam Reynolds told the jury: 'You must decide not whether Robert Costello was killed by Jacqueline Costello, but whether or not she is guilty of murder— or whether she is guilty but was insane at the time.'

The psychiatric evidence was crucial to their decision. The jury heard that Jacqueline was suffering from a psychosis 'causing insanity'. Two psychiatric consultants gave evidence that she was insane at the time of the killing, that she didn't know that what she was doing was wrong, and couldn't have stopped herself doing it.

Dr McCaffrey said: 'Jacqueline was so psychotic that she felt she was doing the right thing. She was actually killing Robert but she didn't realise it. She could not have been persuaded to stop.'

After hearing a number of days of evidence the jury took only twenty minutes to reach a unanimous verdict. A large number of members of Jacqueline's family, and her ex-partner Stephen O'Keeffe, were there to hear it. Jacqueline Costello was guilty but insane. She hugged her brother Patrick, and was taken from the court.

Mr Justice Paul Butler ordered that Ms Costello be detained in the Central Mental Hospital in Dundrum. Then he rounded on the government. 'The criminal insanity laws in this country are not only grotesque, but obscene. Poor Robert was the prime victim, but the accused too is a very real victim,' he said.

'A real stigma is attached to the verdict of guilty but insane. It should be not guilty by reason of insanity. There have been several reports about this. It is quite clear to our policy makers but nothing has been done about it.'

Four years later the judge got his way, when the Criminal Law (Insanity) Act 2006 was passed, and the verdict was changed. But the end result is the same; several years in the Central Mental Hospital. The average length of time that someone will stay in the Central Mental Hospital for a crime such as murder or manslaughter is fourteen and a half years—and this is about two years longer than the time the average lifer does in prison. The other thing that hasn't changed is that Robert—the 'prime victim', the little boy who wanted to live—is still dead.

08 | THE MOTHERS FROM HELL
ABUSE THROUGH THE YEARS

She was the worst mother in the world, she said, and she seemed to take a perverse pleasure in the fact. 'I knew it was my fault, but I was too lazy,' she explained, as Ireland reacted in horror to tales of children going unfed, unwashed and uncared for. Not only were her children half-starved and crawling with lice, she had even, when the mood struck her, forced her eldest son, aged just thirteen, to have sex with her. 'Mammy didn't take care of us right,' cried one of her girls, as she recalled the other school-children refusing to play with her because she smelled.

She was the mother from hell, but sadly she is not an isolated phenomenon. There are some people whose behaviour is so appalling, whose casual cruelty so overwhelming, whose emotions so depraved, that we can scarcely believe they are human. In the previous two chapters we looked at the sad and the mad. Now we turn our attention to the bad.

Psychiatrists might be able to explain how women who abuse their children sink so low, but no amount of psychological theorising can excuse or justify or mitigate their behaviour. These women are bad to the core.

This book is an exploration of violent Irish women, and the behaviour shown in the three cases in this chapter includes some of the most violent abuses it is possible to inflict on another person. No one was ever charged with murder, but a child died—and died horribly—in two out of the three cases. So those women have earned their place in the annals of shame.

The first case goes back thirty-five years or more, and to the quiet, leafy suburb of Dalkey. Cynthia Murphy grew up in the house from hell. Hers was a large family, and she claims that from the age of seven she was sexually abused and raped on a regular basis. She says that four people passed her around as their plaything. Cynthia was not the only member of her household to make that claim: five of the six females brought up in the house claimed that they were sexually abused. It seemed to be part of family life in the Murphy household.

Some commentators have looked at the allegations of Cynthia Owen (she changed her name as an adult to that of her partner) and dismissed them as the ramblings of a fevered mind. False memory syndrome is a very real phenomenon, but there is quite a bit of evidence to substantiate Cynthia's claims, some of it circumstantial, but compelling none the less.

In 1995 one of Cynthia's brothers hung himself after telling one of his sisters that he had been sodomised in the family home. Another brother vanished in 2002, and his body was found under bushes three years later. Gardaí ruled the case a probable suicide. Three weeks after his body was discovered, another member of the household killed herself. She was the daughter of one of Cynthia's sisters, but she thought she was her sister. She left a thirty-seven-page suicide note detailing a whole history of sexual abuse at the hands of her family. There's no place like home.

Cynthia's own story is appalling. Her maternal grandmother was a distinctive figure in Dalkey, always shabbily dressed and smelling foul and unwashed. Her daughter Josephine—Cynthia's mother—had a son before she was married, whose father was reputed to be the man who would later become her father-in-law. Josephine was an alcoholic, which, given her family situation, is hardly surprising.

The family home was a two-bedroom cottage with a single downstairs room. Into that tiny space were crammed fourteen people: two parents and twelve children, eleven of whom were brothers and sisters. The twelfth child thought she was another sibling, but in fact she was the daughter of one of her older 'sisters'.

Cynthia's father was a chimney sweep before he became caretaker of the local town hall. As a boy he had lived in a children's home, where he had been abused. Dr Brian McCaffrey says that while it is not a given that someone who was abused in childhood will go on to abuse, there is evidence to show that those who have been abused are more likely to go on to become abusers themselves.

The Murphy children were regularly beaten and sexually assaulted, says Cynthia. The attacks came from family members, and from outsiders. Neighbours support this picture of a severely dysfunctional family; many remember that the children were shabbily dressed and permanently infested with head lice.

Cynthia was raped for the first time at the age of seven, and for the next several years was at the disposal of four members of the household.

When Cynthia was eleven she discovered she was pregnant. As a slim pre-teen, there was no hiding the growing bump, and people in the neighbourhood did notice; but no one said anything. Ireland in 1973 was a very repressed place. One man remembers discussing the girl's condition with his wife at the dinner table. But no one helped the frightened young girl.

In April of that year Cynthia felt pains; she was going into labour. After a number of hours she gave birth to a healthy baby girl. What happened next was truly barbaric. Her mother Josephine took the child and stabbed her to death with a knitting needle. She didn't just stab the child to death: she butchered her; and she did it before her horrified daughter's eyes. There were at least forty separate stab wounds to the tiny body. The baby died of haemorrhaging from the wounds to her neck.

Her bloody work done, Josephine placed the tiny corpse in a plastic bag, smothered with newspapers to absorb the blood, left the house and walked to nearby Dun Laoghaire, making Cynthia come with her. On the walk they met gardaí on two separate occasions. Josephine Murphy calmly greeted the gardaí and walked on, carrying the bag containing the bloody corpse of the murdered baby. When they reached Dun Laoghaire she dumped the bag in a laneway.

The following day, 4 April, two young boys found the bloody bag, and alerted the gardaí. A full murder investigation was not launched. Infanticide was not given the same priority as the murder of an adult, and the case was quickly pushed aside, half investigated. Forensic evidence was not kept, the files were not updated, and the bag in which the body was found was lost. Gardaí did make an attempt to find the child's mother, by enquiring about any teenagers who were pregnant at the time; but although several people had spotted Cynthia's bump and knew she was expecting, she never made it on to the Garda list.

On 27 April an inquest found that the baby had bled to death due to multiple stab wounds. She was buried in the Holy Angels plot in Glasnevin, along with more than a dozen other babies, and the case was quickly forgotten.

But life went on as normally—or as abnormally—as ever for Cynthia. The abuse continued; the rapes and sexual abuse continued; and in less than four years she was pregnant again.

She was just fifteen when she had her second child, a stillborn boy. In her head Cynthia called him John. She had called her first baby Noeleen. Her mother took the tiny body and buried it in the garden of the house. She didn't bury it deep enough, though, and after a while a little hand poked up through the grass; so the tiny corpse was reburied.

Cynthia eventually got out of the house of horrors and made a life for herself. She met a loving man, took his name, and they settled down and had children together. But her past continued to haunt her. In June 1994 she walked into Dun Laoghaire Garda Station and told surprised officers that the baby found in 1973, twenty-one years previously, had been hers. They could scarcely believe her—she looked too young—but an investigation was launched. Three members of the family were arrested and questioned about the baby's death, but the Director of Public Prosecutions decided not to proceed with a case because of the passage of time and the lack of witnesses.

It was not long after this that Cynthia's brother Martin hung himself, after confiding to one of his sisters that he had been repeatedly sodomised as a child. Seven years later another brother, Michael, disappeared. He too had killed himself, but it would be three years before his body was found in undergrowth near Killiney Dart station.

Much later, on 23 February 2005, Theresa Murphy hung herself, leaving a thirty-seven-page suicide note cataloguing all the horrors she had been put through. Theresa was the daughter of Cynthia's sister Margaret, though she grew up thinking she was one of the sisters.

More than a decade had passed since Cynthia had walked into the Garda station with her extraordinary story, during which nothing had been done. But finally Cynthia achieved something: the inquest into the death of the baby in 1973 was reopened in front of the Dublin coroner. Although Justice Minister Michael McDowell had refused permission to exhume the corpse, this time Cynthia would be present to tell her story.

However, there were several legal issues that had to be resolved, including the fact that some members of her family denied Cynthia's claims, and one took a High Court case in a bid to stop the inquest being reopened.

In November 2006 the inquest was adjourned yet again. Cynthia was furious. 'This is now the fourth time Noeleen's inquest has been adjourned and it is simply not good enough because the Gardaí have had over thirty-three years to solve this case, and bearing in mind that on the night my daughter was murdered my mother, who I witnessed murdering my daughter, came into contact with three members of the Gardaí on two separate occasions within one hour of my daughter being murdered, and that on both occasions my mother was holding the bag that had Noeleen's body in it. That bag was found the next day with Noeleen's body—less than twenty-four hours after she had been murdered.

'Yet my mother was never charged with murder and died peacefully only a few weeks ago, while my daughter died a terrible death.'

The inquest finally got under way in February 2007, twenty-four years after the new-born girl had died. During the inquest some highly graphic evidence of sexual abuse was heard. Some members of the Murphy family supported Cynthia's version, while others maintained it was all a tissue of lies, and claimed that no sexual abuse had taken place in the family home. The case was splitting apart a family already strained to breaking point.

Before her death Josephine Murphy had made a statement in which she denied killing the child. This was read out at the inquest.

Crucial evidence came from two psychologists, who backed up Cynthia's claims. Dr Dawn Henderson said: 'Cynthia is not mentally ill. In my opinion she is reacting in a normal way to a very abnormal and horrific childhood experience.' Her opinion was based on seventy therapy sessions she had had with Cynthia over a three-year period.

'From my professional opinion she was telling the truth about her daughter and sexual abuse. I do not have any doubt about the birth, death and disposal of her daughter. I do not know about the detail, but I'm convinced of the truth of the main events.'

Retired psychologist Fred Noel said that Cynthia gave a detailed account of giving birth. He recalled the horror on her face as she remembered the black afterbirth, and she also gave him details about the second child, who was stillborn.

'She quite clearly had a disturbing and dysfunctional family,' he said, adding that neither he nor Dr Henderson felt that Cynthia was suffering from mental illness. These were not the ravings of a crazed mind.

After hearing all the evidence the jury returned a verdict that the baby found in 1973 was the daughter of Cynthia Owen. Dublin County Coroner Kieran Geraghty asked Cynthia if she had chosen a name for the baby. She told him that she had always called the baby Noeleen, and he accordingly recorded this as her name. The unknown baby buried in the Holy Angels plot now has a name and a family.

Although she never saw her mother charged with murder, the verdict provided some sort of closure for Cynthia. Gardaí dug up the garden of the house where she had been abused, but were unable to find her second baby, John.

In an interesting aftermath the government asked a leading barrister to review official files on the case. Senior Counsel Patrick Gageby was asked to review all available papers to see if there was any basis for a full inquiry into the handling of the death. Cynthia had called for a full public inquiry, believing that the gardaí mishandled the case from the start.

If difficult cases such as this teach us anything it is that lessons are often there to be learned, and that we ignore them. The case of Kelly Fitzgerald is a case in point.

Kelly and her sister suffered a catalogue of physical abuse. Both their parents abused them and they suffered neglect and star-vation, both emotional and physical. This was not like the Murphy household in Dalkey: these girls were not the playthings of their parents. In fact they were a little lower than family dogs in the pecking order. How any mother could treat her children in such a way—and let her husband do it too—beggars belief.

Kelly Fitzgerald was born in 1978, in Battersea, London. She had an older sister, Charlotte, and two younger sisters, Caitlin and Geraldine (five years her junior), as well as two brothers, Kevin and Ruairi. She came third in the family. Her mother had had her first child when she was just fifteen.

Every parent will tell you that they love all of their children equally, but this is sometimes a lie: there are occasionally favourites; and just as often there are children who cause their parents nightmares. But normal people make an attempt to treat all their children equally, and do their best for them all. Favouritism might exist, but the children are rarely aware of it.

The Fitzgerald household was different. For some reason her mother failed to bond with Kelly, and she was neglected right from the beginning. The same thing happened to her sister Geraldine when she came along five years later. The other children seem to have been treated normally and raised normally.

The situation for Kelly and Geraldine was not helped by the fact that their father could be violent. He believed that sparing the rod spoils the child; and his wife did not disagree.

Kelly was just a few months old when she first came to the attention of the authorities. Des Fitzgerald's brother Garry, a social services worker in north London, became concerned that his niece seemed undernourished and small for her age.

He was right; she was admitted to hospital and treated for malnutrition.

When Kelly was ten her uncle became concerned again. 'I wrote to Lambeth Social Services expressing my concerns,' he said. In that letter he described in detail his brother's failures at rearing his children, particularly Kelly. 'I thought that Kelly was suffering emotional abuse. Her parents encouraged her other brothers and sisters, but Kelly was just ignored. What I just can't understand is why they picked on Kelly. She was a happy girl who fitted in well with family life. It was certainly nothing to do with Kelly or her behaviour.'

The social services ignored him. They had no way of knowing how bad things were in the Fitzgerald household. Neither did Garry Fitzgerald. But Kelly's sister Geraldine remembers clearly. She believes the abuse began when she was five. That is how she remembers it, but it could have started when she was younger. She was deprived of food and adequate clothing, and she was demonised by her parents, who isolated her and Kelly from their brothers and sisters, and the two were subjected to daily beatings from their father. 'I was made to sleep outside the back door with the dogs, dressed only in a nightie,' she said.

A year later the social services had to sit up and take notice. Des, Kelly's father, came in and asked the council to take away his child and put her into care. He said that they could not cope with her any longer. She was immediately put on the 'at risk' register.

Des's decision to try and offload one of his daughters incensed Kelly's grandparents, who thought their son-in-law was well out of order. A family meeting was called, at which it was decided that Kelly would move in with her grandparents, which she did, and there was an immediate improvement in her health and well-being.

But the council refused to recognise the arrangement as legally permanent. Had they recognised the arrangement and given her grandparents, or her uncle, guardianship over Kelly, she might have survived her childhood.

Des Fitzgerald was involved in a serious traffic accident in the mid-eighties, as a result of which he lost his leg, which was replaced with an artificial limb. He received £70,000 compensation as a result of the accident and the family decided to use the windfall to change their lives. Des and Sue felt that London was not a good environment in which to raise their children, and now they had the money to do something about that. They decided to move to Ireland.

They eventually found a twenty-eight-acre farm at Tonroe, Carracastle, near Charlestown in Mayo, where they moved in 1990. Although they had Irish roots, neither had any links with the county. Neither Des, then thirty-five, nor Sue, then thirty, had any experience of living on a farm: they were just taking advantage of the fact that property prices in Ireland were still very low at the time, particularly in rural areas. The move left them with a healthy bank balance.

Kelly remained in London with her grandparents when her family moved to Ireland. She continued to thrive, but she did miss her brothers and sisters. Des and Sue were looking forward to an idyllic rural existence, but their daughter Geraldine did not share the utopia.

Lambeth Social Services had contacted the Western Health Board to let them know that both Geraldine and Kelly were on their 'at risk' register, and the health board made some effort to keep an eye on Geraldine. In November 1991, following a visit to the family by a social worker, it was recorded that Geraldine looked 'oppressed and forlorn' and that she had 'very little clothes compared to the other children'. The social worker also noted that she 'sat cowered in a small chair'. The home was squalid and the family were living in primitive conditions.

A few years later, a social worker reported that Geraldine, now aged eleven, weighed under three and a half stone. She was caught breaking into neighbours' houses late at night, wrapped in a blanket, to steal bread; she was falling asleep in school and regularly missed appointments with dieticians and child psychologists. Yet she was left in the house of horrors: no one thought to take her into care.

In December 1991, when BCG vaccinations were being carried out in her school, a number of 'discrete lesions' were spotted on her arms and torso. The following April social workers discussed her case, and said they were concerned that 'her parents may be going down the same path with her as Kelly'.

So how was Kelly getting on? Initially there was very little contact between her and her parents; they did not seem to be eager to keep in touch with their girl, and were apparently content to leave her in London. But she was still their daughter.

'I knew that the time would come when Kelly might want to return to her parents,' said her uncle Garry. 'I treated her as my own daughter, but there was always the inevitable pull back to Ireland and her parents. We were not her parents, and she missed her brothers and sisters. She would never allow anyone to say a bad word against her parents.'

In the summer of 1991 Kelly announced that she wanted to spend her summer holidays in Mayo. 'When she came back to London she said she had had a lovely time,' said her uncle.

Kelly went to Mayo that Christmas, and the following year returned for her summer holidays for the second year running. When she came back to London she told her grandparents and her uncle that she wanted to go to Ireland permanently. Her parents seemed to be in agreement, saying they wanted their 'wonderful little girl home'.

Garry contacted both Lambeth Social Services and the Western Health Board, but got no response from either. Reluctantly he drove to the airport and put Kelly on the flight to Knock.

'Even as she was walking through the barrier I was still trying to persuade her not to go. But Kelly was like any teenager, she knew what she wanted to do, and legally I could not stop her going.'

Kelly settled into life in Mayo, attending the local convent school in Charlestown. Garry rang every week, and he flew to Knock every six weeks or so, to make sure Kelly's parents had not slipped back into their old ways of neglect and abuse. For a while everything seemed to be going well, and Garry believes that Kelly was happy and physically well. Then a spell of very bad weather meant that he was unable to fly to Ireland during December and January. He managed to speak to Kelly that Christmas, but after that, contact was broken. He kept phoning, but every time he rang Kelly's dad would tell him that she was out, or she was too busy to speak to him. The abuse had begun again.

Des had begun to beat his daughter, now thirteen, every day. At one point she confided in her sister Geraldine, asking her to make sure to tell about the abuse if anything happened to her. Des admitted that he used to pull up Kelly's dress and pull down her panties, then use a slipper to beat her every day. He also used a belt on her naked skin.

'Things were all right for a while when Kelly came to live with us,' he said, 'but then she would not do anything for herself. As far as I was concerned she was eating properly and I could not put it down to anything when she began to lose weight. I started slapping her because she was eating a lot of sugar, but it seemed to have no effect. In the end I used to take up her dress and pull down her underpants and slap her with a slipper. Sometimes I used a leather belt.'

It was later discovered that there were also burn marks on Kelly's body, but her mother denied the allegation that she had burned Kelly with a lighted cigarette.

When school resumed after Christmas Kelly did not go back. Her mother contacted the school and said that they were having problems with Kelly, and that she wanted to return to London.

Her physical condition continued to deteriorate.

On 1 February 1993, Des Fitzgerald booked a Ryanair flight from Knock to Stansted, phoning his brother to warn him that Kelly was on her way. She would be accompanied by her older sister Charlotte. Kelly's mother, Sue, as eager as her husband to be rid of the difficult girl, drove the girls to the airport. They had phoned ahead to request a wheelchair for Kelly, who was very weak, and when they arrived at the airport Charlotte ran in to get the wheelchair. She then wheeled her sister onto the plane. Her mother did not even go into the airport to see them off.

Garry Fitzgerald was shocked when he saw his niece that day in Stansted. She was massively underweight, gaunt and unresponsive.

Suzannne Reddan, the Limerick mother who turned murderer when her lover was killed. (© *Press 22*)

Una Black – her friend sold her dog so she knifed him to death.
(© *Collins Photo Agency*)

It runs in the family – Kelly Noble joined her mother, Jackie, behind bars. Both are doing time for taking a life. (© *Collins Photo Agency*)

Happy times – Franco Sacco with his young bride, Anna Maria.
Three years later she would be in court charged with his murder.
(© *Collins Photo Agency*)

Happy times two. Anna Maria Sacco emerges triumphant from the court
with her parents, Lorna and Luigi, after being acquitted of murdering
her husband. (© *Collins Photo Agency*)

Andrew Keegan, 6 (back) and his brother Glenn, 10 (front) larking
with friends before the dark cloud of their mother's depression broke
over them, leaving all three dead in a leafy Dublin suburb.
(© *Collins Photo Agency*)

Jacqueline Costello ignored her son's pleas to be let live, and found herself in the dock charged with murder. (© *Collins Photo Agency*)

Closure at last – Cynthia Owen leaves the coroner's court after an inquest found she was the mother of a baby girl stabbed to death hours after her birth. (© *Collins Photo Agency*)

Peter Murphy, father of Cynthia Owen – was he patriarch of the family from hell? (© *Collins Photo Agency*)

The parents who treated their kids like dogs – Desmond and Susan
Fitzgerald let their daughter Kelly die of neglect. (© *The Irish Times*)

The physician who failed to heal herself – psychiatrist Dr Lynn Gibbs,
who was accused of murdering her teenage daughter.
(© *Collins Photo Agency*)

The funeral of Ciara Gibbs, the talented teenager drowned by her depressive mother. (© *The Irish Times*)

Jesus and the Virgin Mary instructed Mary Prendergast to hack her grown-up daughter to death in Cork. (© *Collins Photo Agency*)

Young mother Jessica Prendergast is laid to rest in Cork, after a frenzied attack by her mother. (© *Provision*)

Kathleen Bell was a little girl in a big woman's body – she didn't have the self-control to stop herself killing her abusive lover.
(© *Collins Photo Agency*)

Dolores O'Neill may or may not have bullied her husband, Declan, but she certainly bludgeoned and hacked him to death in a frenzied attack.
(© *Collins Photo Agency*)

The faces of evil – Linda and Charlotte Mulhall, who killed and dismembered their mother's African lover. (© *Collins Photo Agency*)

Kathleen Mulhall leaving the court after being convicted of helping
her daughters dispose of the hacked-up remains of her lover.
(© *Collins Photo Agency*)

Margaret McCole, the helpful neighbour from hell, who tried to kill an elderly Donegal farmer after stealing his money. (© *Photocall*)

She was only semi-conscious and her condition seemed to be deteriorating rapidly. He rushed her straight to St Thomas's Hospital, where she was put into intensive care.

She was suffering from septicaemia, or blood poisoning, and her ravaged body did not have the resources to combat it. She never regained consciousness, and passed away in her uncle's arms on 4 February.

Within hours a squad car pulled up to the small farm in Mayo and the four remaining children were whisked away and placed in care.

Subsequently Sue and Des Fitzgerald were charged with neglect of their daughter. They were also charged with assault, and assault causing harm, but these charges were withdrawn at the last moment, due to a bizarre legal loophole. Geraldine, then aged ten, was the chief witness to the abuse allegations, and could have testified to how her mother and her father had abused and assaulted Kelly: but her father, as her guardian, was able to refuse to allow her to testify.

Both parents pleaded guilty to neglect. The State was careful not to imply that the neglect had led to Kelly's death. 'Septicaemia could arise in a myriad of ways,' said prosecuting barrister Conor Fahy. The possibility that one of the ways in which septicaemia could have been caused was through the open wounds left by her father's use of a belt on her and her mother's habit of burning her with cigarettes was not explored.

Dr Neil Aiton, paediatric registrar at St Thomas's Hospital, said that Kelly was five foot tall at the time of her death, yet weighed only eighty-five pounds. She was a massive twenty-five per cent underweight, and showed signs of prolonged malnutrition. 'My first impression was that she was a severely ill child. She was dehydrated and looked severely malnourished. There were multiple marks over her skin—lacerations and bruises covering her hips, buttocks, and legs. The marks suggested to me that she had been beaten with something like a belt. There were also scars on her buttocks which were consistent with cigarette burns,' he said.

A shocked Judge John Cassidy found that Kelly's mother was every bit as responsible for the neglect as her father. The maximum sentence he was allowed to impose was two years, but because they had pleaded guilty he sentenced them both to eighteen months in prison. He said at the time he wished it could be more.

The case caused ripples of shock. The health board knew that both girls were at risk, yet they were left with abusive parents. This was a tragedy that could so easily have been prevented. The public outcry led to calls for a full enquiry, and legislation to ensure that it never happened again. Máire Geoghegan-Quinn said in the Dáil, 'The Kelly Fitzgerald abuse case has been one of the most horrific in the history of the State.'

Yet after their release from prison the Fitzgeralds went back to their small farm, where they are now raising two children who were born after they left prison.

An enquiry was held into Kelly's death and a report prepared, but no action was taken, no lessons were learned; and because of that it all happened again. Another mother from hell, via Roscommon, began a reign of terror against her children just a few years after Kelly's death.

The Roscommon abuse case rocked the nation when it came to light at the end of 2008, both because of the appalling catalogue of abuse, and because of the length of time the abuse continued, despite the warning signs. The signs were there, but the system took its sweet time reacting to them. It's as if we had never encountered a situation as horrible as this before.

The woman, who was never identified, in order to protect her children, was bad to the bone. From the day each of them was born until they were all taken into care in 2004, her six children were subjected to appalling neglect and abuse. They had little food and were constantly hungry, only getting dinner twice a week. They went unwashed and were always dirty; they were regularly left alone at home, in a dirty, rat-infested house full of rotting scraps of food; they were often blue with the cold, and their hair was alive with lice. Their mother would just abandon the children and head off to the pub, coming home in the small hours drunk and abusive. She often beat the children.

'Children at school refused to play with me because I was smelly—mammy didn't take care of us right,' said one sister.

'Any food I got to eat was cold, and when mammy was drunk the house was scary. I was bullied at school and children called me smelly. The nits in my hair were crawling down my face,' said another.

But the most horrific tale of abuse came from the eldest brother, the boy who first went to the gardaí. He was just thirteen when his mother forced him to have sex with her.

This happened on at least four occasions. The first time was when his mother returned from the pub, drunk as usual. She called her son into her bed, took off her nightdress and told him to remove his pyjamas before forcing him to have penetrative sex. 'I was crying. She was my mother. Why did she do that to me?' the boy asked in the statement he made to the gardaí.

Admitting that it had happened, the mother said: 'Mine was a house of horrors, with bells on. I can safely say that I was the worst mother in the world.' There seemed to be a sort of pride in this admission, as if it were an achievement rather than a condemnation. But Judge Miriam Reynolds didn't see it that way, and sentenced the woman to seven years. Sergeant John Hynes, who investigated the case, said: 'I don't think we'll ever get the full truth here. I don't think any mother could do what she did.'

In the aftermath of the case, it emerged that efforts had been made to take the children into care years before they were finally removed from their vicious and abusive mother, but that those efforts had been unsuccessful. No lessons had been learned from the Kelly Fitzgerald case, and some children in Ireland are still in danger from their parents.

Josephine Murphy stabbed a new-born infant forty times with a knitting needle because a member of her family had raped her daughter and got her pregnant. Susan Fitzgerald mistreated and neglected her daughter to such an extent that she was a walking skeleton with no resistance when blood poisoning struck. An unnatural mother in Roscommon could just as easily have killed one of her six children. When will the government act to put legislation in place to protect our children?

09 | ALL PSYCHIATRY IS BUNKUM

DR LYNN GIBBS

'Mad or bad?' It's a question that juries are occasionally asked to decide. It's not always an easy question, and in order to answer it facts, legal considerations and opinion have to be taken into account. It requires more from a jury than a regular guilty or not guilty decision.

Traditionally, the division of labour in a trial is very simple: the jury weighs the facts, the judge interprets the law, and the solicitors and barristers make off with the fat fees. But in the case of a plea of not guilty due to insanity, the jury is asked to do more than just judge the facts; they have to interpret them, to provide a meaning for the actions.

Legally, insanity is a grey area, and this is because insanity itself is a grey area. It is not a medical term at all: no psychiatrist will describe a patient as insane. Someone who is mentally ill might be schizophrenic, paranoid, bi-polar or depressed, but they are not insane. And for every defence psychiatrist who testifies that a woman is not responsible for her actions, the prosecution can find one to say the exact opposite. Although psychiatry is based on scientific research and carried out by highly trained practitioners, it is a 'soft' science. Its facts are not the mathematical certainties of physics or chemistry; they are open to interpretation. No wonder it's a legal minefield.

The jury system is a way of imposing common sense on the jumbled mayhem of the legal system. A jury is meant to sift through the conflicting accounts, the partial truths, the self-serving evasions, and decide what actually happened. They are meant to make that decision based on their experiences as twelve men and women of the world. In other words, they should reach a common-sense decision based on the case presented to them.

But sometimes common sense seems to desert them when the question of sanity or insanity arises. The case of Brendan O'Donnell, who in 1994 murdered Imelda and Liam Riney and Fr Joe Walsh, is a perfect example.

O'Donnell was a deeply disturbed individual from a poor rural family living on the shores of Lough Derg in Clare. The court heard that his mother, to whom he was unnaturally attached, had died when he was a child. Brendan was raised by an emotionally distant father, a bully with a strong dislike of his needy son. During his troubled childhood he was physically abused, and by his teens he was constantly in trouble. He was also diagnosed as having psychiatric problems. During one period in juvenile detention he tried to take his own life with an overdose.

After spending some time in England, O'Donnell returned to his native East Clare, where he began living rough, terrorising locals with burglaries and petty acts of vandalism, such as arson attacks on cars. When gardaí tried to talk to him, he confronted them with a shotgun, and they ran. What no one knew was that he was hearing voices in his head, and those voices were leading him down a very destructive path. The devil was talking to him, and what he was saying was not good.

On 29 April 1994, O'Donnell abducted Imelda Riney and her three-year-old son Liam. Within hours he had shot both in a remote wood. A few days later, on 3 May, he abducted Fr Joe Walsh from his home in Eyrecourt, County Galway, and brought him to the same wood, where he killed the priest. Four days later, O'Donnell was caught by gardaí as he tried to abduct yet another victim, this time a teenage schoolgirl.

During the period he was in custody awaiting trial, O'Donnell suffered a couple of mental breakdowns and tried to kill himself. During the trial itself his behaviour was bizarre, and he claimed to be talking to the devil all the time.

After a fifty-three-day trial, and oodles of psychiatric evidence about his state of mind during the killing spree and about the circumstances of his upbringing, the jury still determined that Brendan O'Donnell was not insane, deciding by a ten to two majority that he was guilty of the three murders. The two dissenters thought that he was guilty but insane. (The verdict of not guilty by reason of insanity was not available until 2006.)

But by any sensible definition Brendan O'Donnell was several sandwiches short of a picnic. This verdict highlighted a serious flaw in the insanity plea: some people are just so unsympathetic that a jury does not want to let them off the hook in any way. The jury wants to find them bad, not mad, and will defy the evidence to reach this verdict.

On the other hand, some defendants evoke intense sympathy. Young mothers who, unable to cope with the stresses of life, take the lives of their own children often attract more sympathy than condemnation. Traditionally they are far more likely than a raging lunatic such as O'Donnell to succeed in convincing a jury that they are insane.

This highlights a huge difference in the way we perceive men and women. Statistically, there is not much difference between women and men who kill. Seventy per cent of all children who are murdered are killed by one or both of their parents. Fathers and mothers are statistically almost equally likely to kill their children: while women are slightly more likely than men to commit this particular crime, the difference between the number of men and the number of women who kill their children is minuscule. It is the one crime, apart from shoplifting, where women outnumber men.

But when a father kills his children he is far more likely to be considered an evil control freak acting out of purely selfish motives. As we will see later in this chapter, Dr Lynn Gibbs, a psychiatrist who drowned her sixteen-year-old daughter, was treated with great sympathy by the courts and the media. In contrast, when in 2001 George McGloin stabbed his young daughter to death, then killed himself, he was treated quite differently. The *Sunday Mirror* trumpeted: 'Dad smiled as he knifed his baby girl to death.' The article under the headline goes on to describe how 'evil' George McGloin smiled up at two men who went to the aid of his daughter.

McGloin had been in a relationship with the child's mother, but the relationship had broken up. He visited the child regularly, and had been minding her for several hours before he killed her. That was in November 2001, in Callen, County Kilkenny. When the child's mother arrived to take back the baby he first pushed her, then attacked her. She fought him off, then he attacked the baby before finally fatally stabbing himself.

There was no question of any problems in the past, although an inquest heard evidence that Mr McGloin was unhappy with the break-up of his relationship, and wanted to get back with the mother of his daughter. He received no sympathy in the media, despite the fact that he took his own life—surely an indication of the turmoil and distress he was in.

In the same year, a missing child case came to a tragic end. Five-year-old Deirdre O'Sullivan had disappeared from her mother Christine's house in Douglas, Cork, in December 1999. Her former partner, Christopher Crowley, went on the run with the young girl. Finally, in May 2001, vigilant gardaí tracked him down to a house in rural Tipperary. But when they knocked on the door Crowley shot his now six-year-old daughter with a sawn-off shotgun before turning the gun on himself. The nation was horrified. For eighteen months we had followed Christine O'Sullivan's search for her missing daughter. We had seen her on television appealing for information, and had followed the newspaper accounts of the fruitless search. No one suspected how tragically the case would end.

But in the vast welling of public sympathy, none was found for the killer. Christopher Crowley was described as 'crazed' and 'sick' and 'evil' but never as 'troubled' or 'in need of help'.

It is worth bearing this in mind as we look at the case of Dr Lynn Gibbs. Is our sympathy for this troubled mother misplaced? Dr

Gibbs was a highly experienced and respected psychiatrist, and she was suffering from depression. If anyone knew she was in trouble and needed help, it was Lynn Gibbs herself; and few of us could have found help any more easily than Lynn Gibbs. She could have picked up a phone and called any number of friends in her profession; she could have rung any psychiatrist she wanted, and got immediate attention.

She chose not to. She chose to let her psychiatric condition deteriorate to such an extent that she killed her daughter, and tried to kill herself.

Canadian writer A. E. van Vogt had a theory about highly dominant, truly violent men (and it can equally be applied to women). In his book *The Violent Man* (1962) he maintains that these men 'take a decision to be out of control, in some areas of their lives'. They have an innate sense of their rightness, and a horror of losing face.

In his book *A Criminal History of Mankind* (1984) Colin Wilson expands upon this idea. Some people have an anger within them, and a belief that they are right, and they lose their temper easily if crossed—but that is their decision. A violent man might abuse his wife, leaving her black and blue, but when he goes off to work he doesn't lose his temper with a nagging boss, or with annoying underlings. He knows how to control himself when he needs to, but at times he chooses to be out of control.

You could argue that Lynn Gibbs chose to be out of control when she held her daughter under the bath water. After all, she could just as easily have chosen to pick up the phone and get help.

The Gibbses seemed like any happy family riding high on the back of the Celtic Tiger. They oozed success. Gerard Gibbs was a lecturer in aviation electronics at the Carlow Institute of Technology. His wife Lynn, who kept her maiden name, Hutchinson, for professional purposes, was a doctor of psychiatry, and had a very successful practice. She was a locum psychiatrist with the Carlow–Kilkenny Mental Health Services. The couple had two children: Ciara, sixteen; and Gearoid, three years younger than his sister. They lived in the townland of Killure, near Goresbridge in County Kilkenny. Goresbridge is a small picturesque village nestling on the

Barrow, built up around a two hundred-year-old bridge. It's a beautiful place to drive through, and an idyllic place to live—a place where the relaxed pace of country living is just a short drive from the cosmopolitan streets of Kilkenny. A slightly longer drive brings you to the coast or to Dublin. Country living but close to all the conveniences, as an estate agent might put it. It seemed a wonderful life, but beneath the surface things were not so perfect: the cracks were there and they were beginning to show.

There is no doubt that mental illness can run in families. Whether this is genetic, or whether children follow the behaviour patterns of their parents, is still a matter for debate; but illnesses can recur, generation after generation.

Lynn Gibbs came from a wealthy family; her father was a big farmer. Her mother, Iris, suffered episodes of depression throughout her adult life; and she passed that tendency on to her daughter. According to professor of psychiatry Thomas Fahey, who gave evidence at Lynn Gibbs's trial, the risk of an offspring inheriting a psychiatric condition from a parent is one in five, or even higher. He said that Dr Gibbs maintained a façade of calmness that hid her true nature. 'She is quite self-contained and reserved, but I don't doubt that underneath she is quite an emotional person. All her life her coping mechanism has been to compartmentalise her feelings.'

The shy, introverted and self-contained young woman began to manifest psychiatric problems at quite a young age. The transition from primary school to secondary school caused her some problems. This was not just a change of school; it was a complete change in her life. She was leaving home for the first time and going to a boarding school. At the age of twelve she was prescribed sleeping pills to help her through that difficult transition.

Five years later Lynn experienced an eating disorder, but she came through that. She was also briefly hospitalised for psychological treatment. Then she went to Trinity College in Dublin to study medicine. Her family were wealthy enough to provide her with her own apartment in the city. No grotty student bedsit for her.

Around this time she began going out with a young man who proved to be the love of her life. She was just eighteen when she began dating Gerard Gibbs. He stuck with her through the turbulent few years that followed, and they married after college. But it was not a smooth path from first date to the altar: Lynn continued to suffer periods of depression, and at the age of twenty she experienced a serious episode, resulting in a suicide attempt, which forced her to take a year out from her medical studies. Gerard stuck by her. However, Lynn was already compartmentalising her troubles rather than being open about them. Her younger sister Kathleen never knew of the suicide attempt, for example. Kathleen remembered that when she was nine Lynn disappeared for a few weeks, and when she returned she seemed heavier. Kathleen did not realise at the time that her sister, then eighteen, had suffered a nervous breakdown, and the medication she had received in hospital had caused her weight gain.

When Lynn was twenty-two her mother Iris, then forty-nine, while suffering a severe bout of depression, took her own life in a particularly unpleasant way—by drinking weedkiller. The noxious concoction took three days to kill her. Her mother's death must have had a severe impact on her young daughter, but Lynn bottled up her feelings and soldiered on. This was just two years after her own suicide attempt and she had already lost a year of study.

'But she made a very good recovery and completed her studies, not even interrupted by her mother's death,' said Professor Fahey. Again, the feelings were bottled up. Her mother's suicide was never discussed. Even her husband did not know the details of Iris Hutchinson's death until his wife's trial twenty-five years later.

Marriage to Gerard did lead to years of stability, according to Dr Cleo Van Velsen, another psychiatrist who testified at the trial. Lynn coped with all life threw at her—bringing up two children, a stint in St Vincent's Hospital working with anorexia sufferers, and the death of her father from lung cancer.

Neighbours described the family as happy. People say Dr Gibbs was 'gentle', 'kind' and 'a nice lady'. 'She was quite nun-like, a quiet type who didn't make an impression one way or the other. If you saw her you would hardly remember her,' recalled one local businesswoman. But another neighbour said that Lynn was quite a controlling woman, particularly when it came to her children.

The two young teenagers were not allowed to socialise much, and were rarely seen out.

'Perhaps she was over-anxious, but she seemed to like keeping Ciara and Gearoid at home all the time. You would never see them out. In fact, some people would not have even known they had children,' she said. 'After Ciara's death a neighbour told me they did not even know there were kids in the house.'

Ciara had turned out to be academically very gifted. A student at the Loreto Convent in Kilkenny, she achieved ten As in her Junior Cert. But her parents didn't allow her to take the bus to school, and she was not allowed to use her mobile phone to call friends in the evening. However unusual this might appear, no one doubts that Lynn Gibbs was a loving mother, who put her children before anything else.

As her daughter entered her teens, Ciara began to show signs of the eating disorder anorexia nervosa. This is a condition that most commonly affects teenage girls—they have a distorted perception of their body and believe, despite all evidence to the contrary, that they are fat and unattractive. Typically they begin extreme dieting, which leads to serious health complications. It's a long-term problem, which can take several years of treatment to cure, and often interrupts a girl's education. Even when successfully treated it is a life-changing condition. It is every parent's nightmare.

Until her eating disorder became apparent, Ciara had been the perfect daughter. A slight girl with blue-grey eyes and dark blonde hair, she was an academic high-flyer, just like her mother. In addition to her straight A record, she was attending special classes for gifted children at UCD. She had a flair for mathematics, and was expected to excel in the Irish Maths Olympics the following May. Her school principal, Helen Renehan, described her as 'a beautiful and talented young girl'.

Following her Junior Cert, Ciara went to France on a student exchange programme. It was supposed to be two weeks in a different culture to pick up a bit of the language and expand her horizons, but for Ciara it proved a miserable experience. She hated it. The family she stayed with were very formal, particularly when it came to eating. Ciara came to dread dinner time, and took to skipping the meal. In the odd way that teenage minds sometimes work, this proved to be a 'lightbulb' experience: Ciara realised that she could function without eating. She came home from France with body image issues, and what happened next did not help. Ciara did a deportment course.

Teenage girls are easy prey for these courses, which dangle the carrot of a career in modelling before their gullible noses. At five foot eight, with a slim build and attractive features, this might not have been an unrealistic dream for Ciara. But the course emphasised diet and calorie counting. This, coupled with her experiences in France, led to Ciara developing an eating disorder, and her parents soon began to notice drastic weight loss.

Psychotherapist Leslie Shoemaker later told the court that sometimes, though not always, anorexia can be caused by growing up in a 'perfectionist' environment. 'Anorexia is a complex disorder, but in certain cases it can be caused, maintained, and even recovery can be scuppered by family relationships. You do get a pattern of anorexia sufferers who are children of controlling parents, a mother or a father who is a perfectionist. This pressure to be perfect is a trait in anorexia. Also, if a parent is isolating the child from others, this will also be a factor.'

When Lynn began to notice her daughter's drop in weight it provoked a corresponding anxiety in her. She had suffered an eating disorder in her teens, she had worked with anorexia sufferers in Dublin, and she knew how serious the issue was. She also knew that she had suffered with psychological problems throughout her life, which had resulted in one suicide attempt. Her mother had suffered in a similar way and had ended her own life. Was she looking at the pattern being repeated into the third generation? Was her daughter condemned to the same fate?

'Ciara's weight loss precipitated an arousal of Lynn's own feelings about herself. To her it was a statement about herself, that she had doomed her daughter, that there was something unfixable about her. The enmeshment and confusion with her daughter had reached a level that was psychotic,' explained Dr Van Velsen.

Around this time family members began to notice that Lynn was coming under increasing pressure. They saw the cracks appear, and they began to wonder if they should intervene, but no one realised just how quickly Lynn's mind was crumbling.

Lynn's younger sister, Kathleen Deely, said that she began to notice a change in Lynn around October 2006, a few months after Ciara's return from France. The two sisters had always been close despite a nine-year age difference. Kathleen was well aware of her sister's grave concerns about Ciara's weight loss, and her conviction that she was developing an eating disorder. Kathleen was concerned about Lynn's own condition. Lynn had lost quite a lot of weight herself and said that she wasn't sleeping.

Kathleen and her stepmother Anna visited the Gibbses in their house in Killure in the first week in November, and were shocked at Ciara's drawn and gaunt appearance, and also at the change in Lynn. 'The atmosphere in the house was low,' said Kathleen. This had been sparked off by a row between Lynn and her daughter about her weight loss. Ciara was down to seven and a half stone, a stone underweight for a girl of five feet eight inches, and her body mass index was only seventeen, indicating that she was clinically underweight. Lynn insisted her daughter see a doctor in Dublin about her eating disorder. Dr Gobnait Carney, a specialist in the area, said that initially Ciara gained weight, but she was tearful and resentful about having to see a specialist in Dublin, and she soon began losing weight again. Her condition was causing rows between herself and her mother. During one row she had shouted at her mother: 'I hate you.'

This is typical teenage behaviour, familiar to most parents in the country, but it shocked Lynn Gibbs, who was a reserved woman. Theirs was a family that did not confront one another, and she was unable to cope with the teenage tantrum. She began losing weight herself, and by November had lost at least a stone. 'I was quite shocked. She had lost an awful lot of weight, and looked gaunt and drawn. I definitely thought she had an eating disorder,' Kathleen said, adding that Lynn was not sleeping, and was extremely preoccupied and worried about Ciara's weight loss.

Lynn's stepmother, Anna Hutchinson, agreed. She said that during the summer of 2006 Lynn was pale and getting thinner by the day, while during the visit to the house in November she noticed Ciara had become withdrawn, very gaunt, and had lost a lot of weight. 'She was getting thinner by the day, and I felt I could see she had less energy as the days went by. She seemed always under pressure.' The family were so concerned that they planned to meet on 26 November to discuss the issue. But events overtook them.

In early November, knowing that she was unwell, Lynn took a break from her work as a locum psychiatrist. Others also knew she wasn't well, but no one knew just how serious the problem was.

Anne Ryan, a local activist who worked with those suffering from mental health problems, said: 'It is shocking to think that Dr Gibbs had been working as a locum psychiatrist in the Department of Psychiatry in St Luke's Hospital, Kilkenny, but no one spotted that she was suffering from a serious and dangerous form of depression. Some colleagues and friends who work in the medical profession were aware that she was ill, but could not see she was headed for a psychotic episode that would lead to such tragic events.

'She was working as a psychiatrist for the HSE just a few weeks before the killing. It is worth remembering that psychiatrists are just the same as everyone else. They suffer depression, they commit suicide, they fall victim to alcohol addiction, they self-medicate. They are not superhuman, just because their job is to look after the mental health of others. We cannot forget that.'

A friend of Dr Gibbs, fellow psychiatrist Dr Deirdre Dowdall, said that Lynn had confided in her in the months before the tragedy that she was very worried about Ciara. 'Being a psychiatrist she felt guilty that she had not seen the warning signs in Ciara,' she said. She added that Lynn had noticed the changes in Ciara after her return from the exchange programme in France.

Dr Dowdall was a very close friend. The families often went on holidays together, though they had not done so the previous summer, as Ciara was in France. Dr Dowdall tried to persuade Lynn to get help for her depression, but she seemed reluctant to keep up their meetings, and was always busy with something or other.

Dr Gibbs also confided in Dr Maura Horgan, a consultant psychiatrist and friend, several months before the tragedy. The normally reserved Dr Gibbs broke down in tears as she told her friend about Ciara's weight loss and the worry it was causing her.

Another friend, Dr Marese Cheasly, said that Lynn had been prescribed three different anti-depressants since September, but she had taken herself off all three within a week of prescription, complaining that they did not agree with her. So she was off all her medication, and her psychiatric condition was going untreated.

On Saturday 25 November, Gerard Gibbs took their son Gearoid to Ballypatrick, County Tipperary, to visit Gerard's elderly mother, May. They stayed overnight, a thing they did often. Lynn was going to take Ciara to her special class for mathematically gifted children at UCD, in preparation for Ciara's participation in the Irish Maths Olympics, coming up in a few months. After the class the two were planning to go shopping in the capital.

Ciara had confided to her father that she was going to try and secretly buy a coat for her mother, as a Christmas present from herself and her young brother. Gerard was delighted: despite the harsh words spoken during the recent row there was love in the home. During the afternoon Gerard received a text message from his daughter about the coat. It was the last contact he would have with her.

That evening, after Lynn and Ciara got home, a friend from Dublin, Dr Marese Cheasly, drove down and called in on Lynn. She found Ciara watching television, and the girl appeared happy; but Lynn was deeply depressed. She confided in her friend that she was worried about finances, because she did not know if she would be able to return to work with the HSE. She said that from time to time she thought about taking her own life, but she would never do it. 'She talked about the terrible prognosis for anorexia and how she felt Ciara would never have a career or family because of the anorexia,' said Dr Cheasly.

While she did not believe her friend met the criteria to become an involuntary in-patient, Dr Cheasly said that she was concerned enough to take the decision to phone Gerard Gibbs in the morning to discuss Lynn's condition, and the possibility of getting her into hospital. A little after 11 p.m. she left Lynn and drove home to Dublin. 'I believed she was telling the truth when she said she would not harm herself. If I ever felt she was in danger I would have stayed the night myself, or asked Gerard to come home.'

After Dr Cheasly left, Lynn went upstairs and ran a bath in her en suite bathroom. When the bath was full she went into Ciara's room and woke her daughter. From now on we must rely on the two statements Lynn made to the gardaí a week or so after the tragedy. She remembered little of the night, only snatches and vague recollections. She said that her mood had been low for a number of months, and she had not been sleeping. She thought that Ciara had gone to bed, and she got herself ready for bed.

'I would have run a bath, and I remember calling Ciara and she came into my bedroom. She came into my bedroom and the bathroom. I recall pushing her under the water but I can't recall the steps in between, or what I said,' she told gardaí in her first statement.

'I recall taking her out of the bath. I think she was dead at that stage. I got in to the bath after taking the medication. I went under the water but I wasn't able to stay under. I don't recall when I cut my wrists. I remember being very low. I believed that there was no hope for Ciara or myself. I planned that we both die.'

Lynn pulled her daughter from the bath, then took a number of pills, a mixture of sedatives and sleeping pills, and made an attempt to drown herself. When this was unsuccessful she tried to slash at her wrist and her neck. She collapsed on the floor of her bedroom, near a chest of drawers.

The following morning Gerard Gibbs and Gearoid arrived home early, just after 9.30 a.m. They were surprised to find the gates to the house locked. Once inside the house, Gerard Gibbs walked upstairs and went into the bedroom, then into the en suite bathroom, where he found his daughter lying motionless on the floor beside the bath. The bath was full of water, and lying on the floor was a bloody meat cleaver.

Gerard ran to his daughter and picked up her cold, wet body. Her pyjama top was wet, though the bottom was dry. He ran through to the bedroom and laid her on the bed. Though he knew she was dead, instinct took over and he tried to resuscitate her.

It was then that he noticed his wife was lying on the floor by the chest of drawers. There was blood on her. He picked her up and laid her on the bed beside Ciara. Lynn was alive but unresponsive. He began slapping both their faces to try and revive them. Then he picked up the phone and dialled the emergency services.

Initially gardaí treated the case as suspicious but kept an open mind about how Ciara had met her death. State Pathologist Dr Marie Cassidy examined the body. Ciara had drowned, and there were no traces of anything in her blood which would have led her to collapse or pass out in the bathtub. Although there was blood at the scene, Ciara had no concussive injuries: she had not slipped and hit her head. Gardaí ruled out a suicide attempt, believing that it was impossible to deliberately drown oneself in a bathtub.

There was slight bruising on the back of Ciara's head and on her shoulders. Dr Cassidy said: 'This bruising could be expected of a young female involved in sports, but could also indicate that she was forcibly held under water in the bath.'

Gardaí knew that the investigation was stalled until they had spoken to Dr Gibbs, but she could not speak to them. Immediately after the tragedy was discovered she had been removed to St Luke's Hospital, Kilkenny, and from there she was transferred to St Patrick's Hospital, Dublin, where she was undergoing psychiatric treatment. Gardaí were told that she was unresponsive and unlikely to be able to be interviewed for a number of days. In fact it was a week before she was fully aware that her daughter was dead. During that week she underwent electro-convulsive shock therapy in an attempt to break her out of her unresponsive state.

Meanwhile, Garda technical experts sealed the Gibbses' home and undertook a thorough forensic examination. All possibilities, including that of an intruder, had to be eliminated. It was Wednesday before the family were allowed back into their home.

Ciara's funeral took place on the weekend following her death. On the Saturday evening, 2 December, she was removed to Ballypatrick, just outside Clonmel, the home place of her father, Gerard, and on Sunday she was laid to rest in the graveyard at the village of Kilcash near Slievenamon.

Among the chief mourners were Ciara's father, brother and grandmother. Her mother, still in the private hospital in Dublin, was too ill to attend. Thirty minutes before the Mass commenced the little church was so packed it was standing room only. Classmates brought gifts to the altar, celebrating the life of the 'academically gifted' girl, including her music and maths workbooks, and a tiny pink chair she had made for art class. As the coffin was carried to the historic graveyard beside the church, thirty schoolgirls from Loreto College formed a guard of honour in the bitterly cold wind. Ciara was buried close to Kilcash Castle on the southern slopes of Slievenamon.

For the next several months Dr Gibbs remained in hospital receiving treatment. In May 2007 she was formally charged with the murder of her daughter.

The trial turned into a battle of the psychologists, but it was a battle in which both teams were on the same side. Four respected psychiatrists gave evidence, and the only question the jury had to decide was whether Lynn Gibbs was sane or insane at the time of the killing. Just two years previously the Trial of Lunatics Act had been replaced by the Criminal Justice (Insanity) Act. Now a jury was entitled to find a person not guilty because of insanity, or guilty of manslaughter (rather than murder) due to diminished responsibility. Diminished responsibility was not an issue in this case—Dr Gibbs was either sane or insane.

Opening the case, barrister Brendan Grehan said that there was no difference between the prosecution and defence. 'Lynn Gibbs admits to murdering her daughter, and that she intended to kill her daughter, but is pleading not guilty to the charge by reason of insanity,' he said. 'The case is summed up by her comment made to the gardaí. Effectively Lynn Gibbs had decided in the state of hopelessness that it was best for her and her daughter to die.'

Gerard Gibbs tearfully testified that his wife and daughter had an excellent relationship, and that he and Lynn had an excellent marriage. 'She loved Ciara,' he said.

Dr Tom Fahey, a consultant psychiatrist from London, testified that Dr Gibbs presented a picture of full-blooded depressive illness developing from September onwards and diagnosed a major depressive disorder. 'Lynn Gibbs felt that her daughter was in a state of severe suffering that wasn't going to get any better. It was going to persist and she felt through a type of distorted reasoning that came through her illness that she should act to relieve her daughter of her suffering and take her own life at the same time.

'While she knew the nature and quality of her act, she did not know what she was doing was wrong. In fact, she thought it was right and could not refrain from doing it.'

Dr Cleo Van Velsen, another London psychiatrist, said that the family had never dealt with painful past incidents, such as the suicide of Dr Gibbs's mother. 'Dr Gibbs learnt to compartmentalise things, putting stressors out of her mind. But Ciara's illness preoccupied her, and she became obsessed by it. When she felt her daughter was doomed it was also a statement about herself. I don't think we'll ever fully know what it was that caused the crisis that night,' she said.

Throughout the trial Dr Gibbs remained impassive, sitting between two psychiatric nurses. Dressed in a smart and sober black business suit, she seemed disengaged from the whole process.

The judge was quite clear in his instructions to the jury: 'All the evidence goes one way—that the defendant did not bear criminal responsibility in respect of these tragic events by reason of her mental disorder. If you are to decide anything other than that, you would be saying in effect that psychiatry is bunkum, that you have no time for it, that you don't hold with it.'

The jury took the hint. The nine women and three men were out just twenty-one minutes before returning with their verdict. Court One in the Four Courts was hushed as the verdict was read out. Dr Gibbs herself appeared calm and almost uninterested. She was playing with an elastic band as the six words were read out: 'Not guilty by reason of insanity'.

It was only the second time in the history of the State that this verdict had been returned. The first time, in July 2006, was in the case of John Egan of Naas, who had killed a woman he had never met before, Frances Ralph, as she waited at a taxi rank in Naas with her husband and two friends.

Mr Justice Paul Carney ordered that Dr Gibbs was to be detained in the Central Mental Hospital, Dundrum, where she could receive the treatment she needed. When he left the court family and friends, including a doctor and a psychiatrist who had tried to help

Dr Gibbs before the killing, went over to hug her. Several were crying. Dr Gibbs, who had been blank-faced and unemotional during the trial, smiled as her tearful husband Gerard hugged her. He took her face in his hands and kissed her gently. 'Don't cry,' she said softly. 'It's all over now,' she told her friends.

Outside the court, Superintendent Aidan Roche, who had handled the murder investigation, said: 'As far as the Gardaí are concerned this has been a dreadful family tragedy. The verdict has been a correct one and I can only hope that some day Lynn will be well enough to come home.'

But coming home is not an option for her daughter Ciara. In the outpouring of sympathy for the murderer it is easy to lose sight of the victim. Dr Gibbs was an experienced psychiatrist with access to a network of experienced psychiatrists. Knowing her family history, knowing her crumbling state of mind, she chose to ignore this network of support. The court had heard evidence from her friend Dr Dowdall that Lynn Gibbs had put off meeting her to discuss her problems. Like A. E. van Vogt's violent man, she chose to be out of control in that area of her life, and this decision led to her daughter's death.

Mr Justice Carney's instruction to the jury—that if they ignored the evidence it would be an indication that all psychiatry is bunkum—could be turned on its head. If an experienced psychiatrist and all her experienced friends and colleagues in the business could miss the very obvious signs of an impending breakdown, then perhaps all psychiatry is indeed bunkum.

10 | THE VIRGIN MARY SPOKE TO ME THROUGH THE DRIPPING TOILET

MARY PRENDERGAST

Never take a baby's word on anything—they are notoriously bad judges of character. But perhaps it was not the baby's fault; perhaps his judgement was skewed because the Virgin Mary was using him as a vessel to speak through, when she wasn't communicating through the burbling pipes of the toilet.

Or perhaps it had nothing to do with the baby and the Virgin Mary. A few weeks before the baby started speaking to her, Mary Prendergast had visited the dentist, and he had made a terrible mistake. Instead of using local anaesthetic he had injected her with evil: he had given her a shot of pure antichrist.

Welcome to the broken mind of a paranoid-schizophrenic killer.

When you deal with the world in a rational way, the delusions of someone whose mind has snapped make bizarre and occasionally amusing reading, but if you have to live with those delusions they become far more serious, and far more frightening.

Pretty young mother Jessica Prendergast found this out in the starkest way in July of 2006. Her son had just turned one, and she was planning a little birthday party for him the following day. She was just two months in a new house on Old Commons Road in Cork, and was settling in well. It was 6 a.m., and she was sound asleep in her bed, her baby by her side. Just after dawn broke, her mother suddenly appeared in her bedroom with a carving knife in her hand. Before Jessica could react her mother began viciously stabbing. Jessica was stabbed over forty times. She managed to stagger from the bedroom and stumble down the stairs, but she died on the hallway floor. She was just twenty-one.

The story begins a lot earlier than that fatal day. Jessica was the daughter of Mary Prendergast, who also had a son, Wayne. Mary had suffered psychiatric problems for most of her adult life. Her problems were first noticed in her mid- to late twenties, when her daughter was just a toddler. Many women suffer from post-natal depression after a birth, and it can stretch over months, or even longer, if undiagnosed or untreated. But Mary's problems were far more severe than that.

Consultant psychiatrist Dr Brian McCaffrey said that Mrs Prendergast had had an illness of a psychiatric nature for about nineteen years, during which time she had been admitted to psychiatric institutions on no less than seven occasions.

Typical of those occasions was her committal in October 2001. On this occasion Mrs Prendergast's GP wrote: 'This woman has severe paranoid delusions centred around the government trying to kill her. She is getting messages from the TV. She has confined herself to her house, and is afraid to go out.'

Mary was convinced that the government wanted to kill her, and that they could use household objects such as televisions or microwaves to control her thoughts and cause her harm. Because of her delusions she would not leave the house.

After each of her hospitalisations Mary was released back into the community and her untrained family had to look after her and cope with her problems. On 10 July 2006, Mary was released once more, this time from Cork University Hospital.

By now Jessica had grown up. She had a baby, Jamie Lee, now approaching his first birthday, and she had just moved into a new house, which she was renting. She had been raised in Thorndale, on the Dublin Road, but was now in Blackpool, in the north of the city. She was very happy at Glenna Cottages, Old Common Road. Her partner was away, working abroad, but in regular contact with home.

Everyone described Jessica as a lovely young woman, full of life and love and compassion. It was no surprise that she once more began to look after her troubled mother. She allowed Mary, then forty-seven, to move in with her in the new house, and for a while things went well. Mary continued to take her medication daily, but then she had a dental appointment, and that may be where things began to go wrong. She came off her medication for at least a day, perhaps to prevent the medication clashing with whatever the dentist might give her. According to Mary it was not a normal dentist who saw her. He must have been in league with the forces of darkness. 'She thought that the antichrist had been injected into her at the dentist,' said her son Wayne.

After the dental visit her family began to notice that Mary's behaviour was becoming odd again. This must have been a cause of concern, because she was barely a fortnight out of hospital. If only they had known.

Mary began to hear voices, but this time it was not the television that was talking to her. The Virgin Mary began to hold regular conferences with the troubled Cork woman. The days of a full-blown apparition, such as at Lourdes or Knock, were gone, but the two Marys could still communicate, and their favoured method was through the dripping water in the toilet bowl. Mary Prendergast was convinced that the other Mary was talking to her through the random burbles and gurgles in the bathroom, which was situated right next to her bedroom.

Occasionally the Queen of Peace chose Mary's grandson Jamie Lee as her mouthpiece. Mary became convinced that the child was the new Christ, and he was telling her that she had to kill Jessica.

Jessica had a lot on her mind. She was coping with looking after her baby on her own, and with her new house. She had a troublesome guest, and she had a birthday party to plan. On Thursday 27 July, Jamie Lee turned one. On Saturday there would be a get-together in the house to celebrate the occasion.

But her mother's increasingly erratic behaviour was worrying Jessica. On the Friday, she sent a text expressing her fears to her brother Wayne, in which she said that her mother was 'acting up', which Wayne took to mean that she was behaving strangely again. Neither of them knew how close to the edge their mother was.

That Friday night Jessica went to bed as normal. She slept well, her child nestled beside her; but her mother tossed and turned, unable to sleep. The messages in her head were getting more insistent. Soon she was up and prowling.

As dawn was reddening the city sky, Mary Prendergast got out of her bed in the guest room and crept along the corridor. She went into the bathroom and consulted with the dripping toilet bowl. 'I said to her [Our Lady], when do you want me to do it?' she told the gardaí afterwards. 'She said: "I'll let you know, my love."'

Still in her pyjamas, Mary crept down the stairs to the kitchen and quietly opened the cutlery drawer. She selected one of the longest and sharpest carving knives, closed the drawer, and began silently to mount the stairs. She would be ready when the word came.

At half-past five the message came: 'You can do it now.'

When she pushed open the door of her daughter's bedroom she could see Jessica curled up under the bedclothes, lying on her right side. Beside her, sleeping peacefully, was the baby. She eased her way into the room and raised the knife.

The next few minutes were horrendous. She began driving the knife viciously and repeatedly into her daughter's exposed side. As Jessica woke and turned, the knife plunged into her chest, spraying blood all over the sheets and covering her mother in gore. How long the attack went on is not known, but Jessica was stabbed forty-four times, and suffered over thirty puncture wounds to her chest and neck. The number of cuts and slashes on her hands and forearms showed she fought vigorously for her life.

It appears that after the frenzied assault Mary Prendergast grabbed her grandson and ran down the stairs and out of the house, leaving her dying daughter in a bed of blood. Jessica managed to get out of bed and stumbled to the stairs. She got down the stairs, but collapsed and died within minutes of the assault.

Meanwhile her mother, still clutching her grandson, whom she was convinced was Jesus, ran down the road. A neighbour, Sandra Byrne, was woken by the commotion. She thought she heard the sound of crying and heard the words, 'She's dead. Why aren't you helping me?'

She looked out and saw a woman in pyjamas. The woman was 'panicked and stressed' and had a child over her shoulder. The woman set off at a brisk walk towards the office of a local taxi cab company. The distance was about 300 metres, a three-minute walk. It was just after six when Mary ran into Blue Cabs in Blackpool and told the shocked dispatcher that her daughter had been seriously assaulted. She wanted to order a taxi to take her to the Garda station. Confronted with the woman in her pyjamas, with blood on her face and hair, and on the wailing child in her arms, the staff at Blue Cabs knew this was serious. One of the men working that morning rang the gardaí.

At 6.10 a.m. Garda John Flynn arrived at the taxi office. Quickly assessing the situation, he called an ambulance for Mrs Prendergast and the child, and accompanied them to the Mercy Hospital. 'On the way the woman said something to the effect that her daughter was possessed by the devil,' he said.

Later, Garda Deirdre Murphy arrived and found Mrs Prendergast 'in a shocked state, crying, shaking, and grinding her teeth. There was blood on her left cheek, forehead, hair and left eye.'

Mrs Prendergast told Garda Murphy that the baby had told her that Jessica was 'bad with the devil'. Because of this she had killed Jessica with a knife, but she had kept the baby. She told Garda Murphy that the baby was Jesus, and that is why she had saved him. 'He told me Jessica was the devil. I asked the baby was Jessica dead and he told me she was, and he clapped his hands.'

In the hospital it was found that Mrs Prendergast and her grandson were uninjured, though Mrs Prendergast required medical treatment because she was in a highly excited state.

Almost as soon as the alarm was raised gardaí had arrived at the two-story house on the Old Commons Road. They knocked furiously at the door but got no answer. The door was locked and they had to break it down to force an entry. Jessica's body was lying face down at the foot of the stairs. It was obvious she was dead. The house was sealed, and the state pathologist and the Technical Bureau were called in.

Superintendent Martin Sheehan of Mayfield Garda Station was in charge of the case. Very quickly it became obvious that there was only one suspect, but the investigation was no less thorough for that. Door-to-door enquiries were made, and over the next two days extensive searches were made on the surrounding roads, and even in the river, for the murder weapon, the carving knife Mrs Prendergast had used.

Experts from the Technical Bureau arrived around 1 p.m. and undertook a thorough examination of the crime scene. At 2.30 p.m. Dr Marie Cassidy, the state pathologist, arrived. She performed a preliminary examination of the body at the scene, then the remains of Jessica Prendergast were taken to Cork University Hospital for a full post-mortem.

Jessica's partner returned from overseas, and he and his family took the young baby into their care as the funeral arrangements were made. After a discussion between doctors and gardaí, Jessica's mother remained in hospital under observation.

Despite a detailed search of Jessica's home and stretches of the Lee channels in the area, no trace of the knife was found.

At the funeral a few days later in St Oliver's Church, Ballyvolane, Jessica's father—Mary Prendergast's former partner—asked mourners to forgive the woman who had killed his daughter. Willie Prendergast told mourners of his great love for his daughter.

'She was a child everyone would want—we all miss her desperately. She was a child who always had a smile—she loved her mother,' he said tearfully. 'Jessica forgave her mother—she became a mother herself and brought a child into the world. Jessica was the sort of person that would want people to forgive her mother—she was a special type of child. We just have to look around here and see the friends she made. She is an angel—if ye only knew what Jessica did only an angel could do it.'

Jessica's coffin was greeted in the church by the strains of David Gray's 'Sail Away'. Shortly after the start of the Mass, Jamie Lee, Jessica's son, was carried forward in the arms of a male relation to light a candle for his dead mother.

Parish priest Fr John O'Donovan said: 'She had a great smile and she had her own little ways. She was lovely, but most important of all she was lovable. She was lovable in the way she could wrap her father around her finger and how she could reach out to her mother. She made a place brighter and happier.'

A number of wreaths were placed in the hearse, including some stencilled with tributes such as 'Mother' and 'Jess'. The cortège drove the short distance to Rathcooney cemetery, where Jessica Prendergast was laid to rest.

The inquest into the death was adjourned at the request of the gardaí, who said that Jessica's mother might face criminal charges. Sure enough, in February 2007 she was taken from the Central Mental Hospital in Dundrum to Dun Laoghaire Garda Station, where she was formally charged with murder. As she was living on an invalidity pension of €191 a week, she was given free legal aid.

The trial in the Central Criminal Court in February 2009 was brief. Wearing a sober black jacket over a green top, and looking a decade older than her years, Mary Prendergast pleaded not guilty by reason of insanity. The facts were not in dispute: the jury was told that she had stabbed her daughter forty-four times; the only question they had to decide was whether she was legally sane at the time.

The judge explained that under Irish legislation, for a person to be found legally insane they had to have no knowledge of what they were doing; or they had to know what they were doing but have no conception that it was wrong; or they had to be suffering from a recognised and serious psychiatric condition. He indicated that Mrs Prendergast could be considered to meet some of these criteria.

The chief witness on the opening day of the trial was consultant psychiatrist Dr Brian McCaffrey. He told the jury that Mrs Prendergast had had an illness of a psychiatric nature for about nineteen years, for which she had received treatment on a number of occasions. 'She was convinced that medication was given to her to damage or perhaps kill her,' he said, adding that he diagnosed the accused as a paranoid schizophrenic with very fixed delusions. 'At the time of the events she was suffering from an exacerbation of symptoms. They were actually worse that night.'

The jury agreed. They took just twenty-four minutes to deliberate before returning a verdict of not guilty by reason of insanity. Mary

Prendergast was in tears as she listened to the verdict. Mr Justice Paul Carney, who described the case as 'very distressing', sent her back to the Central Mental Hospital for an indefinite period of time.

After the case it emerged that the family believed they had been badly failed by the health services. A source close to Jessica's father, Willie, told reporters: 'Mary was a very, very sick woman. This awful tragedy would never have happened if she had got the help she needed. The family have been let down by the health system in this country—it is a disgrace.'

The plea of not guilty by reason of insanity is not common in Ireland. Until recently it was not possible to claim diminished responsibility due to mental factors when facing a murder charge, though in the past decade that has changed. Now a jury can reduce a murder charge to manslaughter in the face of psychiatric evidence.

Cases such as the Prendergast case, in which a not guilty verdict is returned, are quite rare and becoming rarer. According to a study published by P. Gibbons, N. Mulryan and A. O'Connor of the Central Mental Hospital, between 1850 and 1995 437 patients were admitted to the hospital after having been found guilty but insane, the old equivalent of not guilty by reason of insanity, most of whom had committed a violent crime while suffering from a major psychiatric illness.

But the number of insanity acquittees has fallen five-fold since the nineteenth century. Acquittees were usually single males from rural areas, aged in their thirties, so Mrs Prendergast did not fit the profile; but the few women who used the defence were typically charged with violent attacks against their own children.

The report concluded that the defence generally results in prolonged detention, the average length being over fourteen years. It will be a long time before Mary Prendergast walks the streets of her native Cork again.

11 | AN EIGHT-YEAR-OLD GIRL IN A BIG WOMAN'S BODY

KATHLEEN BELL

When a man finally gets the courage to get down on his knees and propose to the woman of his dreams he always has some doubts about her reaction. Will she say yes? No? That she needs time to think? Will she laugh at him? No man expects the woman to pull a knife from under her jumper and plunge it repeatedly into his chest.

As Patrick Sammon lay dying in the bedroom of his and his girlfriend's home in Galway, he must have realised his proposal had left something to be desired. But then, during the course of the evening, he had laughed at news that his girlfriend's sister had died, and teased her about her childhood sexual abuse. It had not been a normal proposal.

Nothing about the story of Kathleen Bell was normal. Since her childhood she had been pushed from one horrible situation to another, and she had never learned to cope in an adult way with her problems. As one psychiatrist put it: 'She is an eight-year-old girl in a big woman's body.' To top it all, Patrick Sammon had been beating her for years, and she had finally had enough.

Spousal abuse is a problem in Ireland, as it is in many countries. The world seems to be full of weak men who come home from a day of underachievement and take their frustrations out on their wives and families. In most relationships one partner is more dominant than the other, but this doesn't normally matter: the couple learn to live with each other and within the pecking order. Love brought them together, and the relationship works.

But when the dominant partner is frustrated outside the home, he (or occasionally she) will try to impose their will inside it. If they get away with it, the abuse becomes a cycle, with both partners caught up in the destructive pattern. Alcohol or drug abuse makes the situation worse. Some women let a partner away with abusing them, while others don't. It is down to the psychological make-up of the woman.

If someone has come from a stable and loving family they have a template for how family life should be. They know how one loving partner should treat another, and their partner had better live up to that template. But if they have come from a broken home, and have known nothing but abuse and violence and oppression, they are more likely to end up prey to spousal abuse.

Of course it is more complicated than that, but the truth remains that if someone comes from a deeply dysfunctional background they are more prone to finding an abusive partner. Their life becomes a spiral of ever-increasing difficulties. The abuse can be quite horrendous, and in some cases fatal. In Britain one woman is killed every fortnight, on average, by a partner or former partner.

Our society is becoming more violent by the day. But the biggest increase in violence since 1981 has not come from criminal gangs or disaffected youths: the biggest growth by far has been in domestic violence. And the statistics show that for every twelve women who are killed in a domestic setting by a man, one man is killed by a woman. Roughly ten women are killed each year in Ireland as a result of domestic violence, according to a report by Women's Aid in 2007.

And a little less than one man a year is killed by a woman under similar circumstances.

Not all these cases make a big splash; it's the sensational murders that grab the headlines—gangland assassinations, contract killings, serial killers. The vast majority of murders rarely raise a ripple in the public consciousness, so people don't realise that the bedroom and kitchen are more likely killing grounds than the dark alley or the tenement drug den.

Women and men kill for different reasons. Men kill for gain— either money or status—they kill to cover up; and they kill when their temper explodes out of control. Women tend to kill to escape a situation that would otherwise overwhelm them; or because of psychological pressures.

Occasionally, after suffering months or years of abuse, a woman will get up the courage to fight back, and sometimes she will hit out at those who love her and have done nothing to deserve her ire. There have been several cases of women suffering psychological problems who have lashed out at innocent family members. It is not unknown for husbands to suffer years of torment at the hands of abusive wives.

When women lash out the results can be devastating. This is partly because of the physical differences between men and women. Abusive husbands typically punch or kick their wives. But when a woman attacks, she doesn't use her fists—they would be useless against a stronger man. So she picks up whatever comes to hand. A hammer, a knife from the kitchen, an axe—these are what women lash out with. And the results can be fatal.

This is what Kathleen Bell discovered when she produced a knife and ordered her partner to get out of their house and leave her alone.

Kathleen Bell did not have the best start in life. Her father was a street musician, a very precarious profession. Street entertainers tend to lead a very nomadic life, and do not put down roots—it is not an ideal job if you are hoping to raise a family. In addition, he had a history of violence and alcoholism. Kathleen was born in 1962. She had a sister and two brothers. But her childhood came to an abrupt end when her parents abandoned the young family. They split up and her mother, destitute, went to England.

Records suggest that in addition to the siblings she knew about, Kathleen's mother had two other children who ended up fostered in the UK, and another child who died of meningitis at St Joseph's Orphanage in Clifden.

While her eldest brother was old enough to make his way in the world, Kathleen and her sister and other brother ended up in a large orphanage run by the Mercy Sisters. Kathleen and Mary were then sent to Mount Carmel Orphanage in Moate, County Westmeath, and were effectively separated from their brothers. It was a cold and impersonal place, with very few personal contacts for the girls. Both of them ended up deeply damaged by their upbringing.

Back then the scandals about abuse within institutions such as orphanages and industrial schools had not become public knowledge, and they provided a fertile hunting ground for perverts. It is only in the past decade that we have become fully aware of the number of children's lives that were blighted in the institutions that were meant to care for them and nurture them.

Kathleen, in common with so many others, was abused by those caring for her. Her earliest memory of the abuse is when she was nine or ten, but it may have begun before that. Her abuser, rather unusually, was a female member of staff.

On one occasion Kathleen was running away from her abuser when a nun caught her, and the whole story came out. Back then, people found it difficult to believe that such abuse went on, and children were generally blamed for telling tales, but Kathleen was lucky to have been caught by one of the few enlightened nuns. She told her everything. After hearing about the complaint, the nun did not punish Kathleen; instead, the abuser was removed, and Kathleen never saw her again. But that was not the end of the abuse.

There were several families around the country who took in children from the orphanages for weekends or breaks. Around the time she was ten Kathleen and her sister began spending regular weekends with a family in Dublin. The family were kindly people who did their best for the two young girls. There is no doubt that the weekends were a welcome break from the bleak monotony and casual cruelty of the orphanage. 'They were very kind to us,' said Kathleen. But the couple had a son-in-law, and he was less kind to the two girls. Late at night, as they lay in bed, he would come in and expose himself to them. There were worse incidents as well, which extended over a period of a few years. 'I saw my sister being abused too,' revealed Kathleen. On a trip to England, one of the few occasions when the girls had to visit their natural mother, their mother's new partner abused Kathleen's sister.

The orphanages were not known for producing university graduates. If you were parentless in the Ireland of the sixties and the seventies the best you could hope for was a Group Cert or Junior Cert, and then you were on your own. After leaving the orphanage, Kathleen moved to County Galway, and at the age of sixteen she became pregnant. The father was a youth from Ballinasloe, County Galway. Although she was terrified, and she knew the stigma of having a child out of wedlock in those judgemental days, Kathleen was looking forward to the birth. But she was young and innocent of the ways of the world. Unwittingly she signed papers, and when she gave birth to a little girl she discovered she had signed her away for adoption. She was devastated when the baby was taken from her. 'She was all I had,' she cried.

A friend from her orphanage days, Lilly Broderick, said that Kathleen was 'very disturbed' when the baby was put up for adoption. She took an overdose of tablets, and was brought to hospital in Ballinasloe.

Not long afterwards she got pregnant again, but by a different man. The father this time was Philip Bell, a Derry man who was working in the Republic. By all accounts he was a nasty piece of work, who did not hesitate to use his fists to get his own way. At eighteen Kathleen was a mother, and eventually she married Philip, despite his violent tendencies.

Together the couple had seven children. This was far too many for the troubled Kathleen to cope with, and at one point she went on the pill. The pill was, for many years, a source of controversy in Ireland. It was seen as an erosion of all our values, and the Church violently opposed its use. In fact, until the late seventies it could not be obtained in Ireland, and even when it became available, for several years it was only prescribed to married women. Birth control of any sort was frowned upon, and the only method allowed was the rhythm method, summed up nicely by a marriage guidance counsellor: 'The rhythm method works very well, as long as you are prepared to accept two or three children more than you plan for.'

Philip Bell often beat Kathleen when he felt he wasn't getting his own way. But when she went on the pill he brought in the heavy artillery—the local priest, who came in and laid down the law—and the baby-making machine was back on track.

To help her cope, Kathleen began hitting the bottle and developed a dependency on tranquillisers. These coping mechanisms were worse than useless, and the young mother suffered two nervous breakdowns. She left her husband for a short time in 1986, and her children were later taken into care. On another occasion she attempted suicide, and Mr Bell, who had been working in England, came home and gained custody of the children. Psychological problems were beginning to manifest themselves, and Kathleen began to self-harm.

Self-harming behaviour is a complex issue, and a sign of deep-rooted psychiatric problems. It is not suicidal behaviour. Self-harmers typically cut themselves, particularly on the arms, legs or abdomen, but there is no intent to take their own lives. Often they see the cuts as a way of opening their body to release the demons that haunt them: they think they can cut out the evil they see within themselves. Or it is a way of punishing themselves. It's a warped coping mechanism to relieve emotional pain or discomfort, and is four times more common in women than in men. Although this behaviour is often associated with deeply disturbed psychiatric patients, it is not uncommon among young adults.

Some people glibly assume that self-harm is a cry for help, or a way of calling attention to the sufferer. But this is not true: most self-harmers feel self-conscious and guilty about their wounds and scars, and they often go to great lengths to conceal them. It can often be a sign of anger issues which the person is not able to deal with. Considering her past, this may have been the case with Kathleen Bell—anger at herself for letting the world walk all over her, and anger at her abusers, her parents and her abusive partner.

Another interesting aspect of self-harm is that it is often linked to a history of sexual abuse. According to psychiatrist Dr Brian McCaffrey, who has studied the phenomenon extensively, eighty per cent of self-harmers were abused as children.

Kathleen also tried to kill herself a number of times, according to her friend Ms Broderick.

Eventually Philip Bell left Kathleen and returned to Derry. He successfully applied for an annulment of the marriage. Now, in the eyes of the Church, despite the fact that they had had seven children, the marriage had never taken place. Bell also worked through the courts for a civil separation, and gained custody of the seven children. Kathleen was on her own once more.

Kathleen's sister Mary was also having her own problems. In many ways the lives of the sisters mirrored each other. Mary had married Patrick Sammon, a plasterer originally from Newport, County Mayo, who beat and abused her. They had three children together, but he wasn't a model father. Eventually, in 1988, they split up, Mary moving to England with the children, and Sammon remaining in Ireland.

In 1994, in a strange twist, Kathleen moved in with her sister's cast-off husband. She could not have made a worse choice. As Alex MacClean, a social worker with the Western Health Board, said: 'Kathleen was a typical child of an institutional background. She, her sister Mary, and Patrick Sammon were extremely damaged individuals.'

By the time she moved in with Sammon, Kathleen's self-harming behaviour was well established. And her new man did nothing to help her with the problem. If anything, he made it worse. He would sit calmly and watch her slice her arms, not saying anything. On one occasion he actually handed her a razor blade and egged her on to slice herself. She obliged, gouging a deep wound in her neck.

Kathleen's body was criss-crossed with wounds. One scar on her chest was larger than a surgeon would have left had he been removing a lung, and her arms and neck were covered in slashes and scars. In addition, she had a number of scars that she had not made herself.

Patrick Sammon proved every bit as violent as her former husband. He beat her regularly, but she tried to fight back. On at least five occasions he used a knife on her, and she bore five scars on her body from those fights. In all, she visited the hospital fifty-one times during the course of her relationship with Sammon. Some of the visits were caused by her; some by him. 'Patrick cut my arms with a knife, but sometimes I slashed my wrists myself,' she said. 'I remember once he handed me a razor blade and told me he did not care what I did. I slashed my neck.'

Garda Superintendent Anthony Finnerty confirmed that Ms Bell was a regular visitor to the hospital. In about half the visits she had been responsible for her injuries. The other times it was her partner who bore the blame. In addition, she had called the gardaí between twenty and thirty times in relation to Mr Sammon.

One garda, Peadar Brick of Mill Street station in Galway, recalled that on 27 February 1996, he went to the house and saw Kathleen fighting with Patrick Sammon in the front garden. They were struggling for possession of a poker. 'I saw Mr Sammon punching her in the face with his fist, and I arrested him,' the garda said. Mr Sammon was charged with common assault, and was given a six-month suspended sentence at Galway District Court. On another occasion, he hit her over the head with a kettle. He beat her when she was pregnant, and three days later she lost the baby.

Kathleen agreed that gardaí were regularly out to her house, saying: 'I had to call the gardaí so many times to the house that I can't remember. It could have been around twenty or thirty times. I'd call them when Pat wouldn't get out for me, or had me beat.'

Kathleen was living in Camilaun Park, Newcastle, Galway. Patrick Sammon lived with her, but whenever he got too abusive she threw him out, and he lived in a hostel. That was where he was living at the time of his death; their relationship was going through a rocky patch.

When he was sober they got on great, but when he had drink taken he was a cold and callous monster. There is some suggestion that Sammon thought he was superior to Kathleen, and she was beneath him. She was overweight, scarred, and not very bright. In addition she lacked self-confidence; but she wasn't afraid to stand up for herself, and when the abuse got too much she would order Sammon from the house. 'Sometimes I would try to phone the gardaí, but he would stop me. A number of times he hit me over the head with the phone,' she said. 'When he wouldn't be drinking you wouldn't need the guards. He was the best man in the world without drink, but a completely different person when he was drinking. I hate to talk about it, but he was evil and violent with drink in him.'

Kathleen said that he once stuck a knife in her leg, and up under her chin on another occasion. Her mouth was 'burst', her eye was damaged, and her nose was 'put out' on other occasions. But she gave as good as she got, and once broke Sammon's jaw during a fight. 'I had no choice but to defend myself, because if I didn't I'd be stone dead.'

In the early months of 1997 the couple were getting on all right, according to Kathleen. 'We had our arguments and fights, but things seemed to be all right.'

There was a row when she asked Sammon to pay the rent. He said he had paid it and gave her a receipt to prove it. But it was an old receipt. 'I said: "Get out, Pat, or I'll fecking kill you." But I didn't mean anything by that,' she said.

A few months later there was a far more serious row, which was triggered by some devastating news from England. On 18 June 1997, Kathleen heard that her sister, Mary, who was all she had as a child in the orphanage, had died after taking a fatal overdose of drink and drugs. Patrick Sammon's brother rang with the news that Mary had been dead for nearly two months: she had passed away in the Middlesex Hospital on 28 April.

Kathleen called on her brother, Francis Boylan, to tell him the news. They had been separated when she went to the orphanage in Moate and he was sent to St Joseph's Orphanage in Clifden, but they had re-established contact as adults. Francis found Mr Sammon to be 'the most kind man you could meet' when not drinking, but nasty and possessive when he had drink taken. 'Kathleen never wanted to go to hospital when she was beaten, because she feared she would end up losing her right to see her children, who were living with her ex-husband in the North,' he said.

On the day she went to tell him about Mary's death, she was accompanied by Mr Sammon. 'They argued, and he said: "Now that the bitch is dead I can bring the children back." I think he only wanted his youngest daughter back, but Kathleen wanted them to rear all three of Mary's children together and not break them up,' said Mr Boylan.

That night Patrick Sammon returned to Kathleen's house with her, stayed there for a while, then left when she asked him to. The same happened the next night.

Sammon visited the Shantalla Health Clinic in Galway on Thursday 19 June. He spoke to a social worker, Alex MacClean, about the possibility of getting custody of his youngest daughter. He wanted help to apply to Galway Corporation for a house. 'There had been a history of violence and alcohol abuse in Patrick and Mary Sammon's relationship, and both were frequently admitted to hospital with injuries. Each inflicted injuries on the other, and each would show me the marks to prove it,' Mr MacClean said. He felt that Mr Sammon had kept up a 'veneer of respectability' in both his employment as a plasterer and on the domestic front. But frequently this veneer would crack. His late wife did not have that veneer of respectability, but really the couple were 'six of one, half a dozen of the other'.

On the night of 20 June Patrick Sammon kept ringing and ringing until Kathleen finally agreed to let him visit. He arrived at the house around 11.30 p.m., carrying cans of beer, and the two began drinking. He finished off the five or six cans he had brought, and Kathleen drank around nine cans during the evening. In addition, Kathleen was on tranquillisers: during the course of the day she had taken eight Lexotan and six Zanax, a very high dosage, and more than any doctor would recommend.

Almost inevitably they started arguing. The row was over the three children Patrick Sammon had had with Mary. Sammon wanted the children, but Kathleen suspected he only wanted them to enable him to get a council house. He also annoyed her by saying that now he was free of Mary he could marry her. He seemed completely indifferent to the fact that her sister was dead. The suggestion of marriage at such a time really upset her. 'He said that he didn't give a fuck that my sister was dead,' said Kathleen.

Sammon seemed to have an instinct for inflicting the most psychological pain possible with his barbed words. He teased

Kathleen about the sexual abuse she and her sister had suffered when they were growing up. 'I told him: "She is dead because of you. Get up and go or I'll kill you."'

He laughed and refused to leave. Kathleen said that she would ring the gardaí, but he said he didn't give a fuck about the gardaí. She felt it would be futile to try to phone for help, because that would trigger a violent response from him. It never crossed her mind to ask the neighbours for help.

After this exchange, around 1 a.m., Kathleen got up to use the toilet, but on her way she went into the kitchen and found a knife. 'It was a knife I used to peel spuds. I don't know what made me do it. I told him he was doing my head in and driving me mad.'

In the toilet Kathleen slipped the knife under her jumper, meaning to produce it if she needed to scare Sammon into leaving the house. 'No way did I mean to kill him,' she said. 'I just kept begging him so much to go out of the house.'

When she went back into the room the argument started up again. Sammon still refused to leave.

Then Kathleen told Sammon that she had rung his eldest son in England that evening. 'I told him his kids hated him, they did not want to come back to Ireland, and they blamed him for their mother's death,' she said. 'There was a big argument about this.'

She produced the knife and he began calling her names. He then made a grab for her and she thought he was going to hit her. 'I lost the head and I went for him with the knife. I don't know how many times I stabbed him, as I was freaked out.'

It was not a frenzied attack. She struck him about six times, twice inflicting deep wounds that were caused by using the knife with considerable force. A lung was punctured and an artery nicked. There were some defensive wounds on Sammon's arms, which showed that he tried to block the fatal blows.

'Everything was happening too fast,' said Kathleen. 'It was just like I lost my head and everything went out of control.'

Sammon staggered into the bedroom and she fell on top of him. When she saw him on the ground, she thought he was faking and told him to get up. She realised she had stabbed him when she got off him. Screaming, she ran from the house. But a few minutes later she went back in and phoned a friend, Bernie Ward, asking him to come over straight away because she and Patrick had had a fight. It was now 1.30 a.m.

When Mr Ward arrived he found Patrick Sammon in the bedroom, sitting up against the bed. He saw no blood and when he pulled up his jumper he could 'barely see' the marks, which were 'tiny'. Kathleen was very distressed. 'I don't think she realised how hurt he was.'

She told Mr Ward that she had already called an ambulance and that they had been arguing about her sister, that she wanted him to leave but he wouldn't go. Kathleen asked Mr Ward to tell the gardaí he was passing by and heard her shouts, and to say that Patrick had arrived already wounded. 'I did this because I didn't want to get her into trouble. At the time I thought that if Patrick pulled through his injuries they would make it up,' he said.

The gardaí arrived at 3 a.m. Initially Kathleen stuck to the story that Sammon had appeared at her doorstep with the stab wounds. Bernie Ward, trying to help, confirmed this. But within five minutes of the gardaí arriving Kathleen took one of them aside and admitted that she had stabbed Sammon. She handed over the bloodstained knife.

Initially the gardaí decided to charge Kathleen Bell with manslaughter. When she was charged she said: 'It should never have happened. I am so sorry.' But the Director of Public Prosecutions rejected this course of action, ordering that she be charged with murder instead.

The case was heard in March 1999. The facts were not in dispute: Kathleen Bell admitted that she had used a knife on her lover, stabbing him to death. In fact, she offered a plea of not guilty to murder but guilty to manslaughter. The State rejected this plea, and the trial went ahead, before Ms Justice Catherine McGuinness.

Much of the evidence heard concerned Kathleen Bell's troubled history, and the violent nature of the relationship she was in. Dr Brian McCaffrey, a clinical director of psychiatry at the Eastern Health Board, examined Kathleen three times, and came to the opinion that she behaved like a young child in the body of an adult. 'She is an eight-year-old girl in a big woman's body,' he told the court.

Although Kathleen had been seen by doctors over a period of fifteen years, they were busy professionals covering large geographical areas, and no one had focused specifically on the problems caused by her upbringing. 'I believe I am the first person that Ms Bell spoke to about her horrific history,' said Dr McCaffrey. He felt that he knew her better than anyone else did, as he had interviewed her in detail three times, had studied all her previous case notes, and had listened to her give evidence to the court. During her evidence she said that she still loved Patrick Sammon and regretted what had happened. She said she missed him every day, and wished he was there with her. No one knew the agony she was going through.

Dr McCaffrey diagnosed a behavioural disorder. He also said that the amount of medication she had taken on the day of the killing was excessive, and a factor in her loss of control. 'She went into taking that medication in quite an innocent fashion. She took it as a medication, not as a self-destructive act.'

He explained to the jury that the dose of tablets Kathleen took after she learned of her sister's death would make any ordinary person 'disorientated' and 'certainly drugged'.

The type of tablets she took were tranquillisers or benzodiazapines, similar to Valium but more addictive. The combination of eight Lexotan and six Zanax tablets she claimed to have taken on the day before the killing would have a very marked effect on a normal person. 'I personally do not prescribe either drug, as I consider them too addictive, especially Zanax,' said the doctor. 'The excessive amount of tablets she took combined with the alcohol she consumed on the night would be very toxic.'

He went on to quote from an Irish Pharmaceutical Healthcare Association compendium and an American neuropsychiatry textbook, both of which warned of the side effects of the drugs in even a standard dosage. Rather than calming a person, they could in certain patients have the opposite effect. The Irish book urged extreme caution in prescribing to patients with a personality disorder—a condition from which Kathleen definitely suffered.

She was not a normal person because of her background and history of abuse, the doctor maintained. 'The length of time she suffered physical and sexual abuse was extreme, and later she developed a habit of cutting herself, with major incisions, in a desperate attempt to relieve the internal turmoil she felt. It became quite clear to me that no one had ever sat down and talked to Ms Bell about the abuse. What she needed was somebody to listen to her. I believe she could have been helped.'

He noted a comment from one of her visits to the maternity unit in the Regional Hospital in Galway, which recorded that she was 'over-talkative'. 'She was probably desperately trying to get people to help her, but here were the professionals letting her down.'

Because her first baby had been taken from her for adoption she had a distrust of doctors and nurses, he added. 'She ended up in a pathological relationship with Mr Sammon, who taunted her about her past abuse. It must have been horrific for her. He was throwing abuse at her, yet nobody she sought help from responded. And, consistent with many from abused backgrounds, she said she loved her torturer.'

The psychiatrist said that Kathleen had the features of 'an extreme form of post-traumatic stress disorder,' which lay underneath whole layers of other problems. He said that the drugs and alcohol were a factor in the killing, but not in themselves enough to tip her over the edge.

'Obscene remarks made by Mr Sammon just before he was stabbed reminded Ms Bell of her past sexual abuse and were a major factor in triggering off her loss of control,' he said. 'She did not know how to deal with his taunting about her past. She was trapped. There was nothing new about being trapped—she was trapped for years—but this was the apex of the mental torture and harassment.'

The jury of seven women and five men took just an hour and a half to find Ms Bell not guilty of murder. They accepted her plea of guilty to manslaughter. Her two eldest children, who had travelled down from Derry to be with her throughout the trial, smiled in relief.

Judge McGuinness took the rather unusual step of remanding Ms Bell on continuing bail until sentencing. Normally someone is remanded in custody to await sentencing, but the prosecution and defence agreed with the judge that this was an unusual case, and they would have to explore alternative ways of dealing with it.

Immediately Kathleen began a course of treatment to tackle the problems that were plaguing her life. She began seeing a psychologist regularly for counselling—and the judge told the Western Health Board to pick up the tab. She would continue to see the psychologist weekly for between two to five years, as well as tackling her alcoholism through counselling and AA meetings. The judge delayed sentencing for over a year to see how she got on with the treatment.

Finally, in November 2000, Ms Bell was given a four-year suspended sentence, on condition that she continued to attend weekly counselling sessions and regular AA meetings.

Kathleen Bell did not have to serve a single day for the killing of Patrick Sammon. Perhaps such compassion is appropriate in the light of the years of abuse she suffered. But in her troubled relationship with Mr Sammon she showed that she could give as good as she got, and on one occasion she had broken his jaw in a fight.

It would be interesting to know if a man who killed an abusive and bullying girlfriend would escape so lightly.

12 | ADVICE TO ESTRANGED HUSBANDS—DON'T GO TO SLEEP

DOLORES O'NEILL

I n every part of Ireland there are refuges for women who need to escape violent husbands or partners. We hear horror stories of women being subjected to years of abuse and marital rape, of serious injuries at the hands of those who have vowed to love them until death do them part. There are even stories of children coming into the firing line.

But there are also women who abuse their husbands: we just don't hear about it as much. There are a number of reasons: men are embarrassed to admit to the problem; and they are afraid they will not be believed. This is because they are physically stronger and more powerful, as a rule, than the women in their lives, and society believes they should be able to look after themselves. But what society forgets is that if a woman picks up a frying pan, or a heavy glass ashtray, she can even the odds, and inflict serious damage on her spouse. And some men don't hit back.

It was reflections such as these that caused controversial newspaper columnist Kevin Myers to write: 'Do we really need to ask about the uproar which would have resulted if a man hit his sleeping wife twenty-six times with a plumber's hammer and knifed her twenty-one times, and was only found guilty of manslaughter? We don't. We know that there are half a dozen State-subsidised feminist agencies which would have been shriekingly denouncing the legal system which had come to such a bizarre and grotesque conclusion.

'But for the second time this year our courts have concluded that for a woman to kill her helpless husband in bed is not murder. We know such clemency would never be shown to a man who so killed his wife, for there is an entire assembly of State-subsidised agencies whose sole job is to put pressure on judges and national institutions to ensure a general enforcement of the feminist agenda. One key feature of this agenda is that women—even when they hack husbands to death or blow them apart by repeated shotgun blasts in their beds—are always victims.'

His remarks were sparked by two cases, both concluded in 2004, in which women killed their husbands with extreme violence, and were treated leniently by the courts.

The first case happened in Cork. Norma Cotter and her husband Gary were in an abusive relationship, held together by nothing stronger than alcoholic bonds. Gary was a soldier, and when he came home he expected his wife to be a drinking companion, ignoring their young son. But he didn't react well to drink, and when he had taken whiskey the situation only got worse. He had beaten his wife more than once.

For Christmas 1994 Norma bought Gary a double-barrelled shotgun. In January they went out drinking. He returned home, the worse for wear, and climbed into bed. She stayed out with friends, getting progressively drunker. When she returned home at 4 a.m. she woke her sleeping husband, then threw up violently all over the bedclothes.

He threw her out of the bedroom and went back to sleep. But it had been one abusive episode too many. She got the new shotgun, loaded it, returned to the bedroom and fired a shot over his head. The sleeping man leapt up in terror.

Afterwards she maintained that the first shot had been fired as a warning, and then the recoil of the gun had cocked the second barrel. (Experts testified that this can happen.) If, as she claimed, the gun went off accidentally the second time, she accidentally had a very good aim, because the second shot killed her husband almost instantly.

Norma Cotter was sentenced to life for murder in 1996, but in 1999 an appeal court released her on bail to await a retrial. In the retrial she was found not guilty of murder but guilty of manslaughter, and was sentenced to three and a half years in jail. But she had already served this period, between 1996 and 1999, so in January 2004 Norma Cotter found herself a free woman.

A few months later Dolores O'Neill was given an eight-year sentence—of which she will serve only six—for playing a merry tune on her husband's head with a hammer. He was bludgeoned and hacked to death with a hammer and a carving knife. Her story, which is the subject of this chapter, is what sparked Kevin Myers's outrage: 'this is the second time this year that our courts have concluded that for a woman to kill her helpless husband in bed is not murder. We know such clemency would never be shown to a man who so killed his wife,' he thundered.

Perhaps he is right, but there are two reasons the courts are beginning to show leniency to women in circumstances such as these. The first is that the law now allows a manslaughter conviction if there is evidence of provocation or evidence that a woman acted in self-defence against an abusive partner. The second reason is that we are finally beginning to wake up to spousal abuse.

Spousal abuse is a huge and growing issue in this country. As we saw in the last chapter, it can lead to murder. More commonly it leads to years of quiet desperation, loneliness and pain. Traditionally Irish society is one in which unpleasant things are brushed under the carpet—and some of our carpets are really bulging.

According to Women's Aid, a quarter of all murder victims in the country are women, the vast majority of them killed by a partner or an ex-partner. Women have less to fear from the dark-alley rapist than from the over-zealous and jealous boyfriend.

The fact is that spousal/partner abuse and murder is perhaps the worst category of crime in this country—and few people, it seems, are aware of it.

More than ten thousand cases of domestic violence are reported to the gardaí every year, and the numbers appear to be rising. Nine out of ten cases are assaults on women. Domestic violence occurs across all social classes, in both urban and rural areas.

Willie O'Dea, then Junior Justice Minister, said in the Dáil in 2004: 'It is a sad reflection on our society that some women live in fear of violent attack on a daily basis. The fact that this violence occurs in a family home, a place which should offer security and love, makes the crime even more devastating for the victim.

'We must recognise this fact and not think that because the perpetrator and the victim live together this should be considered a mitigating factor. In my view, the opposite should be the case.

'It is also a sad fact that many people know of women who are living with this fear, yet they choose to turn a blind eye and treat it as a private matter. Domestic violence is not a private matter. It is a matter which should be of concern to all members of society and one which everyone can play a role in bringing to an end.

'The secrecy that surrounds domestic violence only allows it to continue. We all have a responsibility to stop it. Anybody who has had any experience of domestic violence will tell one of the horror and anguish it causes. As a society, we must do all we can to help the victims of domestic violence and to ensure their safety.'

Organisations that help abused women are desperately under-funded, and many victims of domestic abuse are forced to return to violent partners because there are not enough refuge facilities. Ten counties have no dedicated facilities at all. Services aiding women and children are frequently stretched to capacity, with a significant lack of services in the northwest: and there are no refuge beds available in Carlow, Cavan, Kildare, Leitrim, Longford, Laois, Monaghan, Offaly, Roscommon or Sligo, though there are some support services in those counties.

The statistics on abuse are staggering. One woman in five has experienced physical violence, and one in ten has suffered sexual violence involving force, according to the Council of Europe. They say that Ireland has only a third of the capacity it needs to provide refuge for women on the run from abusive partners.

'The nature of domestic violence means the home becomes unsafe. The government have a responsibility to make sure there is accommodation,' says Niamh Wilson, manager of the Domestic Violence Advocacy Service for Sligo, Leitrim and west Cavan (where there are no refuge beds).

Courts are beginning to wake up to the issue too, and the Criminal Justice (Insanity) Act of 2006 has made it easier than ever for a woman to claim provocation if she has been subjected to years of abuse. North of the border the situation is similar, with courts showing leniency to women from abused backgrounds. In fact, there is a strong movement there to change the law to make it easier on such women.

The message is clear: women who kill their abusive partners aren't the same as murderers. This was clearly stated by one Northern victim of abuse, Nicola Henry from Coleraine. She suffered more than a decade of horrendous abuse, and says she feels strongly that women should not be jailed for murdering an abusive husband or partner. 'No woman who has been subjected to abuse over a sustained period of time should have to go to jail,' she said. Kevin Myers would be horrified.

'I definitely think it's too much because when it comes to the worst-case scenario, killing the abuser can be the only way out. With men like that it's terrible. You know there is a chance that he would do it to you; you're always going to feel that it's only a matter of time before he kills you,' she says.

Nicola's husband Alistair was jailed for two years in May 2008, after pleading guilty to making threats to kill her. But because of time already spent on remand, the forty-four-year-old abuser was out walking the streets again in a matter of weeks.

Over the years, Nicola claimed she suffered a horrendous catalogue of both verbal and physical abuse at the hands of her brutal husband. During one particularly harrowing episode, she said, she was locked in a wardrobe for four days and forced to eat her own excrement. In another, her pony tail was 'scalped' from her head and framed in the family home.

Having finally found the courage to leave him when he was sent to prison a number of years ago, Nicola, who has three children, said that women need all the help they can get to extricate themselves from domestic abuse situations. 'I think the law needs to be fair,' she said. 'I thought about killing my husband, I really did, after all he put me through. And I don't think I would have deserved to go to jail for life if I had. Women like me need to be protected.' The problem is, how do we decide who needs to be protected?

Although it is less common, women also abuse their husbands. Kathleen Bell broke her lover's jaw a few years before she drove a kitchen knife into his chest. He was an abusive partner, but was she one also? The case of Dolores O'Neill is even murkier, as we will see.

Statistically, fifteen per cent of Irish women will experience domestic violence of some sort at some time during their lives. That does not mean that these women are all subjected to sustained years of abuse: in some cases the abuse is a once-off or infrequent occurrence. This figure should surprise no one.

But what will surprise people is that six per cent of men will experience domestic violence. That means that for about every three women who suffer abuse, one man is abused. Domestic abuse of men is far more common than most people realise. And within some relationships both partners abuse each other. The comic Italian stereotype of the husband shouting at the wife, and she responding by throwing crockery at him is a harsh reality in many Irish households.

The situation is made so much worse by alcohol. During the trial of Dolores O'Neill much was made of Declan O'Neill's drinking, and of the beatings he administered to his wife. After the trial his family were incensed at what they saw as a completely unbalanced picture of the man. They said that he was bullied constantly by his wife during the course of their stormy marriage. Although the jury were only shown one side of the picture, it is important to consider the whole case.

The marriage of Declan and Dolores was doomed from the start. Two weeks before the wedding, she says, he hit her for the first time. She should have walked away then, but no one walks away two weeks before the big day. Everyone would be talking—the embarrassment would never be lived down. Better to put it down to an aberration, or the stresses of the upcoming nuptials, and put it behind them. After all, he had had drink taken.

She was just twenty-four when she walked down the aisle, and he was just twenty-two. They had the innocence of youth on their side. But more problems arose during the honeymoon. Dolores saw the honeymoon as two weeks alone with the man she loved. They were in Greece, the sun was shining, the beaches golden. Back then Greece was an exotic destination, with none of the yobbish English louts and loud German beach towel hoggers who go there now. It was a very upmarket holiday destination, full of culture and colour. But Declan didn't share Dolores's view of the honeymoon: he saw it as two weeks off work during which he could drink all day and into the night. His drinking was to be a constant bane during their married life. 'I suppose the honeymoon was an excuse to be drinking during the day,' said Dolores. 'He had me over the balcony with his hand around my throat.'

But when they returned to Dublin the young bride must have hoped for some improvement in their circumstances. Surely Declan would stop drinking and knuckle down to work, and the relationship would thrive? He wasn't all bad. He had a sensitive nature, and often took down his guitar and strummed his own songs.

The couple settled into a very pleasant part of the city, Coolamber Park in Knocklyon, an upmarket estate in a leafy suburb. There are no council houses here. Because of the high property prices, many of their neighbours were older couples, well established in life. It was quiet, affluent and sedate, a southside gem where the violence of the modern world seemed a million miles away, and a good place to raise children.

By day Declan worked in sales for a construction plant company. Dolores was a civil servant, working for the Legal Aid Board. She later joined the Equality Authority, where her career flourished and she became a key member of the team.

Within months of the wedding, Dolores was pregnant with her first child, Brian. When he was born she took the normal six months' maternity leave to look after the baby, then returned to work, leaving a relation to mind her baby. But Declan was not happy with this: he wanted a traditional family, with the mother at home looking after the growing children, and the father toiling away to bring in the money. So Dolores agreed to give up her civil service job. 'He loved the idea of coming in and having his meals on the table and the fire lit,' said his wife.

This might have been an idyllic situation, but there was one big problem. Declan's drinking was getting out of control. He would stay out drinking after work, often coming home well after midnight. Thursday nights were the worst, because Thursday was the day he got paid. A substantial portion of his weekly wages would be lodged that night in liquid form down his gullet—very little was being lodged to the bank.

The eighties were bleak years in Ireland, before the Celtic Tiger began to roar. Taxes were high, mortgage repayments were high, and bills had to be paid. Dolores was mortified when they got behind with the bills. More than once their phone was cut off, or their electricity disconnected. You have to fall a good way behind before the utility companies consider such drastic steps, and Dolores came to dread the sound of envelopes falling through the letter box. She would have to argue with her husband for a portion of his wages to keep up with the basics.

Inevitably she returned to work. Her husband might have fancy ideas in his head about the traditional family, but that only worked if there was enough money. There was constant tension between the couple over the mortgage and the bills. On one occasion Dolores wrote a cheque for £25 in a local supermarket and a few days later she was contacted to be told that the cheque had bounced. It was another devastating blow.

Because of their financial difficulties she had to take on a second job, selling Mass cards door to door in the evenings and at weekends. It only paid £2 an hour, but it gave her the little extra she needed to stay on top of things. All the bills were paid from her account.

'Our family's money problems were all down to my husband's drinking,' she tearfully recounted. 'He'd go off on a Thursday when he got paid, and we wouldn't see him until Saturday.'

Alcoholism is not a choice; it is a disease. The alcoholic has no control over their drinking, and consequently none over their spending. Many a man has drunk away a farm or a good business while in the grip of the bottle. Declan O'Neill was following a pattern too tragically familiar in this country.

Dolores remembers one Saturday morning going into the room where he was lying on the bed, still drunk from the night before. 'I asked him for money for groceries, but all I found from his weekly wage was £20 and some small change. I asked him where the rest was, and he accused me of taking it,' she said.

In 1986 the couple had a second child, another boy, whom they named Conor. But the situation did not improve: if anything it got worse. Declan was still drinking regularly, still squandering the family money, and he was becoming more abusive towards his wife as their relationship cooled and they grew distant.

As the boys grew older they became used to the sight of their parents fighting, and to the constant financial strain. The tension in the house was terrible. As they entered their forties the couple's relationship seemed almost unfixable. Dolores suspected that Declan was being unfaithful to her, that he was having affairs. And he had a hair-trigger temper. 'By the end he would strike out for the least thing,' she said.

Her eldest son Brian, a physics student, confirmed that the situation in the home was volatile. He said that he frequently had to intervene in late night rows between his parents. His father stayed out drinking after work, returning home at three or four in the morning, and this had been the pattern for some years. 'It put a strain on their relationship,' he said. 'My father was drinking and coming home late on a regular basis—all the time. Sometimes he would disappear for days on end.'

Dolores was not a meek doormat: she would harangue her husband when he returned home, but when she confronted Declan he brushed her off and went upstairs, putting on his music and blaring it out at full volume.

'I regularly intervened and tried to calm the situation,' said Brian, adding that his father's drinking frequently left the family short of money. One occasion in particular stuck in his mind. His father had come home drunk, and when Dolores had confronted him he had grabbed the car keys and tried to get into the car. 'He tried to drive the car,' said Brian. Dolores and Brian had to pin Declan down and take the keys from him. 'My mother lost her brother to a drunk driver. She felt strongly about it,' he added.

On another occasion he noticed that his mother had a bloodied nose, but she didn't seem to have noticed it, and when Brian pointed out to her, 'she told me that there was a bit of a scuffle and Declan might have hit her by accident,' he said.

'I didn't believe her—not at all. My mother was trying to contain the situation.' But Brian admitted that he had never actually seen his father strike his mother.

Brian said that his father had not really been involved in the lives of himself or his brother for a number of years. 'We got on much better as a family when he was not there. His drinking was out of control.' He said that there was a constant state of tension in the house, with Declan always coming and going, but added: 'I was pretty sure where I stood with him. I kept out of his way. Once he ran out because of the way I looked at him.'

Brian said that his mother was never a violent person, and that she treated her sons well, adding: 'When I was younger she used to tutor other parents on not hitting their children.'

Dolores said that in the last few years of her marriage Declan had become so violent that she was forced to make up stories to explain her injuries.

On one occasion her husband had cryptically warned her: 'I am mixing with people now who can make people disappear.'

Dolores never sought a barring order. 'The stigma of it prevented me,' she explained. 'I wanted his best interests, wanted to help him. I still loved him. Declan knew I still had feelings for him, and he toyed with them. I am sure he was having affairs.'

That is the picture of the O'Neill marriage with which the jury were presented at Dolores's trial.

According to leading psychiatrist Dr Brian McCaffrey, it is typical of abused spouses that they stay with their abuser. He said that most abused partners have low self-esteem and confidence issues, normally stemming from incidents in their childhood. He said that it is very unusual for someone from a stable and happy background to fall prey to a violent partner—they will not put up with abusive treatment. Someone from a happy background will normally only fall into the pattern of accepting abuse from a partner if they become hooked on alcohol or drugs. As Dolores was addicted to neither drink nor drugs, there were probably factors in her upbringing that left her susceptible to abuse; but this possibility was never presented to the jury.

Dr McCaffrey added that abused people do not normally take the violence passively. They fight back, they confront their partner, they pick arguments, and they occasionally hit back physically. The worm doesn't turn suddenly, but rather by degrees. As we saw in the last chapter, Kathleen Bell once broke her lover's jaw in a fight—but she was a big, strong woman. Dolores O'Neill was only five foot two, nearly a foot shorter than her six-foot husband. If she punched him, the only damage she would do would be to her knuckles.

However, there is evidence (which was not presented to the jury) that Dolores did find ways of striking back at her husband. The prosecution took the decision not to focus on the behaviour of Dolores towards Declan, but to fully understand the events of the night of 2 June 2002, we must consider Declan's story.

After the trial Declan's family said that the picture of the marriage the jury was given was far from accurate. They were particularly incensed at the way Declan himself was portrayed. 'Declan was a gentle, loving, friendly and sensitive person,' said his brother Dermot. 'Far from being an alcoholic, he was the one person who could be relied upon to bring everyone home after a function because he never drank anything stronger than Smithwick's or beer shandy.' This was corroborated by the autopsy report. Far from being drunk at the time of his death, Declan had no alcohol in his system.

Declan's family went on to say that he had been keeping an account of alleged abuses by Dolores. This handwritten list, which was found in his car after his death, included a number of incidents, the most recent in March 2002, four months before his death. The entry read: 'In Tallaght Hospital for abrasions to head and leg after flung by car while she was at control.' Another entry in the account reads: 'Hit over head with bottle on at least two occasions.' Interestingly, the account ends four months before Declan's death, and there are no more entries after March 2002—but Declan had left Dolores for a period before their explosive reunion.

Dermot O'Neill said: 'We were stunned to learn that the State prosecution could not or would not use this testimony, which we considered was Declan speaking from the grave. On the witness stand Dolores was given free rein to besmirch Declan's name as she saw fit, in an effort to excuse her actions.'

He claimed that Dolores had rammed her car into her husband's car when her son was with her, and on other occasions she broke an ashtray over her husband's head and ripped the buttons off his shirt. He said phone records would show that she harassed her husband by phoning him up to forty times a day. On one occasion she ripped out his car phone kit. He said she also beat him with a mobile phone charger.

Dermot O'Neill said he had listened to a voice message from Dolores to Declan threatening that she was going to throw acid in his face. 'Declan said that she threatened this on several occasions.' She also threatened that he would have no access to their children.

'It is our family's view that he lived a life of quiet desperation. Regrettably it was Declan's view that any steps he took were futile and tolerating the abuse was his only option. This decision proved to be fatal.' Dermot O'Neill went on to say that his brother was treated for depression 'brought on by the difficulties in the relationship, but his wife saw fit to deprive him of the medication prescribed'.

On one occasion she took his clothes, shoes and work items so that he was unable to go to work or attend a hospital appointment. Family members urged him to get out of the house but he did not want to leave his younger son. Dermot O'Neill quoted from a text message sent from Declan to his sister-in-law saying: 'In my room, waiting for the next attack. I will get over it.' He didn't.

A little over two months before his death Declan left the family home. Whether he finally found the courage to walk away, as his family believe, or whether he found a new woman, as Dolores believed, is an open question. But the insight of psychiatrist Dr McCaffrey is interesting. He says that abused partners do not make a clean break of it. They leave, then come back, then leave again, working up to the final break.

In any case, Dolores said that Declan left the family home in March. He spent two months, she maintained, with a woman he called 'the dominatrix', but on 24 June he returned to Coolamber, determined to give his marriage one last try. She was willing to meet him half way.

Declan suggested that the best way to mark the fresh start would be for the family to take a break. Soon after he moved back home he suggested a weekend in Cork. Dolores agreed, saying: 'I just wanted to try one last time to make it as a family.' Conor would come with them. Brian, who was working part-time in an off-licence, would remain in Dublin.

The trip to Cork was a disaster, right from the start. Before the new motorway was built it was a four-hour trip—longer on a Friday, with serious delays in Mitchelstown and Fermoy. It must have been horrible for young Conor, then aged fifteen, being trapped in a car with his warring parents. Dolores had chosen the music for the trip, bringing a selection of CDs. Declan, who saw himself as something of a music aficionado, did not like her choice of music, and at one point he put on earplugs rather than listen to her CDs. Interestingly, he did not insist on switching to his choice. Perhaps he was less controlling than the court was led to believe.

That night in the hotel Dolores awoke in the early hours of the morning to find her husband kissing her. Perhaps the reconciliation would work. She responded to his affection, kissing him in return. 'I kissed him back and on the shoulder. He jumped up and called me a "fucking bitch, trying to leave your mark on me".' She sat up in bed and asked him what was going on. For reply he struck her, and she spent the rest of the night in the bathroom, cooling her face with a wet flannel.

Whatever went on in the room that night it was loud enough to wake the occupant of the next room. Conor O'Neill remembers hearing a sound 'like a slap' coming from his parents' room. The following morning his mother's face was swollen and bruised. The four-hour journey back to Dublin was conducted in silence. Dolores sat in the back with Conor, leaving Declan on his own in the front of the car. Not a word was spoken all the way.

His son Brian recalls the day they returned. 'I was working part-time in an off-licence and on Sunday my mother arrived to pick me up. I could see, obviously, on her face there was a very large bruise. She asked me not to say anything to Declan about it. She said Declan was opening a door and that he hit her by accident. My mam was just trying to keep everything whole.'

The following morning Dolores phoned in sick to work. Although she had a reputation as a good worker, and particularly good with younger people, her colleagues were used to her absences. During the years there had been many missed days, and some people noticed that she wore long sleeves, no matter what the weather, to conceal her bruises.

That evening was tense. When Declan returned from work he went to his room, and Dolores was trying to limit the amount of contact she had with him. Although she had not done any shopping the preceding weekend, due to the Cork trip, she had enough in the house to cobble together an ample dinner, which she brought up to him on a tray. He was surly. Later she brought him a cup of tea. 'What the fuck are you in here again for?' he snapped.

Later she asked to borrow his car to bring the boys to the cinema. Declan lost his rag. 'Jesus Christ! You're in on top of me again. What the fucking hell is wrong with your own car?' She was low on petrol. He tossed her the keys, and demanded that if she was going out she should bring him back a pack of cigarettes.

That night Dolores gave her two sons some money and brought them to the cinema. It was 22 July, and Dolores and Declan were alone in the house. The only account we have of what went on that night is that of Dolores herself, which she gave during her trial. Quite frankly, her account is flatly contradicted by much of the forensic evidence.

According to Dolores, Declan shouted at her when she brought him the cigarettes. He shouted at her when she brought him more tea. Then she had to disturb him yet again, as she was putting on a wash and went to his room to collect his dirty laundry. She knew that he was close to snapping point, yet she kept approaching him. It's like someone picking at a scab when the sensible thing to do would be to leave it alone.

From here on Dolores's account is at odds with the forensic evidence. Now, forensic findings are facts. Facts are facts—they are what happened. And where her account differs from the facts, she is either lying or her mind was so deranged by the tensions of her life that she misremembered and misinterpreted what happened.

Dolores said that she went to Declan's room for the laundry.

'He jumped up from the bed and started calling me a fucking bitch. He pushed me up against a table.' She says that Declan grabbed her by the throat and forced her up against the wall. He banged her head again and again on the wall. She couldn't breathe, and could feel his grip tightening about her throat. He was shouting, spitting venom into her face, and threatening to give her another black eye.

Somehow she managed to free herself and push Declan away. He tumbled backwards and fell onto the bed. Then she spotted a large plumber's hammer under the bed. This didn't surprise her; Declan had been doing some DIY. 'I just saw the hammer and picked it up. Jesus! Oh God, Jesus!'

From here on Dolores's account is fuzzy. She says she doesn't remember the details of the attack. She knows she struck him with a hammer, but has no recollection of using a knife. Maybe he had the carving knife under the bed as well, for use in his DIY. In any case it was a frenzied attack. Declan was struck on the head twenty-four times with the heavy hammer. Then he was hacked with the carving knife, suffering at least twenty-one stab wounds to his neck. 'I just couldn't take any more. I knew he was going to go for me,' she said.

According to State Pathologist Dr John Harbison it was a serious case of overkill: Declan was long dead as the blows continued to rain down on his head. Dr Harbison said: 'It was a frenzied attack. To me it suggests some derangement. I think the term overkill might be used.'

The pattern of blood spatters on the bedclothes and around the room indicate that at one point Dolores lifted Declan's lifeless head, then let it fall back to the bed. There was a sweeping mark on some of the soiled bedclothes. It was as if she was checking he was dead. But even after that, the attack went on.

Dr Harbison's evidence also contradicts Dolores's account of how the fight began. Declan was lying on the bed on his right side when the first blow was struck. He was attacked from above. He did not have a single defensive mark on his hands or arms, indicating that he never fought back. The clear conclusion is that Dolores sneaked into the room with the hammer and bludgeoned a sleeping man; or that he was awake and caught unawares by the first blow. In either case the result was the same. After the first blow he was unconscious. The next twenty-three blows and twenty-one stab wounds were inflicted on an inert body.

Another finding of the doctor also contradicted the picture painted in the court. A toxicology report on Declan's remains found no traces of alcohol or any other substance. Strange for a man described by his family as a habitual drunkard.

Satisfied that her work was complete, Dolores dropped the knife on the bed, then pulled a duvet over the remains of her husband. Blood continued to seep—because he was dead it was no longer gushing—and the duvet reddened. She went into the en suite bathroom and removed her clothes in the shower. She showered thoroughly, then stepped out and dressed in fresh clothes. She left her blood-soaked clothes and the hammer in the shower.

Then she went outside and got into the car, to wait for her boys to return from the cinema. They returned shortly before midnight, and found her still sitting in the car. She told them to get into the car, which they did, then set out on the twenty-five-mile drive to her sister's house in Ashford, County Wicklow.

'I kept asking her what had happened, but she wouldn't say,' said Brian. 'I had to ask her a number of times before she told us we were going to her sister Ann's house. She just kept saying "No." I kept thinking that Declan had done something—hit her. I asked her was Declan okay. She wasn't answering me.'

When they arrived in Wicklow it was after midnight. Ann Hughes remembers her sister almost 'fell in the door'. Dolores was distraught, and asked Ann to look after her two sons, who were in the car outside. She asked to speak to Ann's husband, John.

'I noticed a mark on her face, like a punch mark. There was a reddish mark on her neck, and later I saw bruises on both her forearms. I asked her what happened. She said Declan had grabbed her by the neck. She said she slapped him to get him away and then he punched her. I could see the mark,' said Ann.

She was aware of her sister's serious marital problems. The house had been re-mortgaged, the mortgage was not being paid and her husband had run up some serious bills. Dolores was worried that they would lose the family home.

Dolores confided in John Hughes, then in her sister. 'She said that she hit her husband with a hammer that was underneath the bed. She then said: "If only I could rewind this." She was like a defeated woman, rather than a battered woman. She looked hopeless. Broken.'

John Hughes said that Dolores was 'out of it, totally devastated and in a horrific state'. It took him about five minutes to calm her down enough for her to tell him what had happened. She said she had 'done a terrible thing to the father of her sons' and that she must be mad. She spoke disjointedly about a trip to Cork and a row.

She told him her husband had caught her by the throat and threatened to give her another black eye. She hit him and he fell back onto the bed. He turned to her and said he was out of there the following morning. Dolores told John that this was when she flipped and hit Declan with a hammer.

But what was the trigger that set off this murderous attack? In the case of Kathleen Bell it was the taunts from her partner about her past sexual abuse. In the case of Dolores O'Neill, was it her husband's threat to leave her? It appears from the forensic evidence that this threat was not made just before the attack, as Declan was probably asleep at that time. It seems more likely he had made his threat earlier in the evening, and this is why Dolores armed herself with a heavy hammer and a sharp carving knife before she went back into his room.

John Hughes rang the emergency services, then went out to break the news to Brian and Conor that their father was dead.

Dolores O'Neill was charged with murder. She pleaded guilty to manslaughter, but the state would not accept that plea. Her first trial collapsed when one of the technical witnesses gave evidence on the stand that was not included in his technical report. The new trial opened in October 2004, and lasted six days. It was not an easy case. A jury of six men and six women had to decide whether Dolores was provoked, and whether she had been acting in self-defence or had deliberately and premeditatively set out to murder her husband, as the prosecution maintained. They took five hours to return a verdict of not guilty of murder, but guilty of manslaughter. Her two boys were there to support Dolores as the verdict was read out.

Mr Justice Paul Carney said that the case had been a difficult one for all concerned. Declan O'Neill's character had been brought into the case, and it was said that he was a 'raging alcoholic', even though the toxicology reports were completely negative for drugs or alcohol. He took the unusual step of allowing the family of the deceased to address the court on how his death had affected them.

Declan's brother Brian said: 'We have lost a member of our family who we deeply loved, and whose character this court is not aware of. What we heard in court was not our brother.' As his siblings wept he added that some of them had lost their jobs because they could not cope with the grief.

Judge Carney said that he was 'bound by the jury's verdict', and that Dolores had never been in trouble before. She was clearly a good mother, devoted to her two sons. However, the evidence 'indicated no resistance on the part of the deceased. It indicated he was asleep or disabled by the first blow. There were no defensive injuries. I am satisfied there was no resistance on his part. He was hit with twenty-four blows by a plumber's hammer, then twenty-one blows of a knife.'

The judge sentenced Dolores to eight years in prison. With normal remission she would be out in six. Some people saw this as a very lenient sentence.

It is interesting to compare the case of Dolores O'Neill with that of Joe O'Reilly. In 2007 Joe O'Reilly was convicted of murdering his wife Rachel. He went out to work on 4 October 2004, then sneaked back and beat her to death with a heavy dumbbell. There are tremendous similarities in the cases. Dolores was devoted to her children. Joe was also a very good father, with genuine concerns about the future of his two children. Joe planned a time when Rachel would be alone in the house, then he struck with violent cruelty. Dolores sent her two children out to the cinema, then violently attacked her slumbering husband.

The chief difference between the two cases seems to be the way the two perpetrators handled the aftermath. Dolores ran to her sister's house in hysterics and admitted everything. Joe kept his cool and proclaimed his innocence long after everyone stopped believing him.

But Dolores will do six years—Joe is behind bars for life. When he lost his appeal in March 2009, the papers gleefully proclaimed 'Evil Joe to rot in jail.'

Maybe Kevin Myers had a point, and men do have it tougher than women when it comes to playing the sympathy card. His article certainly drew a number of letters of support, one of which said that the trial 'spoke volumes about the rights of women and lack of equal rights of men in Irish society. We have no idea why evidence of Dolores O'Neill's history of violent abuse towards her husband was not disclosed in court. Shouldn't we be asking?'

Another summed up the thinking of many. 'Advice to estranged husbands intending to sleep; don't.'

13 | THE ONE THAT GOT AWAY

MARGARET McCOLE

A paradox of murder is that it is both surprisingly easy and surprisingly difficult to kill someone. Many people have learned to their cost how easy it is to end someone's life. A fight in the street, a punch or a kick that hits a thin part of the skull, and a drunken brawler can find himself facing a murder charge. Or a few angry words, hands placed roughly on a lover's slender neck, and the result can be fatal.

Many of the people serving life sentences in Irish prisons are the victims of this human frailty. They never set out to kill. On the other hand, there are many people walking the streets who should be behind bars for murder. Only a stroke of luck saved them; their victim miraculously survived the murderous assault.

We are a resilient species. Just watch two heavyweight boxers knock lumps off each other for twelve rounds: at the end of the bout they embrace, having suffered nothing more than sore heads. And we can survive much more than a few thumps.

On 29 January 2003, five members of the McCarthy Dundon gang in Limerick decided to execute rival gang leader Kieran Keane. They lured him and his nephew Owen Tracey to a quiet spot outside the city, and they shot him in the head. But when it came to Tracey, they hit a problem: the gun jammed. Ever resourceful, they had a plan B. They launched a frenzied attack on him, stabbing him seventeen times. They were determined that there would be no witnesses to that night's work.

They bundled into their van, leaving their victim for dead, but Owen Tracey survived the attack. He managed to get to his feet and stagger away to raise the alarm. After making a full recovery he testified against the men who meant to kill him, and saw all five jailed for life.

Other victims have been equally lucky after being attacked by murderous women. Around the time Una Black was facing trial for the killing of her neighbour in Galway in a row over a dog (see Chapter 2), another woman was lucky not to be facing equally serious charges after a vicious stabbing.

Ciara Byrne, aged twenty-three, of Donore Avenue, Dublin, was handed a community service order for stabbing three men with a pair of scissors outside Tramco nightclub on the Lower Rathmines Road. On the evening of 22 November 2006, a row broke out outside the nightclub between Ms Byrne and her companions. Three members of St Mary's College Rugby Club, including Irish under-21 player Jonathan Sexton, were in the vicinity, and they intervened.

The court heard that Ms Byrne had a pair of scissors in her handbag because she had been cutting a friend's hair earlier. Taking the scissors from her bag, she turned on the three burly rugby players, viciously stabbing each of them. One of the stab wounds was so deep it punctured a lung, but all three victims made full recoveries.

Ms Byrne had not been in trouble before, and was thought unlikely to reoffend. She was given a three-year jail sentence, suspended on condition she carry out 240 hours' community service. She was also bound to the peace for three years. Had the scissors nicked an artery instead of puncturing a lung, she could have been facing a far more serious charge and a lengthy spell in prison.

Stabbing a stranger in a drunken brawl outside a nightclub is very much a male crime. So is beating an elderly pensioner to within an inch of his life, and running off with whatever small money he had in the house; or killing a neighbour in a dispute over land. It was this archetypal conflict that gave John B. Keane the material for his powerful play *The Field*. He based his work on a famous murder in Reamore, County Kerry, in which bachelor farmer Moss Moore was beaten to death in 1959. Dan Foley, a neighbour with whom Moore had a long-running dispute over a few feet of boundary, was suspected of the murder, but denied the charge.

Almost thirty years later a similar attack, this time in Donegal, was described in court as the 'classic, traditional Irish case, involving land and a row about it in a remote area'. What made this case stand out was that the accused was a woman, and Margaret McCole was also lucky not to be facing a murder charge—but in her case it was not for want of trying. The mother of six from Donegal had tried her best to bludgeon to death an elderly neighbour, a man who had come to rely on her.

On the night of Thursday 9 May 1996, an elderly pensioner living in the Inishowen Peninsula was brutally attacked by an intruder to his home. Willie Harrigan, aged eighty-four, was a retired fisherman who also farmed twenty acres in the remote area in the north of Donegal. A bachelor, he lived alone at Magherard, Drung, Quigley's Point, but he had good neighbours who looked out for him. One, Margaret McCole, brought him his dinner every day.

At some point on that Thursday night an intruder broke into Mr Harrigan's house and beat the elderly man badly. The intruder used the traditional favourite of mystery writers, the 'blunt instrument', in this case a claw hammer, and Willie suffered serious injuries to his head, neck and arms in the frenzied attack. According to his niece, Betty Corr, who was home from Boston on holiday, her uncle would need plastic surgery and extensive hospitalisation to recover. 'I just cannot believe that anyone would leave such an old man in such a condition,' she said. 'The injuries and pain Willie has suffered are just sickening. He was left to die like an animal by an animal. He has burn marks around his neck which were caused when his attacker apparently tried to strangle him. His head and face are a complete mess. Willie is unrecognisable. He is a lovely quiet man and thank God he was able to phone his neighbour, Margaret McCole, who raised the alarm.'

The investigating gardaí were equally horrified. 'This was one of the most vicious attacks of its kind we have ever come across. The intruder disturbed Willie and then subjected him to a horrendous beating. He is lucky to be alive.' The intruder, it was thought, might have stolen about £300 from Mr Harrigan during the assault.

But within days it became obvious that Willie Harrigan was not the victim of a burglar preying on elderly and isolated targets. This was more of an inside job. Attention quickly turned to someone quite close to the pensioner.

To tell the story fully, we must go back eighteen months. Willie Harrigan was a lively, sprightly and independent man who lived in a cottage on his own, and who got on well with his neighbours. Although he did not need their help, he welcomed it. One neighbour in particular was very good to him.

Margaret McCole, aged forty at the time, was a mother of six who lived nearby with her husband Oliver, a farmer. She was not from the locality, but had been living in Magherard with her husband for seventeen years. The couple had married at nineteen, and had six children, the eldest aged eighteen when the youngest arrived. Margaret worked in the local hospital as a care worker, looking after elderly women, and was well regarded there. Back home she was also increasingly looking after Mr Harrigan. She cooked his breakfasts and dinners and collected his pension for him. She wasn't the only one looking after the elderly man— a relation also helped him out—but she saw herself as the primary carer.

Shortly after the birth of Margaret's last child, Mr Harrigan visited his solicitor and made a new will, leaving his cottage and his small farm to a second cousin. This seems to have been a trigger to the eventual assault. Mr Harrigan had no idea that his kindly neighbour now looked at him in a different light. Mrs McCole began to put pressure on Mr Harrigan to change his will. She felt that since she was the one looking after him, she should benefit from his estate. The old man eventually came around to her point of view, and he changed his will once more, this time making Mrs McCole the beneficiary. The new will was made a little before Christmas 1995. But Mrs McCole was not the only one he wanted to look after. As the years had gone on he had become increasingly fond of one of his nieces, who was based in Boston. He had gone out to America to stay with Betty Corr and her husband, and she was coming over to Ireland to visit him. She was due in the early summer of 1996, and Willie wanted to give her a gift when she was home. It would prove a costly gift.

After making his will Mr Harrigan asked Mrs McCole to drive him to the AIB branch in Moville, where he withdrew £5,000 for Ms Corr. But Mrs McCole was horrified: leaving that much money lying around the house until summer was inviting trouble—for his own safety he could not do that. She persuaded him to allow her to mind the money, so they drove to her bank, and she deposited the £5,000 in her own account, to be handed over to Betty when she came home from Boston.

The old man was delighted, and thought nothing more of it. With burglaries of elderly, vulnerable and isolated people filling the newspapers every morning, he knew she was right. It was good to have a neighbour looking out for you.

But unknown to Mr Harrigan, Mrs McCole began to withdraw money from the £5,000 she was holding for him. It is not clear what the money was spent on, but it can be surmised that the McColes had a very good Christmas that year, because at the end of the festive season there was very little left in the account. For instance, on 21 December, just four days before Christmas, she withdrew £2,000. It is known that some of the money was spent on furniture, and some on clothing. She didn't drain the account entirely, because on 6 February she was still able to withdraw £700, but by the time the Yanks returned home there was only £20 left. Betty Corr was going to get a very small gift from her uncle.

On the outside Mrs McCole kept up the appearance that everything was normal. She still visited her neighbour, picked up his pension for him and delivered his meals; she brought him into town for his shopping and made herself as useful as ever. But inside she was in turmoil. She knew that the time of Betty Corr's visit was fast approaching, and her deception would be found out.

She went to a building society and tried to get a loan for the amount. She applied for £7,000, which would allow her to comfortably repay the money she had taken. Then Mrs Corr and her husband arrived, and took up residence in a guesthouse nearby. Time was collapsing in on Mrs McCole.

On the evening of Thursday 9 May 1996, Mrs McCole decided to call on Mr Harrigan and come clean. After all, she had applied for the loan, so she could make good the situation. She would explain what had happened and ask him for time to sort it all out. 'The problem was on my mind since the Yanks came home,' she revealed later. But for some unknown reason she decided that she should bring along her husband's claw hammer when she went to call.

What happened next was brutal. Instead of talking calmly to the old man, she took out the hammer and struck him savagely on the head. The most extensive injuries were to the back of his head, indicating that she had sneaked up behind him and taken him by surprise. This might have been why he had no clear recollection of his attacker: she might have let herself in and come up behind him without announcing her presence.

She struck him repeatedly until he fell, unconscious, from his chair to the floor. But this was not enough for her; she continued to rain blows down on the defenceless man, hitting him a number of times on the arms and head, until he was completely still.

According to the medical evidence later presented in court, Mr Harrigan suffered very extensive injuries. Dr Neville Couse, consultant surgeon at St James's Hospital, Letterkenny, said that he had 'extensive lacerations to the back of the scalp', including one laceration 'involving loss of tissue about the size of the palm of a hand'. He also had bruising to his eyes and his neck, and multiple lacerations to his hands. The nail of one finger had been torn off, and Mr Harrigan's right thumb was fractured. He needed a plastic surgeon to deal with the injuries.

Dr Denis Lawlor, consultant plastic surgeon at the hospital, told the court that he had had to treat a 'severe scalp defect'. He said that the most significant thing about the wound was its depth. 'It was right down to the bone. It would take quite a blow to cause the wound I treated. For a man of his age, Mr Harrigan had tremendous reserve to sustain it.'

The process of recovery was slow. Mr Harrigan spent 182 days in hospital before being ready for release, and he never regained his former independence and sprightliness. Months after the assault he needed a stick to walk around, and was visibly frailer than before.

Following the attack, Mrs McCole had the good sense to remove the hammer from the scene. She surveyed her work, and wondered had she done enough. 'Willie became quiet, but was still breathing,' she later told gardaí. 'I did not intend to kill Willie. I am sorry for what I have done.'

But this, like many of her statements after the assault, was self-serving—the whole purpose of the assault was to get rid of the man who could reveal her misdeeds. She quickly scanned the blood-soaked room. There were substantial splashes of crimson streaking the floor, walls, fridge, cooker and ceiling, but these were not what concerned her at that moment. Soon she found Willie's wallet, which contained £340. She pocketed it, then left the house. On the way home she threw the claw hammer over a ditch.

Later that evening, like everyone else in the locality, she reacted with horror to the news that her elderly neighbour had been subjected to a vicious attack. In fact, over the next few days the newspapers even credited her with raising the alarm. Her horror was probably genuine, but its cause was different from that of her neighbours: with Willie still alive, her world was about to crash in on her.

But she maintained an unruffled demeanour. Only a few hours after nearly beating a man to death she calmly called to the guesthouse where the victim's niece and her husband were staying to tell Betty Corr about the attack on Willie. She seemed as shocked as everyone else.

The following day she went with Mrs Corr to the emergency ward at Letterkenny Hospital to visit Mr Harrigan. On the way to the hospital they stopped in Moville, and she went into a bank. A few minutes later she handed Mrs Corr £300, saying that this was money her uncle had intended to give her. She wisely never mentioned the missing £4,700.

Over the next few days the investigation began to home in on the beneficiary of Mr Harrigan's will. Despite her bravado, Mrs

McCole knew the net was tightening, so she tried to get rid of the evidence. She went into Letterkenny and dumped the bloody wallet in a litter bin in a shopping mall. With the wallet gone and the hammer disposed of—and the old man having no recollection of her attacker—perhaps for a few moments she allowed herself to believe it would all work out.

But the investigating gardaí were having none of it. They interviewed her and began to pick holes in her account of the night of the assault and the days following it.

The gardaí had a lucky break when they found traces of Mrs McCole's blood in the kitchen of Mr Harrigan's house. She had cut herself on the night of the assault, and although she had the cut before going into the kitchen it had bled again during the assault, and had left vital forensic evidence. Investigators got another lucky break when they found Mr Harrigan's wallet. In response to Detective Garda Leheney's questions, Mrs McCole denied that she had put the wallet in the mall in Letterkenny, but he kept pressing her, until she asked: 'Are there cameras in the shopping mall?'

Perhaps considering the possibility that she had been captured on film in Letterkenny, she decided to change tack, and told the detective that she had put the wallet in the bin, but she had not taken it from Willie's house. She had found it abandoned outside Letterkenny Hospital. The detective was naturally sceptical, and kept pushing Mrs McCole for a true account of how she had come to have the wallet. Eventually she admitted taking it from Willie's kitchen.

'I found it on the floor following the attack on him, and I thought I might as well have it,' she said. She admitted taking £340 from the wallet before disposing of it.

In subsequent statements she admitted spending £4,980 of the £5,000 given to her by Mr Harrigan for safekeeping. She told Detective Leheney that Mr Harrigan's niece, Betty Corr, had arrived from the United States on 2 May, and she was worried that she didn't have the £5,000 for her. On the day Mrs Corr arrived, Mrs McCole said, she had applied for a personal loan of £5,000 from a building society in Moville.

At first she told gardaí that she went to Mr Harrigan's house on the night of the attack to tell him about the missing money. 'The problem was on my mind since the Yanks came home. I did not intend to kill Willie.'

She admitted going to the house and attacking him with the hammer. She described the attack in detail—how she had struck him on the back of the head, and continued the assault as he lay helpless on the floor. She insisted that she had acted alone, and said that she did not want her husband or family to know of her actions. Investigating detectives were satisfied that in this at least she was telling the truth; she had acted alone that night.

A search party recovered the claw hammer used in the attack over a ditch on the Carrickmaquigley Road, in the spot pointed out to them by Mrs McCole. It was the final nail in her coffin.

Mrs McCole was arrested at her home and taken to Buncrana Garda Station, where she was charged with aggravated burglary. She was released on her husband's bail of £5,000, but subsequently charged with attempted murder.

The case was heard before Mr Justice Quirke and a jury of seven men and five women at the Central Criminal Court in January 1998. The opening day was dramatic; the case was called, but the defendant was not in court. Mrs McCole had done a runner. Her barrister, Brendan Grogan SC, said he could only put her non-appearance down to panic.

The following day Mrs McCole did appear, and she pleaded guilty to four charges, including assault and robbery. But she denied the main charge, the attempted murder of William Harrigan at his home on 9 May 1996.

The jury heard a number of days of evidence, which the judge summed up by saying that both sides agreed that Mrs McCole was desperate on the night of 9 May. Mr Harrigan's niece had returned from the United States and it was to her the £5,000 was due. Mrs McCole had spent all but £20 of it over the Christmas period of 1995.

The prosecution claimed her desperation was induced by greed and that she feared she would lose the house and farm Mr Harrigan had willed to her if it was discovered she had taken the money he had given her for safekeeping. The defence claimed her desperation was born of a deep sense of shame at the possibility that it would be discovered that the money was missing.

Gregory Murphy, barrister for the prosecution, told the jury to consider three things: the element of planning and calculation involved in Mrs McCole's actions; the ferocity of the attack; and the callous abandonment of the victim after she had beaten him. He pointed out that there was a self-serving thread running through all Mrs McCole's statements to the gardaí, and she had tried to cover her back, albeit 'in a rather inept way'. Her actions and accounts after the incident indicated 'a deviousness of mind consistent with premeditation'.

Brendan Grogan, barrister for the defence, pointed out that up to the night of the attack Mrs McCole had been a woman of unblemished character. She had six children, ranging in age from two to twenty, and was employed as a care worker in the local hospital. He said that even the prosecution accepted she had been a very good and caring neighbour to Willie Harrigan.

The jury retired to consider their verdict, as Mrs McCole waited anxiously in the dock, her husband and children with her in court. The jury needed just three hours to decide that Mrs McCole was guilty of all charges. Mr Justice Quirke looked at the woman in the dock, her head bowed and hands clasped, and said: 'I do not wish to cause you pain. I have no wish to cause your family pain— especially your children. But you savagely attacked an elderly and frail man, a man who trusted you, who had bequeathed his house to you, and whom you had promised you would look after for the rest of his days. Your crimes are inexplicable and in many ways so heartbreaking, not least because the latter part of your life had been spent doing good things, especially for elderly people.'

He remanded Mrs McCole in custody until 24 March, when he would pass sentence. This would allow time for psychological and probation reports to be prepared. The judge said that the case was not a normal one, and there were certain matters on which he required explanation and help before sentencing.

When the case came before him in March Mrs McCole was supported by three of her daughters in court; two of the other children remained outside with her husband Oliver. Mr Justice Quirke said that he was entitled to impose a life sentence, but was not going to do so because of Mrs McCole's exemplary life up to that point, her love for her children, and the likelihood that she would not reoffend.

He noted that most of the money stolen from Mr Harrigan had been paid back—the gardaí had been given a cheque for £3,500 for the injured man. He was told by Mrs McCole's barrister that the balance would be paid as soon as it was physically possible to do so.

On the charge of attempted murder, Judge Quirke ruled that Mrs McCole would have to serve seven years in prison. She was sentenced to two years for causing grievous bodily harm with intent, and to another two years for entering Mr Harrigan's house with a hammer and stealing his wallet and £340. The sentences were to run concurrently, which meant she would serve a total of seven years.

The judge described the attack as 'savage' and said Mrs McCole had shown neither regret nor remorse. He said that he would review the sentence in January of the following year, when he would find out if the stolen money had been repaid, and whether Mrs McCole had 'recovered from her denial' about the attack and shown remorse. He was taking into account both psychiatric evidence that Mrs McCole was 'in denial' and an assurance from the defence that the money taken would be repaid shortly.

But in January he confirmed the sentence, saying that Mrs McCole had ignored all chances to show remorse for her attack. Instead, she had chosen to give an interview to the *Sunday World* in which she proclaimed her innocence, and had refused to co-operate with the probation service. 'There is only one conclusion,' said the judge. 'Mrs McCole does not feel she wishes to demonstrate that she is in any way remorseful for the immense damage done to this elderly man. There is not one shred of evidence on which I could justifiably suspend any part of your sentence.'

As Margaret McCole was led away from her tearful children to serve her sentence she could draw comfort from one thing. Had she succeeded in her murderous attack, she would have been facing a far stiffer sentence.

Her victim was also facing his own sentence. Before the attack he had been an active, independent pensioner who enjoyed good health. But as a result of the attack, and the subsequent six months in hospital, medical advice was that he would be unable to live independently and would require long-term care. At least he got the chance to change his will; Mrs McCole was no longer one of the beneficiaries.

14 | **LOSING THE HEAD**
HANNAH O'LEARY

As the two Mulhall sisters went on trial for the brutal murder of their mother's lover, and the subsequent dismemberment and disposal of his body in Dublin's Royal Canal, it was widely reported that this was only the second case in Ireland in which a body had been chopped up prior to disposal.

The previous case dated back to 1963, when a twenty-two-year-old South African medical student, Shan Mohangi, became enraged when his girlfriend Hazel Mullen (aged fifteen) broke off their relationship. He strangled her and then chopped up her body before attempting to burn it in the furnace of the Green Tureen, the restaurant where he moonlighted in the kitchen.

The strange smells coming from the basement aroused suspicion, and he was caught. Put on trial charged with murder, he was found guilty and sentenced to death. But on appeal (and with the death penalty struck off the books in the meantime) he was convicted of the lesser charge of manslaughter. Shan served three years in an Irish prison before being sent back to South Africa. He changed his name to Narutak Jumuna and turned his life around, becoming an important voice in the emerging democracy of that country, and eventually being elected to the South African parliament.

But Shan Mohangi was not the first Irish killer to dismember his victim's body. That honour goes to a family from a scenic seaside village in west Cork, and the murder took place just a few years after the establishment of the Irish Free State.

Patrick O'Leary was a small farmer who eked out a living on forty acres near Rosscarbery in west Cork, a small fishing village nestled in a little cove a few miles beyond Clonakilty. Today the pretty, sleepy village is a pleasant gateway to the yachting playgrounds of west Cork. Back then, tourism was not the big business it is now, and Rosscarbery had to survive on agriculture and fishing.

The O'Leary farm was in the townland of Kilkerran, not on the coast but overlooking the sea. There is a small lake to the south of the townland, and beyond that the wide expanse of the Atlantic. When the wind comes from the south west, as it generally does, you can smell the salt on the air.

Patrick O'Leary had some cattle, and the few horses which were needed to work the land in those pre-tractor days. He managed to support himself, his wife and his family. Times were different then; people were harder. Ireland was just emerging from a war of independence, and an even more brutal civil war, and west Cork had seen a lot of the action. Violence was not uncommon, and a cursory look at the newspapers of the time reveals that many a farmer or business owner ended up on the wrong end of a fatal dose of lead poisoning.

Most of those shootings were as a result of bad blood after the years of civil unrest. But Patrick O'Leary had kept his head down, and no one bore a political grudge against him. He was just a regular farmer, struggling to feed and clothe his family. Though he was not a well-off man, he made ends meet.

By the standards of the day, his family was not that large: he had two sons and two daughters. It was quite common for people to marry late, as he had himself. Sons waited until they inherited before making a move, and single girls were left on the farm if they did not have a dowry.

At the time of his death in 1921 all four of Patrick's children were still living at home, even though they were all grown up. His eldest son, Patrick Junior, was thirty-seven and already set in his ways. A tough, uncompromising man, he lorded it over his siblings. Already there were tensions within the family; he and his younger brother Cornelius (known as Con) had not spoken for several years, and the death of their father did nothing to change that. The two sisters, Hannah and Mary Anne, sided with their younger brother. Their mother, Hannah, tried to stay aloof from the situation, but she did nothing to bridge the gap between her warring children. She was seventy-two the year she was widowed, and no longer a dominant force in the household.

Patrick Senior's will did nothing to help the situation. The farm and his property, valued at £1,100, were left to his wife, but all the family knew that this was a temporary situation: in a few years it would pass to Patrick Junior. Patrick's brother, Con, was left nothing. His sister Hannah was also left out. Apart from £350 that was left to his youngest daughter, Mary Anne (presumably as a dowry), everything would go to Patrick.

Only in the event of Patrick's death could his siblings hope for any share in the property. The only crumb they were thrown was that the will guaranteed them the 'right of support', a country custom that meant they were entitled to live on in the family home and be fed. Beyond that they were on their own, unless their brother passed away.

Over the next few years relations within the family sank to an all-time low: Patrick continued to domineer, pushing around his brother and sisters as if they were chattels. Mary Anne could not take it, and found work as a domestic servant on a neighbouring farm. She rarely stayed in the family home any more; food and lodgings and a small wage were provided in her new position.

Con did not work on the farm—he was employed as a labourer for a neighbouring farmer—but Patrick objected strongly to this. If he had to let Con live on the farm and eat his food, he felt Con should work on the farm—and for no wages. More than once he approached Con's employer, William Travers, and complained that he was keeping his brother away from his rightful place. By early 1924 these complaints were beginning to annoy Mr Travers so much that he gave Con O'Leary notice to quit.

Meanwhile, the older sister, Hannah, was still living at home and acting as an unpaid skivvy for the family. Tensions were so bad that Patrick no longer slept in the house; he had a bed made up in the loft of an outhouse, perched between the potatoes and the animal feed.

But expecting everyone to slave for nothing on his behalf was not the only way in which Patrick antagonised his family. He was a brutal man who felt he never had to account for anything. This was particularly evident whenever he went to a fair. Fairs and marts were an important part of agricultural life at the time: buying and selling livestock and the ability to spot a bargain—then knock another few shillings off the price—were vital skills for any farmer. Fairs were also a great excuse to go on the batter and drink away the profits of the day.

Patrick was known for staying out whenever he went to a fair, and he never accounted for the money to the rest of his family afterwards. This was a big bone of contention. On Saturday 23 February 1924, the family complained to the parish priest about Patrick's behaviour, but the priest did not become involved.

Two days later, on Monday 25 February, Patrick was due to go to the fair in Bandon to sell a colt. He never made it. What happened is uncertain, but the pieces can be put together from the evidence given at the inquest and in the subsequent trials.

The night of Patrick's death was particularly cold. Skies were clear and a wind was blowing from the north. In the middle of the night someone—or more than one person—sneaked up on Patrick as he slept, huddled beneath his blankets. They were almost certainly his brother Con and his sister Hannah. Mary Anne spent most of her nights under the roof of her employer, and his widowed mother was probably too old to play a direct part in the attack, if she knew about it.

From the medical evidence it appears that Patrick was struck with a blunt instrument, probably a hammer or the blunt end of an axe, as he slept. The first blow struck him on the right of the face. He must have then turned over, because subsequent blows fractured his jaw on the left side, broke his nose, and fractured his skull. The attack was ferocious—blood splatters were found on the ceiling above him, and the mattress and blankets were saturated with blood. The head injuries he sustained were so serious that he probably died instantly, or certainly within a few minutes of the attack.

But once he was dead, what were his assailants to do with the body? This is where their plan began to become unstuck. The sensible thing would have been to bury Patrick on the land, or sink his body in the nearby lake, but they apparently decided to cut up the body. It was suggested at the trial that perhaps they hoped the family dog would do the rest.

The body was crudely hacked with a hatchet, and flesh torn off it with a billhook. All four limbs were severed, and the trunk was cut open and eviscerated. The dog probably did feed on the organs, because many parts of the body were not recovered.

A local doctor who was called to give evidence at the subsequent trial, Dr Charles Nyham, explained that because the weather was so cold, and because the trunk had been disembowelled, the body was very well preserved. Decomposition had been slow, and he believed that the limbs and trunk had been stored in the main dwelling house for a number of days after Patrick O'Leary's death. 'Like flitches of bacon, they were kept in the house for a week,' he told Mr Justice William Hanna.

'And did the family live there with the dismembered remains? If that is true they must have been the most hideous of human beings,' replied the judge.

The body was probably stored in the house for a little more than a week—it was ten days after Patrick's disappearance before anything was discovered. During that time the family maintained the fiction that he had gone to the Bandon fair and had not returned.

But on 7 March, a day when spring was finally in the air and a mild southwesterly breeze blew from the shore, a ten-year-old boy discovered a canvas sack. Inside was the head and hacked torso of a man. The boy ran home in a panic. Shortly afterwards, his parents, Mr and Mrs Walsh, went to the scene, and the sight that met their horrified gaze so unsettled Mr Walsh that he subsequently suffered a nervous breakdown and had to be confined to a mental hospital for a number of months.

Gardaí from nearby Clonakilty were quickly on the scene. Sergeant Devoy recalled meeting Con O'Leary at Miltown, nearby, and going to the farm with him. During the brief journey he asked Con about his brother. Con said that Patrick had disappeared a week earlier, but they hadn't made any enquiries because they assumed he had gone to look for work, either in England or in Cork. They were not worried about his well-being.

Arriving at the farm, Sergeant Devoy found that no one seemed greatly concerned about Patrick's disappearance. The sergeant said that a garda at the farm showed him a human arm under a furze bush about forty yards from the house, and a canvas sack, blood-grimed, which contained a human head and torso.

Night was falling by this stage, and he took out his torch to see better. He pointed out the arm to Con O'Leary, who commented: 'It's awful.'

The sergeant then spilled the torso and head from their canvas sack, and shone his flashlight on the head. He asked Con if he knew who the head belonged to. 'He asked me to turn over the other side of the head, then said that yes, it was his brother,' said the sergeant. 'Inspector Troy then asked him could he identify the head, and he wavered a bit. "It's like my brother but I'm not sure," he said.'

The sergeant and the inspector went into the house to question the other members of the family. Mary Anne said that Patrick had been missing for over a week, but she didn't seem overly concerned; neither did Hannah. The sack was brought into the house, and both women were shown the head of their brother. Inspector Troy, who was in charge of the investigation, asked Hannah if she could identify the remains.

Hannah, who appeared remarkably calm, looked at the head, and said that she could not identify it. She expressed no regret about the fate of her brother. Mary Anne was next; she identified the head as that of her brother Patrick, and like her sister she expressed no regret about the calamity that had befallen him.

Con was once more asked, in the light of the kitchen, to look at the head. He seemed less certain about his identification now. 'I'm not sure. It looks like his poll,' he said. As various identifying marks were pointed out to him, he finally showed some emotion. 'I am innocent. My hands are clean,' he bellowed. No one had accused him of anything. It was something of an over-reaction.

The following morning, as light returned, the search of the farm and surrounding properties resumed. It was gruesome work. The loft where Patrick had slept was like an abattoir—but an abattoir that had been hastily cleaned up. The headboard of the bed had been washed, but the dark stains of dried blood were clearly visible in the cracks and grain of the wood. A splash of blood on the ceiling attested to the ferocity of the murderous assault, but an attempt had been made to wipe down the walls. The plaster over the bed was sprayed with blood, and the frame of the bed showed large dark stains. The mattress was missing, but was found out on the farm, reeking of gore. Some of the blankets, torn and shredded, were also recovered.

On a heap of potatoes on the other side of the barn from Patrick's bed, Sergeant Devoy found a heavily bloodstained man's coat. There was a reaping hook, with blood on the handle, in the barn. During the search a hatchet was found: the head was clean, but the handle hadn't been wiped down at all, and the blood had seeped into the rough wood.

One sharp-witted investigator, Garda Reynolds, searching a field behind the O'Leary house, could see Mary Anne and Hannah looking at him very closely. As he approached a hedgerow he noticed that their eyes were following him, and he knew he was on to something. Sure enough, in the hedgerow he found a leg. Just nine yards away he found the second leg.

Body parts and bloodstained bedding and clothing were found within a six hundred-yard radius of the O'Leary house. Part of Patrick's torso was found in a broken-down old hut known as Deasy's Ruin, which was on a neighbour's land. More of the torso was found in a field, less than fifty yards from the O'Leary house, that belonged to the Walsh family. Trousers were found in the undergrowth, and a matching jacket was recovered from a nearby field. These were identified as the good suit of Patrick O'Leary, the suit he had supposedly worn to the fair.

The most gruesome moment came when the family dog ran into the yard with an arm in his jaws. The arm was quickly recovered.

An inquest was held that afternoon, and Con O'Leary gave evidence. He revealed that his brother had been missing for ten days, but no one had been sufficiently worried to look for him. During his testimony it became obvious that there were severe tensions within the family. Con's lack of emotion was also noted.

Con told the coroner that he had last seen his brother around 10 p.m. on the night of Monday 25 February. Patrick had gone to bed in the outhouse as usual. He had retired early, as he was going to the horse fair in Bandon the following morning.

Patrick had been up and gone before Con rose the following morning, and he had not seen him alive again. The last person to see him alive was his sister Hannah, who had made him his breakfast on the morning of the fair. Then Patrick had set off to sell the colt.

But the hole in the story was obvious to all; the colt that Patrick had planned to take to the fair was still in the outhouse on the O'Leary farm. None of the family had any explanation for this anomaly.

More alarm bells rang during the wake. The Irish have always known how to bury a neighbour. A wake would draw everyone from the locality to the house, drink would be laid on—porter and whiskey for the men, and wine or sherry for the ladies—and there would be plenty of sandwiches, pouches of tobacco, gossip, conversation and craic. It would last all night, presided over by the guest of honour himself.

The custom was to lay the corpse out on the kitchen table or in an open coffin. The O'Learys decided on an open coffin for their brother. On the evening of 9 March—two days after the discovery of the body, and only a day after the inquest—mourners trooping into the kitchen of the O'Leary house were confronted by the open box lying up against the wall. This provoked some comment. If ever there was a case for a closed coffin, this was one. But the various bits of Patrick's body were stuffed into the suit that had been retrieved from the bushes, and his torso, the hacked and battered head barely attached, was stuffed into the jacket. With all four limbs severed, much of the torso missing, and the skull mushed to a pulp—not to mention that the corpse was almost two weeks old by that stage—it was a sight that horrified the neighbours. What they could see of the face—the broken nose, the lacerated cheeks and forehead—drew shudders.

Then there was the grieving family. Not even Patrick's mother seemed upset. Much comment was made about the unnatural demeanour of the surviving siblings—they could have been waking a total stranger—but when neighbours said anything Con was quick to loudly proclaim his innocence. At that stage no one had accused him of anything.

When a woman from the adjoining farm, Ms O'Regan, questioned him, he said that he 'freed all the people of Kilkerran of the crime'. Ms Regan's brother then asked Con about his brother, to which Con snapped: 'I am innocent, and so is everyone in Kilkerran. I will go to heaven.' Con's sisters and his mother were strangely silent. Mary Anne's biggest concern seemed to be that the 'foxy' sergeant (Sergeant Devoy) seemed to be paying an unusual amount of attention to her mother, as if he were trying to force some admission from her.

It did not take long for the gardaí to identify the most probable suspects, and within days the whole family were in custody. The headline in the *Irish Times* of the day summed it up perfectly: 'Murder of a Cork farmer—whole family in the dock'.

The first hearing was at Rosscarbery District Court before Judge Crotty. After hearing the preliminary evidence, including the not guilty pleas from the O'Learys, he remanded the whole family in custody, adjourning the case to the Circuit Criminal Court in Clonakilty on 19 June 1925.

But the first dramatic new development happened a lot earlier than June. On 3 May Mary Anne, still well shy of forty, passed away in Mountjoy Prison. Unknown at the time of her arrest, she had been suffering from bowel cancer, and the disease had entered its final stages.

So when the case opened in Clonakilty just three members of the family were in the dock: Con, Hannah and their seventy-five-year-old mother, Hannah. The brother and sister were charged with murder and conspiracy to commit murder; the mother with conspiracy.

When the charges were read out Con and Hannah both pleaded not guilty, but their mother's barrister, Joseph McCarthy KC, caused consternation by declaring that his elderly client was not fit to plead.

William Corrigan KC, barrister for the State, was immediately on his feet to protest: 'Surely notice of this should have been given within the last three months? We have had to wait until this morning for this statement by counsel for the defence. All I have to say is that this is the most extraordinary proceeding. These people have been returned for trial for several months, and now this is sprung on us.'

The judge, Mr Justice Hanna, remarked that the old woman seemed quite intelligent in answering the questions of the Court Clerk, but he adjourned the case for a day to consider the matter. The following morning he put back the case against Hannah Senior, and ruled that the case against both of her children should proceed. Eventually the case against the mother was dropped.

Over the next two days the prosecution laid it all out before the jury—the tensions within the family, the finding of the body parts scattered around the farm, the horrible injuries suffered by Patrick O'Leary, and the bloody state of his sleeping quarters.

The case for the prosecution was that Patrick O'Leary had been murdered by members of his own household, who had decapitated the body, lopped off the arms and legs, and cut up the trunk. Mr Corrigan went on to say that the loft in which the murdered man slept bore all the traces of an abominable butchery. The bedding had been removed, but was found, bloodstained, on the farm. 'When Patrick's disappearance came to be talked about, Cornelius went around saying: "I am innocent, I am innocent. Whoever did this, my hands are clean." But nobody had then accused him of anything. When he protested his innocence, he spoke too soon,' the barrister told the jury.

The defence tried to exclude Garda evidence about interviews with Con O'Leary, saying that the questions had been 'trap questions', but the judge ruled against them. Neither of the O'Learys was called upon to give evidence in their defence.

Despite the lack of a defence, the jury were unable to reach a decision, and the trial had to be abandoned. But it proved to be a short reprieve for the brother and sister. A week later a new trial began, this time before a new jury in Dublin, but again presided over by Judge Hanna. The second trial opened on 29 June 1925.

The prosecution opened strongly, with Mr Corrigan telling the court, 'The prisoners explained the absence of their brother by saying that he went to Bandon horse fair with a colt, but that statement was false, because the colt still remained on the farm.

'The prisoners cut up and disposed of the remains of the deceased man. Their sister Mary Anne, who has since died, might also have had a hand in it. There was the strongest motive of all in this case. The farm had been willed to the deceased man, and we allege that the prisoners, who were disinherited, with an Irish peasant's greed for land, murdered their brother and threw his body to the dogs.'

The trial lasted two days. The defence offered no evidence. The O'Learys' barrister, Joseph McCarthy, wisely decided to keep his clients from the dock—he remembered Con O'Leary's poor performance at the initial inquest, when he wavered in his identification, protested his innocence too much, and was caught out in a number of lies, including the one about the colt being taken to the fair.

Instead he tried to put much of the blame on the dead sister, Mary Anne. When the judge rejected this line of argument, he tried to deflect blame from Hannah, to at least spare her. The court heard that when they were arrested Con O'Leary and his mother had declined to say anything. Hannah had said that she had nothing to do with it, while Mary Anne said: 'I was not there at all that night; ask the woman I slept with.'

Mr McCarthy tried to paint a picture of a family in denial, pride preventing them from washing their dirty linen in public. He said that the prosecution had offered no evidence to tie anyone to the murder and dismemberment of Patrick O'Leary, and the case was entirely circumstantial. He implied that the family had gone to some lengths to conceal what had happened to Patrick, but had had nothing to do with it.

The prosecution rejected this, Mr Corrigan saying: 'If the prisoners had enveloped the family pride in a cloak of silence, why was that cloak not thrown off now and some explanation given of a treacherous and deliberate crime committed in the dead of night?'

After two days the jury did not need much time to find both Con and Hannah guilty of murder. They recommended leniency for Hannah, but Judge Hanna was having none of it.

Donning the black cap, he turned to Con O'Leary and asked the usual question—if there was any reason why sentence of death should not be passed upon him. Con said: 'I had no hand, act or part in the murder.' The judge then sentenced Con to hang. 'I had no part in the murder. I am going to die an innocent man,' Con replied.

The judge turned to Hannah. 'I did not kill my brother,' she said. He sentenced her to death as well, with the date set at 28 July, just four short weeks after the end of the trial.

The state entered a *nolle prosequi* against Hannah O'Leary Senior, and she was released from custody.

An appeal was immediately lodged, which was heard the following week. The grounds for the appeal were mainly legal—no new evidence was introduced. It was claimed that statements made to the gardaí should not have been admitted, as they were made without the witnesses having been cautioned. This was rejected. It was also claimed that there was no evidence given as to who struck the fatal blow, and no evidence given to support the idea that the family had conspired together in the murder. In other words, one member of the family could be guilty and the others innocent, and there was no way of knowing which was which.

'The defence was not allowed to point out to the jury the possibility of the crime having been committed by a member of the family not on trial, the sister Mary Anne who died in prison,' the appeal was told. 'The whole trend of the evidence was that there was a conspiracy of silence among the family. There was a sort of hysteria, and there was a hasty attempt to conceal the body. That would point to members of the family being accessories after the fact, but there was not a scintilla of evidence that they were parties to the murder. The jury was not told the vast distinction that existed between action taken after the murder, and concerted action before that event.

'For all we know Patrick O'Leary may not have been killed in his sleep. He may have lived for several days after being attacked, and he may have been attacked by a stranger.'

Prosecutor William Corrigan rejected this, saying: 'The man disappeared on the twenty-fifth or twenty-sixth of February, and nobody, except members of his family, could have seen him after that. His remains were found in different fields afterwards. Who was answerable for his disappearance? Surely those among whom he lived.

'These people were asked for an explanation, and they gave an untrue explanation. Everything they said was disproved, and the fact remains that the defence was that these people—their brother having been butchered as he lay asleep in bed in an outhouse—because of their family pride, dissected his remains and threw them to the dogs.

'The defence was that every member of the family was concerned in the dissection of the body, by assent or otherwise. But the evidence that the two prisoners had a hand in this abominable butchery and dissection is also evidence that suggests murder, and so the jury found them guilty.'

The chief justice and his panel of judges agreed. The appeal was rejected. Within a day of the appeal being rejected the Governor General of the Irish Free State had commuted Hannah O'Leary's death sentence to imprisonment for life. But Con still faced the drop.

Ireland did not have an executioner, so the British executioner, Thomas Pierrepoint, was brought over, along with his assistant, John Ellis. On the morning of 28 July Con O'Leary, then aged forty, was led from his cell, accompanied by Fr McMahon, the prison chaplain, and the Rev Dr Dargan. Some prisoners struggle, some cry, but Con O'Leary went calmly to his death, walking quietly to the trap and standing there impassively as the noose was placed around his neck. The only drama was supplied by one of the prison wardens: as Pierrepoint, who executed 294 people during his career (his nephew Albert accounted for a further 608), opened the trapdoor and Con was launched to his death, one of the warders who had brought him to the scaffold fainted. He was taken outside, where he received medical attention and quickly recovered.

Hannah O'Leary spent the next seventeen years behind bars. She was released from Mountjoy in 1942, and immediately entered a convent, which had been a condition of her release. She lived out the rest of her days there, finally passing away peacefully in her sleep in 1967. To the day she died she never spoke about the events of that freezing night forty-three years earlier in which her brother passed away a lot less peacefully in his bed.

15 | THE FACE OF EVIL
CHARLOTTE, LINDA AND KATHLEEN MULHALL

'I'll never tell where Farah's head is,' said Charlotte Mulhall. 'I don't think it would make any difference at this stage.'

The heroin addict, street hooker and sadistic killer was speaking from Mountjoy Prison, where she is serving life imprisonment for the murder of her mother's lover, Farah Swaleh Noor. Her sister Linda is inside with her, serving a lengthy spell for manslaughter. Their mother recently joined them for her part in the most grisly and gruesome killing Ireland has seen in decades.

For many people, Charlotte, with her Cleopatra eyes and the cigarette constantly dangling from her lips, came to represent the face of evil. She had savagely hacked a man to death, then chopped his body into small parts and dropped them into the canal. She didn't seem particularly remorseful. 'He was an evil bastard. He broke my ma's ribs with a hurley, her hand with a hammer.'

To dismember a corpse over a number of hours goes well beyond a moment of temporary insanity. It marks you out as one of the depraved. It is the stuff of nightmares—the fictional Freddy Krueger, or Jeffrey Dahmer, the Milwaukee cannibal. But there was nothing depraved about the decision to hack the body: it was purely pragmatic. The Scissors Sisters had to hide what they had done, and they are still hiding it. That's why Charlotte won't say where the head is buried. 'There's nothing to gain either way if I did say where,' she shrugged.

Nothing but closure for Farah's family. But that is not Charlotte's concern. She wants the location to remain a secret. The only trouble is, the Mulhall sisters have shown themselves to be very inept at keeping things secret: that's why they are in prison.

On Thursday 24 March 2005, Paul Kearney was cycling along Dublin's Royal Canal, from Jones Road to Ballybough. As he crossed over Clarke's Bridge (known locally as Ballybough Bridge) he spotted a tailor's mannequin submerged beneath the clear water of the canal. He could see the arm and the torso, wrapped in what looked like a green Ireland jersey. Other limbs seemed to be lurking in the murky slime at the bottom, which was about seven feet deep at that point. Shuddering at the sight, he cycled quickly on. The limbs looked so real, but broken bodies do not lurk under bridges in broad daylight. He put the mannequin out of his mind and went about his business.

It would be another three days before someone else thought that the mannequin looked oddly real, and phoned the police. The Mulhall sister's secret was out. Farah's body had been found.

Farah Saleh Noor was a nasty piece of work. He passed himself off as a Somalian refugee who had fled his own country in fear of his life after members of his family had been butchered. The truth is that he was an economic refugee from Kenya, looking to better himself in a wealthier nation. At one time Europe and America had been the destinations of choice for economic refugees, but with the economy booming in Ireland more and more people sought refuge here.

Sheilila Said Salim left his wife and three children in Kenya, paying $1,600 to a human trafficker to get to Europe. The man arranged for Salim to get on a flight from Mombasa in Kenya to Rome, then on to Ireland, and Salim touched down in Dublin Airport on 30 December 1996.

He was Sheilila when he boarded the plane, but by the time he reached Ireland he was Farah Swaleh Noor, a Somalian national. He claimed to be aged twenty-nine (he was actually thirty-one).

He applied for political asylum, and was put in emergency accommodation.

As gardaí later found out, his story was a tissue of lies. His father was Somalian, but Farah was Kenyan. He had married young, and had three children: Somoe was seven, Mohamed six and Zuleh five when their father ran out on them. He had told his tearful family that he would fly out and make his fortune, then send for them, but he secretly admitted that he had no intention of ever seeing his wife or children again. He had heard stories that some countries in Europe were soft touches when it came to refugees: if you turned up and told a convincing enough sob story you would be allowed to stay, you would be given a free house and cash every week, and you wouldn't have to work. Party time!

Applying for asylum, Farah explained his lack of documentation. 'I had no time to get these documents before I had to flee Somalia.'

There are a number of international procedures in place for dealing with refugees. One of the rules is that you apply for asylum in the first country in which you touch down. But Farah had not applied for asylum in Italy, because the system there is a lot tighter than the system in Ireland, with less economic support for refugees. In any case, it is possible that Farah went to England first, then on to Italy, from where he flew into Ireland.

Farah had a good sob story, which he wrote in tortured English in the asylum application form. 'From 1990 the war start to spread. I decided to go back to Mogadishu and see my family. When I reach Mogadishu I went to my family house. The door was open, when go inside nobody was in. The only thing I saw was the dead body of my wife, she was having a bullet in her chest. I don't know where's my family, are they alive or dead? When I reach Kismayo I saw a lot of people which they were leaving the country with a big boat. I rush there and I ask where's the boat going? One of them tell me is going to Kenya.'

After a couple of years in a refugee camp in Kenya, where conditions were appalling, he said, he paid over money to a trafficker who got him to Ireland. 'Before the war I was having a very good life but the war affect me very much. I don't know what to do because the war destroy my house and I don't know where's my family, are they alive or dead? Somalia will never be like before. No hospital, no houses, no water, no animal, no light, no road and no food. So I will be very happy if you allow me to stay in this country.'

The process took over two years, and Farah's application was initially rejected, but that decision was reversed on appeal. He was very happy: he was in. He was legally entitled to be here, and he could claim social welfare payments.

Friends said that Farah was very proud to be legally living in Ireland. He got on well with people, was happy, and was a big supporter of the Irish soccer team—he had several Ireland jerseys. On 21 August 2003, Farah applied for Irish citizenship, and that application was still being considered at the time of his death.

It would appear that Farah was a good-natured chancer—and our country is full of those, so he should have fitted in. But there was a darker side to his personality. He was a heavy drinker who could easily get through a few bottles of vodka in a day. He also dabbled in drugs, including cannabis, cocaine, ecstasy and possibly even heroin. There is no evidence he was an addict; just an occasional user.

In August 1997 Farah met a Chinese girl in an amusement arcade in the centre of Dublin. She was only sixteen, and had a learning difficulty. Farah came on strong, approaching the girl and asking her to be his girlfriend and have his babies. It was an unusual chat-up line, and the girl declined; but she did go back to his flat with him, and Farah forced her to have sex. It was the only time they had sex, but the teenager discovered she was pregnant. Farah had no interest, and cut off contact with the girl. It would be several years before, in a drunken daze, he called to her flat to see his son for the first time.

'Farah was not violent to me,' said the girl. 'We had a nice relationship. I was with him for nine months, and I only had sex with him once. When my child was born Farah never saw him. I think he was six years old when Farah first saw him.' That was on 20 March 2005, just a day before Farah met his end. Later, pressed about her relationship with Farah, the girl admitted that he had been a brute during their brief time together.

Less than a year after meeting the Chinese girl Farah met another girl. She was a third-year student, and he bumped into her on her sixteenth birthday. Within three months she was pregnant. Their child was born in March 1999. Initially Farah was a devoted father, but within three months his behaviour had reverted. He started drinking again, and he began hitting his young girlfriend. Over the next few years the abuse got worse and worse: beatings became a daily occurrence, and he began to rape his young partner. She tried to leave him twice, but came back both times. Eventually, in 2001, she plucked up the courage to leave for good. She got a barring order against Farah, and obtained full custody of their son.

Despite the barring order, Farah continued to stalk his former partner for a number of months. But then, in late 2001, he contacted a recruitment agency where he was registered and told them to take him off their books. He was moving to Cork.

Farah had a new woman in his life. She was a decade or more older than him, and she was married with children, but she left her husband to follow her young lover to Cork. Her name was Kathleen Mulhall.

Kathleen Mulhall was in her forties. For twenty-nine years she had been married to John Mulhall, and they lived in a small corporation house in Tallaght. They had married in 1972 and their first child was born three years later. Their last was born in 1988. The early years of her marriage had been hard. John had been a tearaway as a teenager, and was a heavy drinker, and a mean drunk. He beat her regularly. Unlike many of the men in this book, he battled the bottle and won; he gained control over his alcoholism, and got a job. For twenty-five years he was a fitter with City Glass, working alongside two of his brothers. He drove a company van, but also had a motorbike. John was devoted to his children—three daughters (Charlotte, Linda and Marie) and three sons (James, John and Andrew). But the children were growing up in one of the rougher parts of Tallaght, money was tight, and they got in with a rough crowd. Two of his sons ended up doing time, as did two of his daughters, Linda and Charlotte.

John was a hard-working man, and probably the most stable part of the topsy-turvy world of the Mulhalls, but in the mid-nineties he had a brief affair, and Kathleen never forgave him. Their relationship never recovered, although they stayed together.

Kathleen met Farah in Coco's nightclub in Tallaght in the summer of 2001. It was her daughter Marie who introduced them. The mother of six fell for the African, and almost immediately they began having an affair. Early the following year she separated from her husband John. She took a barring order out against him, claiming he was beating her again, and he had to leave the family home in Kilclare Gardens, Tallaght.

To Kathleen's surprise the children sided with John, and moved out with him. John moved in briefly with Linda, then moved on to his son John Junior, bringing the youngest children, Marie and Andrew, with him. He was very bitter that Kathleen had abandoned three decades of marriage for her new flame, and he never really spoke to her again, though his devotion to his children never wavered.

Kathleen was blamed for the end of the marriage, and family and friends shunned her. After a few uncomfortable months living with Farah in Tallaght the couple decided they needed a fresh start. They headed for Cork, and John moved back into the family home with his kids.

Over the next two years Kathleen and Farah lived at seven different addresses in the southern capital. Farah had friends in the city, as he had lived there before. Kathleen, who did not have a job, spent the days moping around and drinking, subsisting on benefit money and rent allowance. Farah had more initiative. As well as signing on, he worked in construction jobs. As he could not drive he got around on a black mountain bike.

The couple did a lot of drinking, and went to house parties thrown by other Africans living around the city. Everyone remembers that Farah called his much older girlfriend 'the boss'. Kathleen was in her late forties, and was a harsh looking woman. Her long hair was still black, but her face looked weathered.

At one point Kathleen's daughter Linda, with her then boyfriend, moved to Cork, and the couples socialised together. Towards the end of 2003 Kathleen and Farah were living in a flat in a three-storey terraced house on the Lower Glanmire Road. One night the gardaí and an ambulance were called. When the landlord arrived she found blood splashed in the living room and the hallway. Kathleen promised to clean up the flat. A week later, when she came for the rent, the landlord noticed that Kathleen was covered in bruises. Noor was up to his old tricks.

In the various flats and apartments the couple rented during their two years in Cork there were complaints from neighbours about noise, drunkenness and fights. Once Kathleen became pregnant, but she lost the baby. The beatings she claimed to be receiving from Farah could have been responsible. He was a man who regarded women as objects to be used, and he was frequently violent in his relationships.

Both Charlotte and Linda kept in contact with their mother through this time, and both sisters travelled down from Dublin to visit more than once. One neighbour recalls: 'I remember the two girls visiting, but I took them to be her sisters. They were rough and in my opinion they were hookers. There used to be fierce rows between them all. I remember once Farah was shouting at them, that they were all tramps and prostitutes, and they responded in equally colourful language.'

Interestingly, when the same man heard that Farah's body had been recovered from Dublin's Grand Canal, he 'straight away thought of the three women. I think they would be well able to do that. They were very rough.'

A measure of Farah's personality can be read into his boast of having once killed a girl. The death of Raonaid Murphy was a high-profile case, which to this day has not been solved. The pretty southside teenager, aged just seventeen, was stabbed to death one evening as she was returning home. Farah claimed to the Mulhalls that he had killed the girl, and would not hesitate to kill again. His claim is extremely unlikely: gardaí investigated his story and dismissed it.

Around December 2003 Farah enrolled in a FÁS course on computers, and he did well: he wasn't much good on the computers, but he showed up regularly and got on well with everyone. After that course Farah did another, this time on sales. This time his attendance was more patchy, and in September 2004 he dropped out. He told people he knew that he had got a job in construction in Dublin. On 14 September the couple moved back to Dublin.

An expert at using the system, Farah claimed emergency accommodation because of his refugee status. He was put temporarily in a B&B in Tallaght with Kathleen, but after a few weeks she applied to move out, claiming she was frightened of him. She moved to Drumcondra. However, she told other people that she was getting on great with Farah. He had re-registered with the employment agency in Dublin, and was signing on.

Kathleen found a flat at 17 Richmond Cottages in Ballybough, and in December the couple moved in. She began building bridges with her family, regularly visiting her sons in prison, as well as seeing Charlotte and Linda.

Linda was thirty by now, and a mother of four. She had had her first child when she was eighteen, and for the next number of years she and her partner lived in a house in Tallaght. They had three more children, but in 2000 they decided to separate. She was devoted to her two boys and two girls, but their father was not in the picture any more.

After the break-up of her relationship she moved on to a violent and sadistic partner, who took great pleasure in inflicting pain on the family. There was an allegation that he was abusing three of the children, and in 2003 the Health Board took all the children into care.

Linda and her partner moved to Cork, where they socialised occasionally with Kathleen and Farah. Then they decided to relocate to Manchester, but the move did not work out, and in January 2004 they returned to Dublin. At this point their relationship was going through a rocky patch and they were fighting a lot. Linda agreed to co-operate with the gardaí and the Health Board in prosecuting her partner for child abuse. As a result, her children were returned to her, but on 10 February 2004 she placed them into voluntary care.

Linda left her partner at this stage, and went completely off the rails. She was evicted from her council house because of anti-social behaviour, and she spent the next few months moving from one homeless hostel to another. She was drinking heavily, and now she began to take heroin. She made a number of suicide attempts, slashing her wrists.

But in May Linda's children were returned to her. The family were accommodated for a while in a homeless unit in the Coombe area of Dublin, but were evicted because of Linda's continuing anti-social behaviour. Her father John, always devoted to his children, agreed to let Linda return to the family home in Kilclare Gardens, Tallaght. Here she remained for the next few years, and living with her father did give her some stability. She struggled with her drug and alcohol problems, and John Mulhall was able to help her with the children, otherwise she would have lost them again.

Meanwhile the court case against her ex-partner came and went. He was convicted of cruelty to the children, and jailed for four years. But the evidence that emerged in court was truly frightening. On one occasion he had made Linda's eldest boy, then aged ten, strip down to his underwear and had beaten him repeatedly with a belt, then with the flex of a nightshade. Then he went into the next room, where he attacked the boy's nine-year-old brother, picking him up and throwing him to the ground, and hit the boy's face off the wall. Then he went into the third room and beat Linda's eight-year-old daughter. Finally, he returned to the first room, where the ten-year-old was cowering under the bed. The man flipped the bed over and dragged the boy out for another beating, only stopping when exhaustion kicked in. He also beat Linda regularly.

It is quite possible that Linda's exposure to this continuing violence gradually desensitised her. She became inured to violence, and was not capable of the same horrified reaction that most people feel when confronted by blood and gore.

Her younger sister Charlotte was a tougher cookie altogether. Just twenty-two at the time of the killing, she was a seasoned troublemaker. She first came to the attention of the gardaí at the age of seventeen, when she was arrested for stealing money from Bewley's Café in the Square, Tallaght, but was let off with a warning. A few months later she was given similar lenient treatment after a public order offence. A few years later she was put on probation after being arrested for throwing cans at the home of an ex-boyfriend of Linda's, who had committed the unforgivable crime of moving on to someone else.

In all Charlotte had been arrested eleven times and charged on fourteen occasions for a variety of offences, including being drunk and disorderly, threatening behaviour, assault and causing criminal damage. She was also charged with loitering for the purposes of prostitution.

Charlotte was a street walker, at the bottom end of the sordid business of prostitution. She engaged in anonymous sex acts around Baggot Street to support her growing heroin habit. She never had a job, and turned to prostitution in her late teens to earn some extra cash. She worked regularly in Lad Lane on the Grand Canal, and was always busy. She was young, voluptuous, and although she had a hard face she hadn't the worn and weathered look of many of the other street walkers.

In fact, when her mother Kathleen returned to Dublin from Cork, Charlotte brought her down to these regular haunts, and introduced her mother to the world of prostitution. Their first visit was after a night of heavy drinking, when Charlotte brought her to Lad Lane and showed her how things operated. Although Kathleen was forty-nine, and looked years older as a result of her hard life, she took to life in the streets, and frequently went touting for business when cash was low.

Charlotte was not in a long-term relationship. She seemed to change boyfriends as regularly as other people change their socks. She went through a succession of boyfriends, and had a preference for Africans and Eastern Europeans. Although at the time of the murder she was living at home with her father and Linda, it was not unknown for Charlotte to take off and disappear, sometimes for weeks or months.

Kathleen, Linda and Charlotte had all been involved in abusive relationships. They were all heavy drinkers and at least occasional users of drugs. They lived hard lives at the bottom of the economic heap. Psychologists say that it is possible to become desensitised to violence by repeated exposure to it—which is why so many returning Vietnam veterans in America ended up living in the underbelly of society and drifting into crime. Several high-profile killings in America were committed by returning vets whose values had been scrambled by repeated exposure to brutality.

Drugs are another contributory factor. Psychiatrist Dr Brian McCaffrey says that drug use can trigger psychotic states in people, and these states can return after the person has stopped using drugs. In the early days of the drug LSD he was involved in research into its therapeutic uses, and he has seen people suffer flashbacks long after they have come off the drug.

But while drugs and drink are contributing factors, a trigger is needed before a person turns murderous. Only seriously violent career criminals, who act for money, kill without a trigger. Everyone else needs something to spark the violence, said Dr McCaffrey.

Farah may have seen it coming. According to his friends he was troubled in the weeks leading up to his death. He told one friend, Ali Suleiman Abdulaziz, that he was scared, but he would not say why. 'I said to stay away from people who took drugs,' said Ali.

On 20 March 2005, Charlotte asked Linda if she would like to go out for the day and meet their mother. It was the day before Charlotte's birthday, and she wanted to get in the mood with some drinking. Linda was reluctant as she didn't want to leave the children, but her father said that he would mind them, so the two girls went upstairs to get ready, knocking back some vodka to kick things off.

In mid-afternoon they caught a bus into the city centre, and Charlotte called her mother. Kathleen was in high spirits, walking along Upper O'Connell Street with Farah. They agreed to meet outside McDonald's. It was hard to miss Farah and Kathleen—the athletic African in his bright Irish jersey, and his much older white girlfriend. As soon as they met, Kathleen noticed that Linda's lip was swollen from a new piercing. Farah suggested going to a shop to replace the piercing with one in a superior metal, to reduce the swelling. But on the way they stopped at an off-licence to buy a bottle of vodka. They also bought three Cokes to use as mixers.

On any normal day drinking on the street would get you arrested, but this was the tail-end of the St Patrick's Day weekend, and so many people were strolling around drinking from cans that the foursome blended in and drew no attention to themselves.

The four people ambled slowly along the street until they reached the boardwalk that runs along the Liffey through the centre of Dublin, a lovely place to stroll, or to sit and watch the world go by. They picked a bench and sat down. Linda had about ten tabs of ecstasy on her, and she slipped one to Charlotte. Their mother spotted the drugs being passed between her daughters, and she asked for one as well. The only person who declined was Farah—he was quite happy with the vodka.

Under the influence of the drink and the drugs the girls became a bit giggly. But later the atmosphere subtly changed. Farah began bickering with Kathleen, and Linda tuned out by listening to music on her mobile phone.

Suddenly Kathleen said it was time to move on. Darkness was descending, so they decided to return to the flat Kathleen and Farah shared at Richmond Cottages, Ballybough, in the north inner city. But on the way, unsteady on his feet with the drink, Farah accosted a young boy. In his drunken state he was convinced the boy was the child he had fathered with the Chinese girl when he first came to Ireland. 'This is my son,' he shouted as he grabbed the little boy. 'That's not your son, you bleeding eejit,' said Kathleen. The girls managed to drag him away from the terrified boy.

By 6.30 p.m. the four had reached the small ground floor apartment. Kathleen and Farah were now arguing freely. The girls ignored them, putting on music and settling down with cans of lager. Kathleen poured a glass for Farah, but unknown to him she crushed one of Linda's ecstasy pills into the drink. Perhaps she wanted him to mellow out.

Unfortunately, that is not what happened. Whether it was the drink, the drug, or his bullish personality, Farah seemed to lose his inhibitions and to become aggressive and sexually predatory. Little by little he began to come on to Linda.

Linda recalls: 'Me and Charlie [her name for Charlotte] were having a laugh. I was sitting on Charlie's lap on the settee. Farah was sitting beside me and Ma was on the arm.'

Farah moved closer to Linda, then pulled her to him, placing his arms around her waist. She tried to pull away without causing a scene, but his grip was too tight. 'It did not feel right. He pulled me closer to him, sort of touching on Charlie's lap and his knee. His arm went from my back onto my shoulder and he pulled me close to him. He said something in my ear. I did not understand him, but I knew it was dirty. It was something he should not have said to me. It caused me to shiver.'

Charlotte told Farah to take his hands off her sister. But he took no notice, pulling her closer and continuing to whisper in her ear. He called her a creature of the night, and said she was just like her mother. 'Get your hands off me!' Linda shouted. But he wouldn't. He ignored Kathleen's attempts to get him to calm down and leave Linda alone. Charlotte was fuming, her anger building.

Farah's refusal to let go of Linda was the trigger that sparked his murder. All three women knew he was a violent man, who became impossible to manage when he had drink taken. He was young and strong, and could physically impose his will.

Linda tried to stand up. 'I was trying to say: "Get your hands off of me," but his hands were still around my waist. I really don't think he could see me ma and Charlotte. I was now standing beside the sink and Farah was standing in front of me.

'I was trying to push Farah's hands from my waist. I said to me ma as I tried to push his hands away: "He would sleep with your daughter as quick as he would look at you." Charlotte was saying: "Get your hands off her. She is nothing like me ma. Get your hands off Linda." Farah would still not get his hands off me.'

Suddenly Charlotte spotted an orange Stanley knife, used for cutting carpet, on the kitchen draining board. She picked it up and slashed at Farah's throat. Shocked, he let go of Linda and staggered. The blade had nicked an artery, and he was losing blood fast. Charlotte said that her mother then handed the two girls weapons. 'Me ma just kept saying to me and Linda: "Please kill him or he is going to kill me." She just kept going on about it. Me ma gave me a knife and she gave Linda a hammer. I don't know where she got them. I cut him on the neck on the side. I was facing him.'

Farah staggered and fell back into the bedroom, his head hitting the bunk bed before he collapsed to the floor. At this point Linda joined in the attack. 'I picked up a hammer from the sink and hit him on the head, loads of times; a good few times. He fell on to the ground and I hit him again. Charlie stabbed him.'

Charlotte said: 'I cut his neck. Linda hit him with the hammer, this was in the bedroom. I can't remember everything. I stabbed him in the neck. I don't remember how he died in the bedroom, but he was dead.'

Charlotte made a number of cuts using the Stanley knife, then switched to a bread knife. There is no suggestion that their mother helped in the attack. By all accounts she egged them on at the start of the attack, then stood back and watched, taking no active role.

Farah suffered horrendous injuries. Both his lungs were punctured, his kidneys were ripped and his liver perforated. Several of the stabs could have been fatal on their own, but the cumulative effect was such that Farah would have died almost instantly. He also suffered extensive head injuries, but as his skull was never recovered we will never know the extent of these. However, there were deep marks on the floor from the hammer blows, indicating that Linda was using all the strength she possessed in the assault.

Finally, their blood lust satiated, the girls put down their weapons and surveyed the scene. In her confession to the gardaí Linda recalls the scene: 'Charlie said: "Is he alive, is he alive? I thought he was coming at me." Farah was lying on the ground and Charlie said to me ma that he was dead. Me ma said: "Get him out, get him out." We were all screaming at this stage.'

The two girls dragged the corpse into the small bathroom. There is disagreement about who first got the idea to dismember him. Charlotte said that it came from Kathleen, but Linda claimed that Charlotte said: 'We will chop him up.'

The butchery took place in the small, poky bathroom of the flat. There was no room to move, and scarcely space to do the work they had in mind. But they felt they had no choice, and they got to work. Charlotte sat on the toilet seat, while Linda positioned herself in the shower. Kathleen stayed in the kitchen and chain-smoked through the night.

The girls had limited tools at their disposal, and no knowledge of anatomy. Even cutting up a chicken neatly takes some skill and the right knife; but dismembering a whole body is a specialist job. Charlotte began by trying to sever one of Farah's arms with the bread knife, and Linda began banging at the legs with a hammer, hoping to break the bones and make the job easier. It was exhausting work. The Stanley knife, so good at slicing through flesh, was useless at severing cartilage and bone. The job took hours. The girls switched positions frequently, and swapped implements. Both also took more ecstasy, and the drug kept their energy levels up for their bloody work.

When someone dies they stop bleeding. The heart is no longer pumping, so nothing is pushing the blood out of the body. There might be seepage, but that's it. However, if you start smashing a body with a hammer, and hacking with a bread knife, blood goes everywhere. A healthy man of Farah's size would contain about twelve pints of blood. That's a hell of a mess.

The two women spread towels to contain the blood, but to little avail. The tiny bathroom resembled a slaughterhouse. The distinctive coppery smell of the blood, mingled with the odours released as the guts were sliced, was overpowering. Linda would later say that the smell would not go away. 'I think about it every night.'

Both sisters were covered in blood. But they made efforts to keep on top of the situation, frequently wiping the blood from their faces and hair. Dismembering a body requires anatomical knowledge, and the girls had none. They had no plan, and no idea of what they were doing—they just hacked and hammered and hoped for the best.

At one point Linda decided to remove Farah's penis. 'Me ma had told me already that he had raped her and I said: "He won't rape me ma again." I cut his private parts off, the long piece, not the balls,' she told gardaí. This hints at a sexual element to the killing—that it was Farah's advances towards her, rather than her fears for her mother, that triggered off the murderous assault.

After five hours of hard work Farah's body was in eight separate pieces of various sizes and weights—and one penis. It was a very amateurish job. The largest piece was his upper torso. During the process of cutting the torso, Farah had been disembowelled, revealing his intestines and internal organs, the smell from which contributed more than anything else to the noxious atmosphere in the small flat. His lower torso still had the hip joints fully intact, though both legs had been severed. After the legs were taken off the women had managed to remove the thigh bones and broke them up further. The arms were hacked off beneath the shoulder, a difficult job because of the network of muscles, tendons and sinews around the shoulder, not to mention three big bones, the humerus (or upper arm), the scapula (shoulder blade) and the clavicle (collar bone).

Finally, they removed the head. This was not easy, and the two women took turns. Linda found it particularly traumatic and could not look as she hacked, sliced and hammered. Eventually she put a towel over Farah's face as she hammered the neck, trying to dislocate it from the shoulders. 'I had the towel over his head, over his face, and kept using the hammer. It would not come off. Both of us had to take turns with the hammer. I did not think about chopping it up but Charlotte said to do it,' said Linda.

It was now not far off midnight. Linda rang her father John at 11.41 p.m. and told him what had happened. She was drunk, high on ecstasy, and panicky, and he found it difficult to understand her. A few minutes later he rang Kathleen, who confirmed the story.

Meanwhile, the sisters worked away, packing the body for disposal. They also began furiously trying to mop up as much of the blood as they could. At the end of an hour the flat was probably as tidy as it had ever been during their mother's tenancy.

At 1.30 a.m. John Mulhall arrived at the flat, rang the doorbell and walked in. The smell still lingered, mingled with detergent. But the flat appeared clean. He saw his daughters and neither of them was covered with blood. He began to relax—this was a fantasy of their drug-crazed minds. 'Where's Farah?' he asked. Linda told him the body was in the bedroom. He went in but could see nothing. 'He's not in there,' he said.

Linda told him to look again. When he re-entered the bedroom he spotted a full black bin liner in the corner. He walked over and looked in. Then he turned and ran from the flat, throwing up on the doorstep. He got into his van and drove off. As far as he was concerned they were on their own.

Realising they could not lug a full bag of body parts—weighing more than twelve stone—they decided to repack everything. All the parts were put in separate plastic bags. These were then placed into sports bags for easy and discreet transport. The head was put in a suitcase, which they took into the back garden and left there overnight. This was Linda's idea. 'I decided we were not throwing the head in. I said it to Charlotte so that it would not be identified.'

If only they had used the same foresight in disposing of the rest of the body. The most sensible thing would have been to leave various bits in different parts of the city, spread widely around, and removing all clothing to eliminate any potential clues. But they didn't have a car: and you can't hop on a bus with a leg under your arm.

So instead they had to dispose of the body within walking distance of the flat. Linda carried the lighter bits, while Charlotte carried the heavier sections. Kathleen walked with them, but did none of the carrying. They walked the five minutes to the Royal Canal, which flows through the north inner city. The dumping ground they chose was under Clarke's Bridge, near Ballybough: they would climb down the bank, open the sports bags and throw the body parts into the water.

Flesh and bone is heavier than water, and a body will normally sink unless the lungs are full of air. Farah's lungs had been punctured and were flooded with blood. Nothing was going to float. It is only several days after a body has been submerged, when the gases involved in decomposition build up, that a body floats back to the surface. Perhaps the women believed that the canal would carry the body parts far away from the spot, but canals are not rivers; there is no strong flow to the sea.

It took several trips to bring all the parts to the canal. When the job was finished, they turned their attention to the flat. Blood had soaked into the carpets, lino and wooden skirting boards, and the carpet closest to the bunk bed was saturated. The towels they had used in their earlier clean-up had left bloody streaks on the floor.

Out came buckets, mops and cloths. The clean-up lasted all night. They did a good job, but it was a cosmetic job: when gardaí later began the detailed forensic examination, large amounts of small blood specks were found on a number of surfaces. The clean-up left extensive traces of the terrible violence that had been done in the flat that night. Finally, as dawn was approaching, they faced the decision about what to do with the head. 'We were just cleaning up for hours. We had everything in the flat cleaned up then we went up to the Watergate Park and buried the head,' explained Linda.

It was a bizarre job. After cleaning the flat, cleaning themselves, and resting from their exertions, they left the house around 11 a.m., carrying a sports bag containing Farah's head. By now the three women were ravenous, so they walked into a Gala supermarket on Summerhill Parade, still carrying the head. They ordered three salad rolls at the deli counter, which they ate on the street. Then they made their way into the city centre, and caught a bus to the Square shopping centre in Tallaght. This was familiar ground to them: they had grown up in Tallaght, and both sisters still lived there with their father. The Square was where Charlotte was first arrested, for stealing.

Instead of immediately getting rid of their burden, they went into the shopping centre and walked around, looking at the clothes shops. Eventually they left, and walked to Sean Walsh Memorial Park in Tallaght. 'Charlotte knows the park,' said Linda. 'We were walking around for ages. We sat down on a rock. We were looking for different places, where the bench was. Charlie started digging holes with the knife. The hole was not very deep. I had the head on me back and I said to Charlie: "Get this off me." Charlie took it out of the bag and put it in the hole. The head was still in the black bag. Charlie filled the hole. I could not do it.'

Kathleen then took the knives and the hammer, and threw them into a pond in the park. Then they went home: Kathleen to Richmond Cottages, and Linda and Charlotte to their father's house in Tallaght. That evening they burned the sports bag.

Kathleen began to tell people that Farah had left her for another woman, who was pregnant. She told others he was missing, and she was worried about him. She was covering her tracks—though she retained his bank card, and used it a few times. As late as May she asked at a Community Welfare Office if they had any way of getting an address for Farah, as she had not seen him in some time and was very worried.

John Mulhall, whose devotion to his children never wavered, helped get rid of some of the bloody carpets, towels and other items from the flat. He used his company van, and disposed of them well outside the city.

For ten days the three women lived in a state of panic, wondering if they had got away with it, and initially it looked as though they had. On 30 March Farah's body was discovered, but it was so badly decomposed that it could not be identified. Gardaí put out public appeals, but with little success.

In early April Linda got a notion into her head to revisit the site where Farah's head had been buried. She dug up the clay with her bare hands, picked up the decomposed head and put it into a black plastic bag. She walked to the nearby Killinarden Park and put the bag in some thick bushes. The following day she went back to the park with her son's school bag, into which she transferred the head, and then went home. She rang her mother to tell her that she was going to dispose of the head properly. Her mother didn't want to know.

Linda walked to Killinarden Hill, about forty minutes away. She climbed over a locked gate into a large field, and walked about 300 feet to the back of the field. She sat down on the grass, close to the ditch, and took the bag off her shoulder. 'I'm sorry, Farah, I'm sorry,' she said, then downed a small naggin of vodka, took out a hammer, and began bashing the bag. She kept banging until the skull was completely shattered. Then she dug a small hole and tipped the fragments into it.

The skull was never found, despite intensive searches.

Meanwhile Charlotte and Kathleen got on with their lives. Both women met up with Russian men, and both began new relationships within weeks of Farah's death. Kathleen's new man was just twenty-two, and spoke barely a word of English, but the relationship was not exactly based on intellectual compatibility;

two months into the affair Kathleen didn't even know her lover's name. Life goes on.

Kathleen moved out of the apartment, but she didn't move far—only to a flat upstairs. The new tenant at Number 1 noticed a 'big blue ring' on the floor at the bathroom door. She would have been shocked to know this was caused by a combination of cleaning chemicals and Farah's seeping blood and brain matter. There was no carpet under the double bed in the bedroom (Kathleen had lifted it up, and John Mulhall had disposed of it). There was an unpleasant smell of sewage in the flat, which could have been caused by flushing skin and bone fragments down the toilet.

Gardaí were getting nowhere with their investigation. Because of the missing head they went down the wrong route, looking into ritualistic aspects of the killing. But on 16 May a friend of Farah's contacted them to say he was worried that the unidentified body from the canal might be his friend's. It was the first time the name had come up in the investigation, and it was put on a list with other possible names.

Over the next month the name Farah Swaleh Noor kept coming up, and gardaí began to look into the background of the asylum seeker. Then came the breakthrough. On 11 July 2005, gardaí made a positive identification. Thanks to a combination of tip-offs and forensic evidence, they now knew that the body in the canal was that of Farah Noor. The final piece of the jigsaw came from a very unlikely source.

John Mulhall Junior contacted the detectives and told them that he knew whose the body was, and who had killed him. Detectives were immediately dispatched to Wheatfield Prison, where John and James spilled the beans on their sisters and their mother. Their motive remains unclear: perhaps they were looking for a transfer to an easier prison, or for a reduction in their sentences. In any case, they told the detectives in detail about the killing, right down to Linda's decision to cut off Farah's penis.

It was the breakthrough the gardaí were waiting for. Once they knew who was dead, it was only a short step to charging his killers. A very short step, as it turned out. Linda was the first to crack, making a statement admitting her involvement four days later.

Charlotte was tougher—she lied with ease, but not always consistently, and claimed to have had nothing to do with the murder. Linda was charged with murder in September, but it was not until October that Charlotte, who had recently discovered she was pregnant, admitted her involvement. Their mother did a runner, disappearing to England.

John Mulhall took the situation very badly. He had done his best all his life for his family. He had worked steadily at his job and tried to bring up his children as best he could. But his wife had left him, two of his sons were doing time, and now two of his daughters had been charged with murder. Where had it all gone wrong?

On the evening of 8 December Linda, under the strain of the murder charge hanging over her, exploded with pent-up fury, accusing her father of never having done anything for the family. He calmed her down and left the house, driving aimlessly around the city for a while before pulling into Phoenix Park. He parked his van and took a rope out of the back. Scribbling a hasty few words on the back of a €50 euro note, leaving all he possessed to his daughter Marie, he climbed a solid oak tree and knotted the rope. Then he slipped the noose around his neck and jumped.

The trial of the Scissors Sisters was a media sensation. It is hard to remember any trial, except perhaps when Mary Cole was accused of drowning two young children in her care, that attracted such interest. Charlotte and Linda were not beautiful women, but they were striking. They both appeared in court each day heavily made up, with dark eyeliner giving them a Cleopatra-like air. Charlotte had a natural arrogance in her stance, and a sort of defiance in her face, that reinforced that image.

The media quickly dubbed them the 'Scissors Sisters', despite the fact that scissors played no part in their atrocities. However, it was a catchy name—a name shared by an American pop band—and it stuck.

The trial, in October 2006, lasted nine days. Charlotte was now a mother, having given birth to a baby boy in May. She seemed indifferent to the proceedings, sitting impassively through the evidence, and slipping out during breaks to have a cigarette and read her magazines. Linda appeared equally impassive. But

Charlotte's composure broke on the fifth day, when the statement she had made to the gardaí about her involvement was read out. The court adjourned for the day to allow her to recover.

Linda had a lucky break in the trial. Her barrister, Brendan Grehan, told the jury that there was no evidence before the court that her hammer blows had killed Farah. Of course there wasn't; maybe her decision to move the skull to a safer hiding place had been a clever move. He added that Linda had been terrified of Farah when he grabbed her and would not let her go.

Barrister Isobel Kennedy, acting for Charlotte, said that the younger Mulhall sister had initially denied any involvement in the murder to protect her sister, the one person she was 'utterly devoted to'.

The jury were expected to return a quick verdict, but after a number of hours, when they had not reached any agreement, Mr Justice Paul Carney dismissed them for the evening. The following day they still could not reach agreement. At lunchtime he told them he would accept a majority verdict. They asked for clarification on the legal definitions of self-defence and provocation, then retired once more, but they still could not reach a decision and were sent home for a second night.

On the afternoon of the third day the foreperson of the jury told the judge they were deadlocked, and unable to reach a verdict. But he was having none of it. 'You are not the only jury in the building deliberating for this time. There are five children who have a vital interest in this, as you know, and we're anxious to reach a conclusion. If you're in any doubt as to the evidence you should resolve it in favour of the accused and if there's any further help I can give you I'll be delighted to do so.'

That evening the jury returned, still deadlocked. 'We're talked out. The air upstairs is blue and we wish to come back to this tomorrow,' said the foreman. The jury went home for another night, and came back the following day to begin deliberating for the fourth day. If this went on, the jury deliberation ran the risk of being as long as the trial itself, but on the afternoon of the fourth day of deliberations the jury were finally able to deliver a verdict.

The court was thronged. Linda, wearing a chocolate leather jacket over a white blouse and navy jeans, glanced up as the jury returned. Her sister, dressed in black trousers and a black vest top, and carrying a copy of *A Million Little Pieces*, a novel by James Frey about drug addiction, seemed impassive and stony-faced.

Two of her brothers, James and John, and her sister Marie were in the court. Charlotte didn't even flinch when the verdict of guilty of murder was read out. She faced automatic life imprisonment.

Linda also stared ahead, showing little emotion, as her verdict was read out. She was found guilty of manslaughter. As they were being led away their brothers ran over and hugged them. Finally the mask slipped and both women shed a tear.

'Thank God it's over,' whispered Linda.

She was eventually sentenced to fifteen years, a very harsh term for manslaughter. Mr Justice Carney said that he had had the option of imposing a life sentence, but he had taken into account the jury's finding that she had been provoked into the attack on Farah.

Kathleen was nowhere to be seen. She had disappeared, and was reputed to be living in England. Finally, in February 2008, she voluntarily surrendered to gardaí. She had dyed her hair blonde, and was living under the name Kathy Ward. (Ward was her maiden name.)

In February 2009 she faced nine charges: that she withheld information, helped clean up a crime scene, five counts of giving false information over Mr Noor's whereabouts, and two counts of pretending she did not know his whereabouts. She was planning to contest the charges but, dramatically, she changed her plea as the ~~ca~~se was called, and pleaded guilty to helping clean up the crime ~~scen~~e to protect her two daughters. Mr Justice Carney sentenced ~~her to~~ five years in jail. She is now behind bars with her two ~~daughter~~s.

~~The siste~~rs share a block in the Dochas Centre at Mountjoy. ~~Kathleen~~ had a very hard time, but has settled in. Charlotte is ~~a disrupt~~ing force in the centre, constantly in trouble. She got ~~hold of il~~licit drink and drugs at her son's christening in the ~~centre; sh~~e got into trouble when she exposed herself to a group of ~~school c~~hildren on a tour of the prison; and at one point she was photographed holding a knife to another prisoner's throat. When the tasteless picture was smuggled out of the prison and got into the papers, Charlotte was transferred to Limerick Prison as a punishment. She remained there for nine weeks, during which time she was unable to see her young son. She was later transferred back to the Dochas Centre, but could not stay out of trouble. She gave an in-depth interview to a journalist, and was back in hot water. As well as being in trouble with the authorities, some of her fellow inmates might not be too happy to know what she thinks of them. 'The only one I fell out with is Kelly Noble, fucking little bitch that she is. I have a lot of sympathy for Jackie [Kelly's mother]. It's Kelly more so than anyone else. Kelly will start the trouble and then leave her ma there to face the music and go and lock herself in her cell,' she said.

She is no more impressed by Catherine Nevin, the 'Black Widow', who hired a man to gun down her husband Tom at their pub, Jack White's in Brittas Bay. 'I can't stand her. She's only a fucking bitch. She's writing a book up there. She's the only one in the prison that's allowed a computer in her room. Everyone else in the prison, everyone's room gets searched. She has so much stuff it's unbelievable.'

Sharon Collins, the Ennis woman who tried to hire a hitman over the internet to kill her lover and his two sons, is another who draws her scorn. 'It doesn't take you long to suss her out. She's a very manipulative woman.'

Only her young son seems to draw out her soft side. 'He's really coming on grand and his speech and all is brilliant. He's the only thing that keeps me going.'

Charlotte Mulhall is one of the most recognisable wome Ireland, and for all the wrong reasons. If women such a Robinson and Sonia O'Sullivan are proof that women ar as good as men, Charlotte, Linda and Kathleen Mulh of the opposite. These women are every bit as bad a